Toward a Science of
DISTRIBUTED LEARNING

Toward a Science of
DISTRIBUTED LEARNING

EDITED BY

Stephen M. Fiore
Eduardo Salas

AMERICAN PSYCHOLOGICAL ASSOCIATION

WASHINGTON, DC

Published by
American Psychological Association
750 First Street, NE
Washington, DC 20002
www.apa.org

To order
APA Order Department
P.O. Box 92984
Washington, DC 20090-2984
Tel: (800) 374-2721
Direct: (202) 336-5510
Fax: (202) 336-5502
TDD/TTY: (202) 336-6123
Online: www.apa.org/books/
E-mail: order@apa.org

In the U.K., Europe, Africa, and the Middle East, copies may be ordered from
American Psychological Association
3 Henrietta Street
Covent Garden, London
WC2E 8LU England

Typeset in Goudy by World Composition Services, Inc., Sterling, VA

Printer: Data Reproductions, Auburn Hills, MI
Cover Designer: Berg Design, Albany, NY
Technical/Production Editor: Kathryn Funk

The opinions and statements published are the responsibility of the authors, and such opinions and statements do not necessarily represent the policies of the American Psychological Association.

Library of Congress Cataloging-in-Publication Data

Toward a science of distributed learning / edited by Stephen M. Fiore and Eduardo Salas.—1st ed.
        p. cm.
    Includes bibliographical references and index.
    ISBN-13: 978-1-59147-800-3
    ISBN-10: 1-59147-800-6
    1. Distance education—Computer-assisted instruction. 2. Computer-assisted instruction—Social aspects. I. Fiore, Stephen M. II. Salas, Eduardo.

LC5803.C65T68 2007
371.3′58—dc22   2006032590

British Library Cataloguing-in-Publication Data
A CIP record is available from the British Library.

Printed in the United States of America
First Edition

To Paul and Mary Fiore, whose passion for knowledge served as an inspiration to their family.

CONTENTS

CONTRIBUTORS

Alan R. S. Ashworth III, PhD, Air Force Research Laboratory, Brooks Air Force Base, TX

Bradford S. Bell, PhD, Cornell University, Ithaca, NY

Brian Bell, New Jersey Health Care System and Cognitive Engineering Research Institute, Mesa, AZ

Kenneth G. Brown, PhD, The University of Iowa, Iowa City

Scott R. Chaiken, Air Force Research Laboratory, Brooks Air Force Base, TX

Nancy J. Cooke, PhD, Arizona State University and Cognitive Engineering Research Institute, Mesa, AZ

Stephen M. Fiore, PhD, University of Central Florida, Orlando

Barry P. Goettl, Air Force Research Laboratory, Brooks Air Force Base, TX

Jamie C. Gorman, PhD, New Mexico State University and Cognitive Engineering Research Institute, Mesa, AZ

Arthur C. Graesser, PhD, University of Memphis, TN

Eddie Jerden, Development Dimensions International, Bridgeville, PA

David H. Jonassen, PhD, University of Missouri, Columbia

Joan Johnston, NAVAIR, Orlando, FL

Steve W. J. Kozlowski, PhD, Michigan State University, East Lansing

Kurt Kraiger, PhD, Colorado State University, Fort Collins

Richard E. Mayer, PhD, University of California, Santa Barbara

Rudy McDaniel, PhD, University of Central Florida, Orlando

Harry Pedersen, New Mexico State University and Cognitive Engineering Research Institute, Mesa, AZ

Eduardo Salas, PhD, University of Central Florida, Orlando

Mark E. Van Buren, Corporate Executive Board, Washington, DC

Robert A. Wisher, U.S. Department of Defense, Arlington, VA

ACKNOWLEDGMENTS

The creation of this volume was partially supported by Grant F496200110214 from the Air Force Office of Scientific Research, by Grant SBE0350345 from the National Science Foundation, and by Grant N000140610118 from the Office of Naval Research. Many people contributed to this volume in differing ways. First and foremost, we thank the publishers at the American Psychological Association for supporting such a multidisciplinary edited volume. Their effort through this challenging process has surely produced a superior volume, and we sincerely appreciate the support. Second, we thank the faculty and staff of the Institute for Simulation and Training at the University of Central Florida for their continued and tireless efforts in providing a culture of scholarship and service in support of multidisciplinary science. Additionally, Stephen M. Fiore thanks his many mentors who encouraged an appreciation of multidisciplinary approaches to understanding. This includes the outstanding faculty at the University of Pittsburgh's Learning Research and Development Center who instilled an appreciation of diverse scientific knowledge in pursuit of understanding the process of learning.

Toward a Science of
DISTRIBUTED LEARNING

1

MOVING US TOWARD A SCIENCE OF DISTRIBUTED LEARNING

EDUARDO SALAS AND STEPHEN M. FIORE

The world is getting smaller. This is such a trite colloquialism—one echoed in countless conversations during the 20th century to convey the ease with which the human race could traverse the globe. Although formerly used to convey the idea of both geographic and communicative travel, in the latter portion of the 20th century this phrase truly took on a different meaning. It was now possible to engage in instantaneous virtual traversal such that one could easily project a presence across the globe. Distance no longer matters as long as the information network is in place—a fact of modern life that brings us to the rationale for this volume. Government, industry, and academia are all taking advantage of this to achieve some form of superior performance whether this is manifested as gains in learning, productivity, or national defense.

Through the implementation of technologies such as distance learning or training, various organizations are rapidly adopting tools and techniques

The views herein are those of the authors and do not necessarily reflect those of their affiliated organizations. This chapter was partially supported by Grant F49620-01-1-0214 from the Air Force Office of Scientific Research to Eduardo Salas, Stephen M. Fiore, and Clint A. Bowers and by Grant SBE0350345 from the National Science Foundation to Eduardo Salas and Stephen M. Fiore.

to adapt the way they do business. With this increase in use comes the concomitant question of how to best implement such technology. Answering such questions requires a pragmatic scientific approach—pragmatic in the sense that it requires scientists to recognize that they are trying to solve real world problems and scientific in the sense that it is theory based and attempts to achieve "understanding" in addition to finding solutions. This latter point—that the power of science needs to be better focused on helping to solve societal problems (see Stokes, 1997)—is echoed in policy discussions throughout Washington, DC, and in associated meetings across the United States. In this chapter, we briefly outline the rationale for this volume and provide an overview of the questions and associated issues we set out to address within the context of distributed learning and training.

RATIONALE FOR A VOLUME ON DISTRIBUTED LEARNING AND TRAINING

In today's dynamic work environment, modifications to industrial operations and rapid advances in technology have created an unparalleled demand for training. Simultaneous with this has been a rapid advance in technology for the delivery of training along with an infusion of technologies into academic settings. Because of this, traditional classroom learning and training approaches have been increasingly supplanted by distance-learning efforts. As such, within organizations, in both the military and industry, distance learning and distributed training are becoming prevalent. For the purposes of our discussion, we use the term *distributed learning and training* (DLT) to generally describe learning or training that takes place while the student or trainee is geographically isolated from either the instructor or his or her peers. We choose this terminology because it covers the three primary areas in which learning at a distance may occur: (a) e-learning in organizations, that is, any type of learning facilitated using network or digital tools, (b) distance learning in academia, and (c) distributed training in the military.[1]

Distributed Learning and Training

As evidence of the ubiquity of DLT programs such as e-learning in organizations, a recent survey published by the American Society for Training and Development (ASTD) noted that approximately 95% of the respon-

---

[1]In chapter 2, Kozlowski and Bell describe in more detail the differing forms of DLT and the types of technologies used in these environments.

dents had used some form of DLT with their current employer (Ellis, 2003). Flexibility and cost-effectiveness are argued to be driving the increasing use of such technologies, with some estimating that more than $10 billion would be spent annually in the United States alone on DLT in the beginnings of the 21st century (Moe & Blodget, 2000). Estimates vary, but a number of large organizations have claimed to have experienced tremendous savings in their training through the implementation of DLT (e.g., Dow Chemical was reported to have saved more than $30 million, see Brayton, 2001; and IBM was reported to have saved $200 million in the training of their sales force, see Evans, 2000). Within military environments, the cost savings were reported to be nearly $300,000 a year for the National Guard (see Wisher & Priest, 1998). More recently, in a review of DLT within the military, the U.S. General Accounting Office found substantial cost and time savings associated with implementation of such programs:

> The Army's Battle Staff Noncommissioned Officer course conversion to an Advance Distributed Learning format resulted in a $2.9 million annual cost avoidance while maintaining student performance [and] the Air Force developed CD-ROM training for hazardous material incident response for [Department of Defense] firefighters and law enforcement personnel that reportedly resulted in a significant increase of certified responders and a projected $16.6 million cost avoidance. (U.S. General Accounting Office, 2003, p. 12)

Finally, in academia, distance learning spending in the United States alone is well into the billions, with projections for future spending approaching $10 billion (Moe & Blodgett, 2000).

Nonetheless, the ubiquity of such learning environments does not necessarily match their efficacy. In academia, the use of online learning has been explored from the perspective of the learner and the characteristics determining effective learning outcomes. Along these lines, researchers have begun to understand the characteristics of success and failure for students in online courses. For example, Wang and Newlin (2000) found that online activity was proportional to success in the course. Additional research suggests that self-efficacy related to course content and to technologies related to online learning is necessary for effective performance in distance learning courses (Wang & Newlin, 2002).

In organizations, an additional issue to consider is the degree to which the participants actually prefer such approaches to learning. For example, some data suggest that classroom training is preferred with more than half of those surveyed by ASTD, stating that they preferred the classroom over distance learning (ASTD & The Masie Center, 2001; see also Phillips, Phillips, & Zuniga, 2000). To address this issue, organizations have implemented blended learning environments to provide both a reduction in cost and trainee desire for face-to-face meeting time. Indeed, a substantial number of organizations have implemented these forms of hybrid training programs (Sparrow, 2004) involving a mix of online or technology-enhanced learning with face-to-face teaching. For example, an IBM report indicated that the company has been able to reduce its training costs significantly while enhancing learning outcomes using DLT (Mullich, 2004).

Metascientific Theme

Despite these differing forms of DLT implementation, the underlying component is that people and/or content are separated by time and/or distance. This produces a host of psychological, technological, and social issues surrounding learning in such environments. Although research has begun on understanding this phenomenon on differing levels, much is yet to be learned. To address this problem, we conceptualized this volume within the scientific framework presented by Stokes (1997). In his book on basic science and technological innovation, Stokes discussed science policy from the vantage point of the history of science and humankind's quest for understanding. He described how current science policy, largely shaped by Vannevar Bush's (1945) report, "Science, the Endless Frontier," is increasingly at odds with the needs of society. In this treatise, Stokes outlined the tension that inherently arises from dichotomizing basic and applied research, a dichotomy codified in the Bush report. Stokes eloquently argued that the quest for fundamental understanding, which is historically the purview of basic science, and the consideration for use, traditionally the domain of applied research, are not mutually exclusive categories of science. Instead, when viewed from an historical perspective, these approaches have a long and productive commingling in a variety of research domains. Using Louis Pasteur's groundbreaking and significant studies in microbiology as the quintessential example of what he labeled "use-inspired basic research," Stokes outlined how science and science policy can benefit from considering research not along a single continuum of basic versus applied but within a matrix crossing a quest for fundamental understanding with a consideration of use (see also Fiore, Rubinstein, & Jentsch, 2004).

We provide this introduction to Stokes's (1997) work because it is a cogent means with which to describe our approach in this volume. In particular, the domains covered in DLT exemplify the tension that exists between the basic–applied research dichotomy. On the one hand is the view that to truly understand learning and learning processes, only pure, basic research can be used to disentangle the multitude of issues surrounding such a fundamental scientific issue. On the other hand is the view that DLT is merely a new method of information delivery, and thus pure, applied research is all that is necessary to ensure gains in educational efficacy.

Indeed, some argue that this latter view has dominated DLT research, and too often at the expense of developing a true science of DLT (see Salas, Kosarzycki, Burke, Fiore, & Stone, 2002). We argue that DLT can best be understood by considering it under the rubric of "use-inspired basic research." Specifically, although distance technology is indeed a means of information delivery, a small but significant number of researchers have been exploring fundamental issues in learning but within the context of DLT.

In the present volume, we bring together representative members of this small group of researchers who pursue a quest for fundamental understanding, but with a well-specified consideration for use. These researchers have been exploring DLT issues from a theoretically driven perspective while simultaneously considering the eventual use of this knowledge (e.g., educational or industry applications). In short, although this technology offers tremendous promise, and is already being widely used in academia, industry, and the government, the scientific and pedagogical implications of such instruction are unclear. As such, our overall goal with this volume is to begin to truly shape a science of distributed learning that has both theoretical and practical value.

STRUCTURE OF VOLUME

There are a number of areas in which DLT is making an impact: in industry, academia, and the military. As discussed, colleges and universities are increasingly offering online or blended learning environments, and public and private organizations are just as likely to offer distance training. Similarly, the military is steadily transitioning its training to online settings as well as implementing sophisticated distributed simulations for enhanced training. Thus, the issue of learning and training at a distance cutting across these domains requires that we address a multitude of differing questions, ranging from the macro to the micro. Rather than focusing on one at the expense of the other, we chose rather to present a representative cross-section of these questions to convey some of the current and influential ideas affecting DLT. Furthermore, after reflecting on cognitive psychology, technology, training, and industrial–organizational psychology's approach to use-inspired basic research, we have noticed an important increase in attempts to blend these issues. As such, we wanted to provide a focused avenue through which to present these questions and provide the beginnings of answers. Thus, in conceptualizing this volume, we set out to bring together researchers who would be able to help us begin to chart the course for a science of learning in distributed environments.

Within this broader context we set out to consider a set of questions enabling an understanding of learning in distributed environments. In essence, the field needs to better understand why DLT may or may not be superior to co-located learning and training. What pedagogy can we adapt, and what pedagogy must we create, for these new learning environments? Both general and specific questions were generated for this volume, and these were developed to help the field move forward in addressing some of the broader issues and problems within DLT.

First, more generally, we considered why there is still such a focus on technology in this area. As Mayer (1999) noted, technologies have always been introduced to the learning environment, typically along with exaggerated claims as to how learning will be greatly enhanced. As such, in conceptualizing this volume we thought at a more global level in consideration of the learner-centered approach (Mayer, 2001) and chose to present a set of what we believe are promising ideas in DLT. We chose these approaches not because they address technology in the learning environment but because of their attention to the learner's cognitive processes when interacting in technology-based learning environments. The goal is to begin laying the foundation for the principled application of technologies in DLT. Second, and still generally, we asked, Where are the broad-based theories that can help us manage the tremendous complexity of distributed learning environments? All of the contributors were asked to discuss the underlying theoretical principles driving their research. Third, and more specifically, we asked, Where is the research producing our understanding of knowledge in DLT? In industrial–organizational psychology, discussions of knowledge, skills, and attitudes are ubiquitous, yet invariably it is the skills and the attitudes that are discussed. Therefore, we included some focus on the nature of knowledge, writ large, potentially derived in DLT environments (e.g., knowledge surrounding teamwork, knowledge associated with problem solving). Fourth, and related to our third question, we asked, Where are the cognitive principles in DLT? To address this, we invited contributions from researchers who have been researching and/or developing important areas of cognition within the context of DLT (e.g., metacognition, narrative). Next, we briefly discuss the specific sections within this volume.

Part I: Theoretical Models Emanating From Distributed Learning in Organizations

In the first section of this book, we present a representative sample of the theoretical models addressing distributed learning within organizations. We have assembled a set of researchers who have effectively integrated organizational, technological, and cognitive issues. These authors discuss how constructs emerging from the cognitive and the learning sciences can help us to better understand organizational learning and training.

First is a chapter by Kozlowski and Bell, who present a comprehensive framework of learning principles and concepts along with associated technological issues, all to be considered within distributed learning environments. As they illustrate, the field can greatly benefit from consideration of theory that can integrate the design, delivery, and use of DLT. Next is Brown and Van Buren's chapter, in which they discuss theoretical issues surrounding social capital within an organizational context. They suggest how to leverage the technologies inherent in networked organizations so as to help overcome some of the negative consequences arising from distributed interaction. Here, we see how this concept can be seamlessly blended with organizational learning and performance in today's increasingly networked settings. Finally, we have a chapter by Kraiger and Jerden; they articulate some of the foundational issues with respect to learner control and demonstrate important findings with a meta-analysis of training research that has examined this. Furthermore, on the basis of this analysis, they present an extended model of the potential differing forms learner control can manifest in organizational contexts.

Part II: Distributed Teams and Distributed Team Training

In Part II, we present a set of team training concepts and theories that are representative of the complex factors that must be addressed when considering distributed learning and interaction at the interindividual level. As such, we have team researchers discussing how the burgeoning field of team cognition (Salas & Fiore, 2004) and its associated training concepts need to be explored in distance and distributed learning environments.

First is chapter 5, by Goettl, Ashworth, and Chaiken, in which they address how fidelity (i.e., faithfulness to the operational context) within distributed training environments alters the learning experience. They based their arguments around distinctions between fidelity at the cognitive level and the more prevalent notion of physical fidelity. As they discuss, although these differing forms of fidelity play an important role in distributed training, their use and the timing of their use must be based on sound learning principles. Next, in chapter 6, Fiore, Johnston, and McDaniel discuss how the narrative form, a concept emerging from many differing disciplines, can be productively used within distributed training environments. As they illustrate, distributed simulation-based exercises lend themselves to narrative analysis, suggesting that automated assessment and feedback delivery mechanisms can be developed by relying on the narrative form. Finally in chapter 7, Cooke et al. discuss how geographic distribution alters team process and performance within a complex military task setting. As they illustrate, team processes are altered in differing ways by distribution and understanding this effect is critical as distributed interaction becomes more prevalent.

Part III: Cognitive Processes and Products in Distributed Learning Environments

In Part III, we offer a sample of what we describe as *cognitive processes and products*, for which we must account if we are to fully understand DLT. In this final section, the chapter authors discuss experimentation and theory so as to better integrate cognition and learning within distributed environments. We chose three specific topics that are viewed as pressing in the sense that they represent areas of inquiry in which well-articulated theory can make a tremendous impact on DLT.

First is chapter 8 by Mayer, who discusses the use of multimedia in learning environments, a use that is ubiquitous and almost synonymous with DLT. As Mayer outlines, such technologies can better augment the learning process by supporting the learner's attempts to construct knowledge associated with the domain being studied. Second is chapter 9 by Jonassen, who addresses a specific learning issue given its ubiquity in real world situations: problem solving and how problem-solving processes need to be taught within DLT. Third is chapter 10 by Wisher and Graesser, who discuss not just interactivity but a more specific form of interactivity: questioning. In particular, as Graesser and Wisher note, questions occur substantially less often in the classroom compared with settings such as those experienced during tutoring. The epistemological issue is how this important component of interaction can be better understood so that it can be incorporated into distributed learning environments.

Concluding Chapter

In our closing chapter to this volume, we discuss some of the broader science policy issues surrounding federal funding and how this volume can be used to strategically contribute to a science of learning in distributed environments. Our goal is to stimulate thinking at a higher level so the multiple communities involved in the science of learning can better conceptualize how the field can move forward using the contributions from this volume.

CLOSING REMARKS

Our understanding of distance, distributed, and even blended learning (i.e., a mix of traditional and distance learning) environments is greatly overshadowed by the rapid rate at which they have been implemented. If academia, industry, and the military are spending billions of dollars annually on the design and delivery of distance learning and distributed training, then clearly the scientific community should support this movement by providing theory-based empirical research findings on this topic. Indeed, our professional responsibility is to investigate emerging issues, produce empirical findings, and offer those findings to help guide the field—not only in the principled application of DLT but also in areas still requiring scientific investigation. For that reason, our volume fits within policy notions of use-inspired basic research and focuses entirely on theoretical and empirical aspects of DLT research. We have selected authors who can discuss important topic areas in distance learning theory, methods, and applications, and each chapter contributes to an overall understanding of major DLT issues.

We believe that progress toward understanding what comprises learning in DLT environments requires more and better concepts, information, data, methods, and theories. We sincerely hope that the content of this volume begins to meet this need and encourages expanded research and theory development in this important area.

REFERENCES

American Society for Training and Development & The Masie Center. (2001). *E-learning: "If we build it, will they come?"* Alexandria, VA: American Society for Training and Development.

Brayton, C. (2001, October 1). The learning curve: The fragmented e-learning industry rallies around a new business case: The value chain. *Internet World.* Retrieved January 30, 2002, from http://www.iw.com/magazine.php?inc= 100101/10.01.01ebusiness1.html

Bush, V. (1945). *Science: The endless frontier.* Washington, DC: United States Government Printing Office.

Ellis, R. K. (2003, November 17). E-learning trends 2003. *Learning Circuits.* Retrieved February 20, 2005, from http://www.learningcircuits.org/2003/ nov2003/trends.htm

Evans, S. (2000, May 15). Net-based training goes the distance. *The Washington Post.* Retrieved February 20, 2005, from http://www.washingtonpost.com/ac2/ wp-dyn?pagename=article&node=&contentId=A58362-2000May12

Fiore, S. M., Rubinstein, J., & Jentsch, F. (2004). Considering science and security from a broader research perspective. *International Journal of Cognitive Technology, 9,* 40–42.

Mayer, R. E. (1999). Instructional technology. In F. T. Durso, R. S. Nickerson, R. W. Schvaneveldt, S. T. Dumais, D. S. Lindsay, & M. T. H. Chi (Eds.), *Handbook of applied cognition* (pp. 551–569). Chichester, England: Wiley.

Mayer, R. E. (2001). *Multi-media learning.* Cambridge, England: Cambridge University Press.

Moe, M. T., & Blodget, H. (2000, May 23). Corporate e-learning—Feeding hungry minds (Part 4, pp. 225–290). *The knowledge web.* Study conducted by Merrill Lynch & Co. Retrieved February 25, 2004, from http://internettime.com/itime group/MOE4.PDF

Mullich, J. (2004). A second act for e-learning. *Workforce Management, 83,* 51–55.

Phillips, J., Phillips, P. P., & Zuniga, L. (2000). Evaluating the effectiveness and the return on investment of e-learning. *What Works Online: 2000, 2nd Quarter.* Retrieved February 21, 2005, from http://www.astd.org/ASTD/Resources/eval_roi_community/return.htm

Salas, E., & Fiore, S. M. (Eds.). (2004). *Team cognition: Understanding the factors that drive process and performance.* Washington, DC: American Psychological Association.

Salas, E., Kosarzycki, M. P., Burke, C. S., Fiore, S. M., & Stone, D. L. (2002). Emerging themes in distance learning research and practice: Some food for thought. *International Journal of Management Reviews, 4,* 135–153.

Sparrow, S. (2004). Blended is better. *Training and Development, 58,* 52–55.

Stokes, D. E. (1997). *Pasteur's quadrant: Basic science and technological innovation.* Washington, DC: Brookings Institution.

U.S. General Accounting Office. (2003). United States General Accounting Office report to congressional committees: Military transformation, progress and challenges for DOD's advanced distributed learning programs, February 2003 (Report No. GAO-03-393). Washington, DC: Author.

Wang, A. Y., & Newlin, M. H. (2000). Characteristics of students who enroll and succeed in Web-based psychology classes. *Journal of Educational Psychology, 92,* 137–143.

Wang, A. Y., & Newlin, M. H. (2002). Predictors of Web-student performance: The role of self-efficacy and reasons for taking an online class. *Computers in Human Behavior, 18,* 151–163.

Wisher, R. A., & Priest, A. N. (1998). Cost-effectiveness of audio teletraining for the U.S. Army National Guard. *The American Journal of Distance Education, 12,* 38–51.

I

THEORETICAL MODELS EMANATING FROM DISTRIBUTED LEARNING IN ORGANIZATIONS

2

A THEORY-BASED APPROACH FOR DESIGNING DISTRIBUTED LEARNING SYSTEMS

STEVE W. J. KOZLOWSKI AND BRADFORD S. BELL

There has been steady growth in the use of distance learning and distributed training over the past decade (Salas & Cannon-Bowers, 2001), with some estimates suggesting that nearly 80% of all companies use some form of distributed, computer-based training (Kiser, 2001). Although a variety of factors are stimulating this rapid growth in the use of distance learning and distributed training, two factors have been key in

This chapter is based on research sponsored in part by the Air Force Office of Scientific Research (Grant F49620-01-1-0283); S. W. J. Kozlowski and R. P. DeShon, principal investigators; and Battelle Scientific Services (Contract DAAH04-96-C-0086, TCN: 00156). The U.S. government is authorized to reproduce and distribute reprints for governmental purposes notwithstanding any copyright notation thereon.

The views and conclusions contained herein are those of the authors and should not be interpreted as necessarily representing the official policies or endorsements, either expressed or implied, of the Air Force Research Laboratory, the Army Research Office, or the U.S. government.

the growth of what we refer to collectively as *distributed learning systems* (DLS). One factor has been the practical benefits—lower cost, rapid deployment, and flexibility—associated with training systems that transcend space and time and enable training anytime and anywhere. Another factor has been the advances in technology and connectivity. The penetration of computer technology into all facets of the workplace, the substantial increases in computing power and speed, and the interactivity enabled by the explosive growth of the Internet have provided a ready infrastructure for delivering distributed training. Indeed, the literature on distance learning and distributed training, both popular and academic, has been dominated by discussions concerning technological innovations and cost savings (Bell & Kozlowski, 2006; Kozlowski & Bell, 2002).

As is often the case, the factors stimulating the attractiveness of DLS have a negative side effect. One consequence of the heavy emphasis on practical benefits and technology is that researchers and practitioners alike have paid far less attention to critical instructional design issues surrounding distributed learning. The purpose of such systems is to promote learning, yet the tendency is to design distributed learning around the media and supporting technologies rather than the underlying instructional goals and objectives of the training. This is not surprising given that there is currently no well-developed theoretical framework to guide training design for distributed systems (Salas, Kosarzycki, Burke, Fiore, & Stone, 2002). However, for DLS to be optimally effective, trainers and instructional designers must integrate learning models with instructional design practices (Schreiber, 1998; Welsh, Wanberg, Brown, & Simmering, 2003). It is critical, therefore, to develop a theoretical framework that can be used to guide DLS design. In the absence of such a framework, many organizations have discovered that their DLS, although practical and cost efficient, are suboptimal or even ineffective for developing critical knowledge and skills. As Hamid (2002) noted, the growing consensus is that "after the initial excitement, many e-learning initiatives have fallen short of expectations" (p. 312).

The purpose of this chapter is to present a theoretical framework to guide DLS design and enhance the effectiveness of distributed learning. The framework we develop provides theory-based principles for specifying DLS design to achieve specific instructional goals. In contrast to much of the extant literature in the areas of distributed training and distance learning, our theory views the identification of desired instructional goals and associated learning processes—not technology—as the point of departure in DLS design. We believe these goals and learning processes should drive DLS design because they elucidate the optimal instructional experience, clarify critical instructional features, and determine the technologies most appropriate for delivering the features.

DESIGNING DISTRIBUTED LEARNING SYSTEMS

Recent reviews of DLS research (Bell & Kozlowski, 2006; Welsh et al., 2003) and the DLS design process (Kozlowski & Bell, 2002), as well as the opening chapter of this book, highlight the need for a conceptual foundation that provides a solid empirical basis for the derivation of scientific principles to guide instructional design for DLS. To a substantial extent, progress in this area has been impeded by researchers' preoccupation with an important pragmatic concern: the bandwidth–cost trade-off problem. That is, much of the research is driven by an examination of the degree of bandwidth and interactivity required for distance learning or distributed training to approximate conventional instructor-led classroom training. Although we acknowledge that this is an important practical concern, its primary attention to cost and technology factors has misdirected attention away from the need for a conceptual foundation—one driven by learning processes and mechanisms, not technologies—to guide the design of DLS.

The dilemma is that elements of the technology infrastructure are already in place or anticipated (e.g., the penetration of computer technology, enhanced connectivity, intranet and Internet access), the economic logic to harness the technology for training is compelling (e.g., upward of 80% of training costs go for indirect support rather than directly to training), and the push to practice is rapidly diffusing early efforts (e.g., there are many well-publicized e-learning efforts and initiatives in industry, education, and government). Thus, the availability of flexible technology, compelling economic drivers, and benchmark practices of early adopters are shaping the emerging nature of DLS. As a consequence, distance learning and distributed training programs are often driven by technology in terms of availability and cost rather than by instructional goals linked to desired cognitive and behavioral competencies.

The availability of technology and cost factors drives the selection of delivery media. Instructional issues typically receive little or no attention in this selection process. In fact, Govindasamy (2002) noted that most learning technology vendors "deliberately distance themselves from pedagogical issues" (p. 288). Existing instructional content (e.g., manuals, lecture-based course materials), when available, is often simply mapped onto existing technology, a practice known as *repurposing*. That is, distributed learning technology choices are driven by what the organization has available, not what the training program requires. Because performance-relevant instructional goals are not the primary drivers of system design, attaining desired knowledge and skills as outcomes is more a matter of chance than intent. Moreover, there are two alternative outcomes that may be more likely. On the one hand, this technology-driven logic can yield training that is *inefficient* because it invests in more advanced technology than is necessary for delivering the desired skills. On the other hand, it can yield training that is *ineffective* because it fails to use technology with sufficient capability or bandwidth to deliver an instructional experience that develops desired knowledge and skill competencies (Govindasamy, 2002). This is, in essence, the core of the bandwidth–cost trade-off. From our perspective, the current approach can yield only trial-and-error research and practice that attempt to map the boundaries of the trade-off unsystematically. In the long run, it is likely to be a slow and costly approach.

Our position is that the best way to start to resolve this problem is to begin with a theoretical foundation that is driven by instructional goals and learning processes, not technologies. Training needs derived from the performance domain are used to identify desired instructional goals, which in turn implicate particular cognitive mechanisms and learning processes. Next, targeted cognitive mechanisms and learning processes guide the identification of instructional features that specify the type of content that should be delivered, how much immersion is desired, the necessary degree of interactivity, and how much communication bandwidth is essential. Desired instructional features then guide the selection of appropriate technologies and the design of a theoretically grounded instructional experience. Technology selection is appropriately located at the endpoint of the design process as a tool to ensure the delivery of an instructional experience that has been calibrated to fit training needs and instructional targets. The proposed approach can, in the short term, prescriptively suggest bandwidth targets that are likely to approximate the perimeter of the bandwidth–cost trade-off and, in the long term, can better focus research in an effort to more precisely map the trade-off curve. We believe that this approach will yield a more timely and cost-effective research agenda to enhance the design of DLS.

THEORETICAL FOUNDATION

We begin by developing a model that links instructional goals, desired knowledge and skill competencies, underlying learning processes and mechanisms, and necessary instructional design foci that deliver targeted skills. The model is designed to link the complexity of the instructional goal (basic to advanced knowledge and skills) to the types of instructional characteristics necessary to stimulate underlying cognitive–behavioral mechanisms to achieve the targeted instructional outcomes. It is important to note that because instructional goals and associated knowledge and skill competencies are sequenced from basic to advanced, higher level competencies subsume more fundamental knowledge and associated learning mechanisms. This model and its conceptual linkages form the theoretical core of our approach.

In the second step, we develop a typology that identifies categories of instructional features that contribute to different aspects of the design of an instructional experience. This approach is different than the more typical focus on technologies and the delivery features they possess (e.g., Noe, 1999). Our focus is not on technologies per se, although different technologies—singly or in combination—are implicated by these instructional features. Instead, the idea is to first focus on the key features that enable the design of an instructional experience. The selection of technologies becomes relevant later, when the DLS infrastructure is constructed. The central conceptual characteristic distinguishing instructional features within categories is the information–experience richness of the instructional experience (low to high). As a general rule, greater information–experience richness necessitates wider bandwidth and greater cost.

Next, we integrate the theoretical core and the instructional feature typology. This integration provides a basis for prescriptive guidance to predict how information richness along particular instructional feature dimensions is linked to accomplishing desired instructional outcomes at different levels of knowledge and skill complexity. Thus, this integrative typology links our theoretical core to desired instructional features, thereby providing a theoretical foundation for the DLS design.

Finally, we map instructional features to discrete technologies to help guide the technology selection process. Although there are many ways of delivering different instructional features, we highlight several examples of how specific technologies can be used to deliver instructional experiences of varying levels of information/experience richness. Our goal in this final section is not to provide a complete mapping of features to all available DLS technologies but, rather, to provide several illustrative examples of the capability of specific technologies to deliver a feature-rich instructional experience. This logic underlying this mapping process can be extended beyond our examples to ensure that the technology selection for the delivery of an instructional experience is a consequence of theory-driven instructional design. We believe that by calibrating DLS delivery technologies to fit instructional goals and learning requirements, our approach will deliver cost-efficient yet effective training experiences. Moreover, we also believe that by helping to identify pragmatic concerns that are least likely to be in doubt and areas that necessitate further research, our approach will guide research toward the derivation and validation of principles for guiding the design of DLS. We now develop the rationale of this approach in more detail.

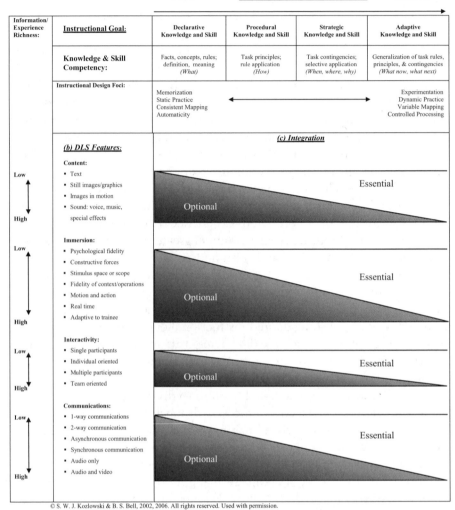

Figure 2.1. A model linking instructional objectives, trainee competencies, and instructional features. From *Enhancing the Effectiveness of Distance Learning and Distributed Training: A Theoretical Framework for the Design of Remote Learning Systems* (p. 44), by S. W. J. Kozlowski and B. S. Bell, 2002. Copyright 2002 by S. W. J. Kozlowski and B. S. Bell. Reprinted with permission.

Instructional Goals, Competencies, Learning Processes, and Instructional Design Foci

This model within the overall framework forms the theoretical core of our approach. As shown in the uppermost section of Figure 2.1, labeled *(a) Knowledge and Skill Complexity*, its foundation is provided by *instructional goals* that are sequenced on the horizontal dimension from basic to advanced knowledge and skill complexity. This developmental sequence is in conformance with contemporary theories of skill acquisition that postulate the progressive development of *knowledge and skill competencies*, from facts to principles to contingencies to generalization (Anderson, 1982; Ford & Kraiger, 1995; Kozlowski, Toney, et al., 2001). Learning processes for acquiring this progression of competencies differ qualitatively such that the acquisition of basic knowledge necessitates encoding and is memory intensive, whereas advanced knowledge and skill acquisition requires higher level self-regulatory and metacognitive processes with an emphasis on integrating cognitive and behavioral skill. As a result, the differing learning processes that underlie different instructional goals along the developmental continuum implicate different *instructional design foci*. For example, at the basic end of the continuum, instructional design needs to stimulate rehearsal strategies and memorization under consistent practice conditions, whereas at the advanced end of the continuum, instruction needs to stimulate exploration and experimentation; variability in instructional stimuli and responses; and active, controlled reflection during practice.

The most basic instructional goal in the sequence is the acquisition of declarative knowledge, which entails basic domain content. It focuses on knowledge of the definition and meaning of important domain facts, concepts, and rules (VanLehn, 1996). It represents basic domain content or knowledge of "what." Learning this competency involves repeated exposure to the relevant content, effortful attempts to encode the material into memory, and evaluation of current competency through tests of recall and retention as learning indicators and aids.

Through practice and experience, declarative knowledge begins to be proceduralized (Anderson, 1982; Ohlsson, 1987). Procedural knowledge represents understanding of "how." This process occurs with continued practice (repetition) beyond initial successes at reproducing certain behaviors. In addition, knowledge about situations, responses, and outcomes is integrated into the knowledge to form context-specific rules for application (Ford & Kraiger, 1995; Glaser, 1994). Proceduralized knowledge, therefore, can be described as a set of condition–action rules, such as "If Condition A, then Action B" (Anderson, 1983). With experience, condition–action rules are compiled or chunked together. As a result, as knowledge is proceduralized and compiled, individuals not only are better able to determine when knowledge is applicable but also are able to apply what they know more automatically and efficiently.

As knowledge and procedures continue to be compiled, more elegant task strategies emerge. Cognitive resources are freed by the internalization of behaviors, and those resources can be devoted to strategy development and self-regulation of action initiation and performance. As individuals develop strategies and a better understanding of task situations, they integrate this knowledge into more complex mental models. The mental models of experts contain diagnostic clues for detecting meaningful patterns in the learning or transfer environment (Glaser, 1989; Kraiger, Salas, & Cannon-Bowers, 1995). These richly interconnected knowledge structures allow experts to determine *when, where, and why* their knowledge applies. That is, they understand the conditions, timing, and rationale that yield effective task performance. Development of strategic knowledge requires variable practice and experimentation so that individuals can develop a complex network of structural relationships among important task concepts in the domain (Bell & Kozlowski, 2002; Kozlowski, Toney, et al., 2001).

Finally, the most advanced instructional goal is the development of adaptive knowledge and skills, which are closely tied to the development of strategic knowledge and skills. However, whereas strategies are used to react to changing circumstances in a particular task context, adaptability involves generalizing and extrapolating knowledge to novel situations or tasks (Hatano & Inagaki, 1986; Holyoak, 1991). It represents knowledge of *what is happening now* and *what one should change next* to resolve the new problem or situation. Adaptability requires metacognition, which involves processes such as analyzing the situation, monitoring and evaluating one's learning progress, and controlling how to allocate one's resources and the prioritization of activities (Flavell, 1979; Schmidt & Ford, 2003). Meta-cognition enables an individual to recognize not only when a situation has changed but also when to discontinue a problem-solving strategy that would ultimately prove unsuccessful (Larkin, 1983). Adaptability involves dynamic replanning and the ability to pull together task-relevant knowledge to create an innovative, creative, and effective task approach. The development of adaptive knowledge and skills typically occurs well into the knowledge and skill acquisition process (Kozlowski, Toney, et al., 2001). Individuals must have relatively complete mental models of the knowledge domain, and these mental models need to contain not only valid causal relationships but also error information that is gathered from variable practice and experimentation. Existing knowledge and behaviors must also be internalized because the greater the internalization, the more cognitive resources are available for executive (metacognitive) functions (Kanfer & Ackerman, 1989).

To summarize the theoretical core, we assert different instructional goals involve qualitatively different learning processes, and appropriate learning processes have to be stimulated by the DLS to accomplish the instructional goal. This provides the basic logic to guide DLS design. A fundamental aspect of the sequence of instructional goals is that *complex competencies build on the foundation of basic competencies.* From a training systems perspective, one key implication of this aspect of the model is that training for advanced instructional goals must ensure that (a) trainees possess basic domain competencies or that (b) provision has been made to target more basic competencies prior to targeting advanced ones.

Distributed Learning System Features

As we have noted, the literature on distance learning and distributed training has been dominated by a focus on technologies, with technologies then driving the form of distributed instruction. Table 2.1 catalogues the broad range of technologies that have the potential to be used in distributed learning and describes typical applications and examples. Although this approach can provide useful interventions, instructional design is ad hoc, and the technology is not tailored to deliver an instructional experience linked to a model of learning. The instructional foci derived from the model shown in Table 2.1 have the potential to be delivered in myriad ways by means of different technologies or sets of technologies. Thus, the purpose here is to look past the technologies per se and to focus instead on the kinds of instructional features—embedded in the technologies—that can be used to stimulate targeted instructional foci, thereby shaping the learning process.

Our typology of (b) *DLS Features*, appears on the left-hand side of Figure 2.1. It classifies DLS features into four primary categories that index the richness of domain content, immersion, interactivity, and communication that can be delivered by DLS. Within categories, features are organized from low to high with respect to the richness of the information or experience they can create for trainees. The first category, *content*, concerns the richness with which basic information (declarative knowledge) is delivered through the system to trainees. In its most sparse form, information is conveyed as text. Text is quite flexible and is a near-universal capability in most DLS. Additional features, such as still images and graphics, images in motion, and sound, can be added to basic text to enrich the information stream. It is important to recognize that more information is not necessarily richer information. Multimedia elements enhance learning only when they help the learner understand and make sense out of the material (e.g., Mayer & Anderson, 1992). The second category focuses on features that influence *immersion*, or sense of realism. This category concerns the extent to which the training captures key psychological characteristics of the performance domain (i.e., psychological fidelity) and, beyond that, draws trainees into the experience—that is, creates a micro- or synthetic world that captures their attention and subjects them to important contextual characteristics relevant to the performance domain (i.e., gradations of the physical fidelity of the experience; Schiflett, Elliott, Salas, & Coovert, 2004). This category is particularly important with respect to simulation design (e.g., distributed interactive simulation [DIS] and distributed mission training, DMT), because

TABLE 2.1
Distributed Learning System Technologies

System	Primary features	Examples
CD-ROM DVD	• Integrates text, graphics, animation, audio, and video. • Computer-based delivery allows trainees to interact with content by typing responses, using a joystick, or using a touch-screen monitor.	• Colorado Springs Fire Department has created digital simulations of fires on DVDs. Depending on decisions that trainees make throughout the program, the fire either gets better or worsens. • Dow Chemical places many of its training programs on CD-ROM so that employees can participate in the training where and when they want.
Interactive video	• Instruction is provided one on one to trainees via a monitor connected to a keyboard. • Trainees use the keyboard or touch the monitor to interact with the program.	• Federal Express has an interactive video curriculum that covers courses on customer etiquette, defensive driving, and delivery procedures. Employees control the content they view and where and when they participate in the training.
Web-based training	• Can allow communication between trainers and trainees and among trainees. • Online referencing. • Testing assessment. • Distribution of computer-based training. • Delivery of multimedia. • Trainees can use hyperlinks to interact with the program.	• CIGNA uses Web-based training programs to deliver training to its nurse consultants distributed around the country, many of them in rural areas. • General Electric has created Web-based environmental, safety, and health training in 17 languages to ensure compliance among its operating locations distributed around the world.
Virtual reality	• Provides trainees with a three-dimensional learning experience. • Trainees move through the simulated environment and interact with its components. • Trainees in different locations can be linked in a simulated environment.	• Ford Motor Company uses virtual reality simulations to train new employees in its Vulcan Forge unit. Employees are fitted with a head-mount display that allows them to view the virtual world and they handle tools that are the same size and weight as those that they will use on the job. The virtual environment allows employees to learn the potentially hazardous job in a safe environment.

(continued)

TABLE 2.1 *(Continued)*

System	Primary features	Examples
Intelligent tutoring systems	▪ Refers to instructional systems that utilize artificial intelligence to provide individualized instruction. ▪ Trainee performance is analyzed to provide feedback and coaching and also to generate future scenarios and instruction.	▪ The U.S. Navy uses an intelligent tutoring system in its officer tactical training. The system uses simulation and provides an automated evaluation of each student's actions. The system has enabled the program to be offered as self-study, and learners receive 10 times more hands-on experience than before.
Electronic performance support systems	▪ Computer applications that provide skills training, information access, or expert advice upon request. ▪ Often used as an employee assistance device, but can also be used as a training tool.	▪ American Express uses an Electronic Performance Support System to train its customer service accounts staff. The system helps employees to deal with problems by structuring information, coaching them, prompting for required information, and serving as a reference for information on company products and policies.
Distributed interactive simulations (DISs), synthetic task environments (STEs)	▪ Low-fidelity, PC-based simulations of real world tasks. ▪ Linked by a standard interactive protocol, dispersed simulations can be linked together to emulate teams and teams of teams performing in a real-time virtual environment or microworld.	▪ The U.S. military uses a variety of DIS and STE platforms to model team performance and conduct research on team effectiveness research (DDD, TEAM/Sim, AEDGE). As the psychological fidelity of these simulations improves, DISs and STEs are increasingly being used as basic training tools for military team effectiveness.
Distributed mission training (DMT)	▪ High-fidelity simulations of real world tasks, replicating operational equipment, procedures, and task demands. ▪ Both "real" and constructed or virtual entities create a complex and rich performance context. ▪ Linked by a standard interactive protocol, simulations located worldwide can be linked together to emulate teams and teams of teams performing in a virtual task environment.	▪ The U.S. military has experimented with a variety of DMT systems to gain experience and lessons learned for the development of this training technology. Examples include ROADRUNNER '98, SIMNET, and JEX. By allowing trainees to participate in a common, but complex and diverse battlespace, DMT systems allow the honing of high level skills, safely, and at low cost.

Note. From *Enhancing the Effectiveness of Distance Learning and Distributed Training: a Theoretical Framework for the Design of Remote Learning Systems* (Final Report; Contract No. DAAH04-96-C-0086, TCN: 00156), by S. W. J. Kozlowski and B. S. Bell, 2002, Research Triangle Park, NC: Battelle Scientific Services. Copyright 2002 by Battelle Scientific Services. Reprinted with permission.

it provides a basis to identify features that help scale the immersion potential of lower to higher fidelity synthetic task environments (STEs) and task scenarios. The presumption is that psychological fidelity in terms of central constructs, processes, and performance measures provides an essential basic foundation for learning and that gradations of physical fidelity add contextual realism that further grounds the instructional experience to important cues and contingencies present in the performance domain (Kozlowski & De-Shon, 2004).

Up to this point, the two categories of features that have been discussed are common to all instructional systems and represent important instructional design choices that shape the instructional experience. The next two categories, however, are unique to DLS in that they enable distribution of instruction by means of communication media, and they shape the nature of the distributed instructional environment by determining the type of interaction that can ensue. They are the features that make the learning experience "distributed." The category labeled *interactivity* considers characteristics that can influence the potential degree and type of interaction between remote instructors and students; among distributed student peers; and, potentially, among multiply distributed student teams or collaborative learning groups (e.g., Bouras, Philopoulos, & Tsiatsos, 2001; Collis & Smith, 1997). The potential range of interactivity is dependent on communication bandwidth, which is considered as a separate category. However, the interactivity category presents a set of design options in its own right. Given that instructors and students are distributed in space (and potentially in time), the issue here concerns the degree to which learning is centered on the individual learner in relative isolation, or whether learners are to be linked into clusters to enable teamwork or collaborative learning.

There is a growing theory and research literature indicating that training for teamwork skills—coordination, communication, and adaptability—necessitates a team context (Cannon-Bowers, Tannenbaum, Salas, & Volpe, 1995; Kozlowski, 1998; Kozlowski & Bell, 2003). Thus, instructional design for some applications of distributed learning—especially those using STEs such as DMT and DIS involving teams and teams of teams—must incorporate considerations of team interaction as it relates to training desired performance competencies. In addition, there is an emerging literature on collaborative learning suggesting that appropriate instructional supports can help learners to teach each another and that learners can learn more and better under collaborative learning conditions (e.g., O'Donnell, 1996; Rosenshine & Meister, 1995). Given the distance or potential absence of instructors, collaborative learning principles may have the potential to augment instruction and to supplement instructor guidance for DLS. How such principles could be applied would be constrained by whether students were independently distributed—necessitating remote collaboration—or whether they were distributed in cluster sites, allowing face-to-face collaborative learning.

The last category, features that influence *communication* richness, concerns the issue of communication bandwidth. Conventional face-to-face instruction places experienced instructors and students in spatial and temporal proximity. This enables the expert instructor to evaluate student learning in real time by monitoring student reaction cues (e.g., nodding vs. a puzzled face) and testing for comprehension (e.g., asking a probing question). It also allows students to share views, perspectives, and comprehension with each other. However, when students are distributed in space (and potentially in time), real-time access and processing of such latent communication cues are dependent on the bandwidth of the communication link (Guzley, Avanzino, & Bor, 2001). Also, even at its highest bandwidth (e.g., synchronous, real-time, audio–video link), latent cues and strategies for managing instruction, conversation, and exchange are degraded: Field of view is reduced, the ability to gesture is limited, facial expressions are eliminated or constrained, auditory cues are diminished, tools and artifacts are difficult to share, and shared information is delayed or decoupled from its context. On the one hand, these concerns regarding communication richness have formed the primary focus of research evaluating the effectiveness of distance learning relative to conventional face-to-face classroom instruction (e.g., Faux & Black-Hughes, 2000; Huff, 2000; Meisel & Marx, 1999; Wisher & Curnow, 1999). The essential question is, How much communication bandwidth is necessary to approximate the same instructional quality across environments? On the other hand, other literatures concerned with remote collaboration or computer-mediated communication suggest some positive aspects of lower information richness (e.g., asynchronous, time delayed, text only) that may enhance information exchange, at least for some individuals. For example, status differentials are reduced, responses can be more thoughtful, and introverted or culturally dissimilar individuals may be more likely to participate (see McGrath & Hollingshead, 1994; McKenna & Green, 2002). In addition, communication can entail more than person-to-person conversation, and production blocking can be eliminated. DLS will often necessitate information and data exchange exclusive of conversation. Thus, any way one considers the issue, communication bandwidth is an important consideration in the design of DLS.

Integrating Instructional Objectives, Competencies, and Features

Implications for DLS design that are provided by the integration of these two conceptual models are shown in the core of Figure 2.1 and labeled *(c) Integration*. Each DLS feature category is associated with a rectangular area demarked into two zones that correspond to the applicability of the feature(s) on the vertical dimension of *information/experience* richness to the targeted *instructional goal*, *competency*, and *instructional design foci* along the horizontal dimension. The key conceptual contribution is the diagonal demarking the two zones that posits the applicability of the instructional features to targeted instructional goals. The diagonal signifies the hypothesized degree of information–experience richness (i.e., bandwidth trade-off) required to achieve targeted instructional objectives. The white zone corresponds to features that are essential to meeting the desired instructional goal. The shaded zone corresponds to features that are optional, at the cost of additional technology and bandwidth. Although additional features may augment the instructional experience, they may not be necessary and may yield cost inefficiencies.

For example, when the targeted instructional goal is declarative knowledge, the diagonal references text as the primary content, psychological fidelity as the key immersion feature, single participants as the interactivity target, and one-way communication as the enabling link. In other words, the leading edge of the diagonal maps the most parsimonious, instructionally effective, and cost-efficient features that should drive the specification of delivery technologies for the targeted instructional objective. Additional features—at the cost of greater bandwidth and more advanced technological infrastructure—may augment the instructional experience, but the trade-off of cost efficiency relative to any increment in instructional effectiveness is an open question. Moving away from the leading edge of the diagonal into the shaded area suggests the potential degree of inefficiency. In contrast, when the targeted instructional goal is adaptive knowledge and skill, the leading edge of the diagonal references the highest degree of information–experience richness (and the subsumed lower level features) to accomplish the objective. That is, failure to use sufficient information–experience richness will likely yield ineffectiveness relative to achieving the targeted instructional goal.

The purpose of this model is to specify how instructional goals can be used to guide the selection of essential instructional features needed to provide an instructional experience of sufficient richness to achieve targeted objectives. Once the necessary instructional features have been identified, the next step is to select a technology system or infrastructure that can deliver the desired level of information–experience richness. We discuss this final stage of the process in the next section. The diagonal in Figure 2.1 represents the hypothesized bandwidth trade-off. It is likely that—rather than a linear diagonal—the boundary or leading edge defining the essential and optional features is a nonlinear curve. Precise specification of this curve will necessitate targeted research to test and map the boundary. However, in the interim the model can serve as a prescriptive and predictive tool for specifying cost-efficient and effective instructional features and delivery technologies for achieving particular instructional goals. We now turn our attention to the process of selecting a delivery technology that can provide the necessary instructional features.

Linking Instructional Features to Distributed Learning System Technologies

The final stage of the DLS design process involves mapping the necessary instructional features against potential delivery technologies. All too often, the selection of DLS technologies has served as the first step in the design process. The theory-based approach we advocate, however, views technology selection as an activity that concludes the DLS design process. Technology simply serves as the medium by which to deliver the instructional experience necessary to stimulate critical learning processes and develop targeted knowledge and skills. Thus, competent technology selection can occur only when one has first specified the goals of instruction and identified the level of information richness necessary on each of the four features to achieve those goals. Examples of specific technologies that can be used to achieve different levels of information–experience richness on the four distributed learning features are provided in Table 2.2.

This goal of the table is not to present a comprehensive mapping of instructional features to DLS technologies because technological combinations or variants create the potential for a vast number of unique DLS applications that can have very different capabilities. Instead, the table is designed to illustrate the level of information richness that can be achieved on each of the four critical instructional features using different types of technologies. We also highlight the specific technological features that implicate the ability of these systems to offer different levels of information richness.

If one focuses on content, one sees that the lowest level of information richness is provided by printed material, which contains only text and images. As one moves up the information richness continuum, there is Web-based text, which has the potential to include motion, and then at the highest levels there is interactive, live instruction, which combines text, images, motion, video, sound, and special effects. Because the technology uses a multimedia format there is an opportunity to present information so that it targets multiple sensory modalities (e.g., visual, verbal; Clark & Mayer, 2002; Mayer, 2001). Presenting content through multiple sensory channels can enhance learning, although it is important to avoid overload because learners have a limited cognitive capacity (Mayer, 2001; Paas, Renkl, & Sweller, 2003).

Video-based programs provide the lowest level of immersion, offering basic psychological and physical fidelity. Immersion is enhanced by programs

TABLE 2.2
Illustrative Examples Linking Distributed Learning System Features
to Specific Technologies

Level of information/ experience richness	Distributed learning features			
	Content	Immersion	Interactivity	Communication
Low	Printed material (text, images)	Video (basic psychological and physical fidelity)	CD-ROM (individual oriented)	Web-based text presentation (1-way, asynchronous communication)
Medium	Web-based text presentation (text, images, motion)	Web-based interactive media program (psychological fidelity, potential for human–computer interaction)	Web-based program with group support systems (trainee interaction)	Online learning communities (text-based, 2-way, synchronous communication)
High	Interactive, live instruction (text, images, motion, video, sound, special effects)	Virtual reality (high psychological fidelity, motion, action, adaptive)	Distributed interactive simulation (multiple participant/ team oriented)	Video conferencing (video-based, 2-way, synchronous communication)

such as Web-based interactive media programs, which create interactive content, but there is a significant jump in the level of immersion offered by virtual reality programs. Virtual reality offers a three-dimensional representation of the environment and provides an opportunity for realistic human–human or human–machine interactions. The result is high levels of both psychological and physical fidelity. With respect to interactivity, at the high end of the continuum is DIS, which is a PC-based, networked simulation that allows individuals to participate in hands-on exercises with other participants or teams. The programs typically simulate real-world environments and allow real-time communications and interaction, although the level of immersion is typically low because of a two-dimensional representation of the environment (Schiflett et al., 2004). In Web-based environments, moderate levels of interactivity can be achieved by incorporating group support systems—such as chat, bulletin boards, or Webcams—

that increase the level of interactivity over individually oriented programs, such as CD-ROM programs.

Many Web-based programs use one-way, asynchronous communication because information is being provided to the learner, but the learner does not have an opportunity to communicate with the instructional system or other learners. To provide an opportunity for social learning in Web-based environments one can use online learning communities that allow learners to communicate with one another through text-based messaging (Johnson & Huff, 2000). When social learning is critical for achieving desired instructional goals, as it often is in team-based learning environments, more information-rich communication technologies, such as video conferencing, can be used. Video conferencing offers not only an opportunity for learners to communicate verbally but also an opportunity to send visual signals, which may be important when visual cues are critical to learning or task performance.

Although the previous examples consider the distributed learning features individually, it is important to recognize that these features combine to create an instructional experience, and it is likely that the level of information richness required on one feature is not entirely independent of that required on other features. For example, if a high level of immersion is necessary for learning, then the content will likely need to be presented through multiple sensory modalities. Similarly, if a high level of interactivity is desired, then it is also likely that two-way, synchronous communication systems will need to be used. Thus, it is important to consider these interconnections and to use a technology that can deliver the level of information richness necessary in all categories. This may necessitate the blending of different technologies to gain access to necessary features.

CONCLUSION AND IMPLICATIONS

The growing use of distributed, technology-based training systems by organizations is both exciting and potentially problematic. Recent advances in technology have facilitated the development of a host of new and innovative training tools, such as virtual reality and interactive media, and have allowed organizations to devise training programs that transcend boundaries of space and time. At the same time, however, both research and practice surrounding DLS have been driven largely by pragmatic concerns, such as the bandwidth–cost trade-off, and many critical instructional issues surrounding DLS have received little or no attention. In effect, the availability of flexible technology, compelling economic drivers, and benchmark practices of early adopters have shaped the emerging nature of DLS. As a consequence, there currently exists the potential for organizations to develop DLS that are ineffective for developing employee knowledge and skills. At best, organizations are likely to underutilize the instructional capabilities of distributed learning and, therefore, greatly limit their potential return on investment.

We have addressed this problem in this chapter by developing a theoretical framework that can be used to guide the design of DLS. In contrast to most of the extant literature, the framework is driven by instructional goals and learning processes, not technologies. We argue that DLS design should begin with the identification of desired instructional goals to identify specific cognitive mechanisms and learning processes. Targeted cognitive mechanisms and learning processes then guide the identification of the instructional features and content necessary to stimulate knowledge and skill development. Finally, desired instructional features guide the selection of appropriate technologies and the design of a theoretically grounded instructional experience. We believe this approach to DLS design will ensure the delivery of an instructional experience that has been calibrated to fit training needs and instructional targets, thereby producing a more effective and efficient DLS.

Implications for Future Research and Practice

Research Implications

Given the limitations associated with the logic that currently drives DLS design, we believe the theoretical framework described in this chapter provides instructional designers and trainers with a valuable prescriptive tool. The theoretical framework provides a conceptual foundation for principles that can provide guidance at critical stages of the DLS design process. Nevertheless, the framework is preliminary, and it is important to conduct research to validate, evaluate, and refine it. Empirical work is needed to validate the proposed linkages between instructional goals, instructional design foci, and technology features; to evaluate how the fit between these conceptual dimensions influences DLS effectiveness; and to refine the framework and its underlying principles.

One potential area of research focus in this regard is the leading edge demarking the boundary between essential and optional instructional features given a particular instructional goal and associated learning processes illustrated in Figure 2.1. Although the conceptual mapping represents the boundary as a linear diagonal, differences in information richness across the DLS features are not likely to exhibit smooth linearity in practice. Instead, it is more likely that specific DLS features will vary in their incremental contribution to information richness; some will add much, whereas others may add relatively little at any particular point along the knowledge and skill complexity continuum. Thus, the leading edge is more likely to be represented by a curve, one with discontinuities for particular DLS features.

We believe that in the absence of precise mapping data, the linear assumption inherent in the model is reasonable. However, the leading edge represents the cost–bandwidth trade-off and, to the extent to which one is interested in maximizing impact while minimizing cost, the boundary needs to be more precisely mapped for different DLS features. Inherent in this process is the need for research to provide a more precise evaluation and cataloguing of the instructional information–experience richness of different technologies. Research is also needed to explore how information richness may interface with other characteristics that define the instructional experience. For example, some researchers have focused attention on issues such as cognitive load or information processing (Clark & Mayer, 2002; Mayer, 2001; Paas et al., 2003). It is likely that information richness has implications for information processing and the cognitive load of trainees in that greater information richness is likely to necessitate more information processing, placing a larger cognitive load on the trainee (Kalyuga, Chandler, & Sweller, 1999). Researchers should also examine how different strategies, such as segmenting (allowing time between segments of material) or synchronizing (present corresponding visual and verbal information simultaneously), can be used to reduce cognitive load in information-rich learning environments (e.g., Kalyuga et al., 1999; Mayer & Moreno, 2003).

In the interim, however, we believe the model is a valuable prescriptive tool for specifying cost-efficient and effective instructional features and delivery technologies for achieving particular instructional goals. The theoretical framework we have developed can, in the short term, help guide distributed learning practice and, in the long term, stimulate a focused research agenda that will produce empirically grounded scientific principles to guide DLS design and ensure DLS effectiveness and efficiency.

Research Extensions

Beyond the focus of this model—integrating instructional goals, learning processes, and the design of DLS technologies—other theoretical issues are relevant to enhancing DLS design and thus are deserving of further consideration. For example, one set of issues that are particularly relevant concerns the integration of instructional supports that can be embedded in DLS design to further enhance the instructional experience. Some of these instructional supports are similar to those used in traditional learning environments (e.g., feedback), but the way these instructional supports are designed and implemented may be influenced by the unique characteristics of distributed learning environments. Hamid (2002), noted, for example,

> In an e-learning situation, a student is prone to frustration because of the technical skills required, the isolation, and because an online class lacks the built-in conventions. User frustration can be minimized

through embedding support and feedback features such as chat rooms, active links, and perhaps by providing a time management system. (pp. 314–315)

Parush, Hamm, and Shtub (2002) considered metacognitive issues in the context of distributed learning, suggesting that it is important to build in functions that can support or enhance metacognitive activities. They added a learning history function in their study that facilitated learners' ability to review and evaluate past performance. The issue of metacognition in synthetic task environments also was highlighted by Fiore, Cuevas, Scielzo, and Salas (2002), who focused on the importance of metacognition for training individuals for distributed mission teams. As another example of an instructional support strategy, work by Paas (e.g., Paas & Van Merriënboer, 1994) has considered the use of "worked examples" in computer-based training to reduce the level of cognitive load experienced by trainees.

Our own work in this area of providing instructional supports in technology-based training has focused on learning processes and how the focus and quality of self-regulation can be leveraged by means of instructional design and supports (Kozlowski, Toney, et al., 2001) to prompt active learning (Smith, Ford, & Kozlowski, 1997). Some of the more effective active learning tools include the use of mastery-oriented versus performance-oriented goals to prompt more effective learning and adaptation (Kozlowski, Gully, et al., 2001); prospective adaptive guidance that guides the learner to make appropriate choices about what to study and practice given current levels of learning (Bell & Kozlowski, 2002); and the synergistic combination of instructional, motivational, and emotional control elements that prompt more effective self-regulation and learning in the open, learner-controlled environment that typifies technology-based and distributed training (Bell & Kozlowski, 2003). The point is that the area of instructional supports is wide open for theory development and research, and it is an important adjunct to the basic theoretical foundation we have developed in the chapter. The next step in our systematic research effort will be to integrate it with the framework presented in this chapter.

Implications for Practice

Influencing the practice of DLS design is the target of our approach, with principles to guide practice falling directly from our theoretical framework. Thus, the basic application of the model begins with the specification of desired instructional goals, targeted knowledge and skill competencies, and associated learning processes that then indicate the types of instructional foci or experiences needed to develop the targeted skills and the sets of technologies that can deliver a corresponding instructional experience.

The application of this approach clearly will necessitate a multidisciplinary effort. Organizations or training design firms will need to use the services of instructional designers, educational psychologists, cognitive psychologists, and other specialists expert in the *science of learning* who are working in partnership with computer programmers, Web designers, and other technology and media specialists expert in the *art of creating an experience*. There is a pressing need for more cross-disciplinary interaction; achieving a balance between these design foci is critical.

Finally, we believe that those developing return-on-investment models will need to consider the effectiveness of distributed learning from an instructional standpoint. That is, to what extent does a DLS deliver targeted knowledge and skill competencies? The dominant focus on operating costs has produced what appear to be large return-on-investment estimates, but if learning is not considered then it is difficult to determine whether the program is really having the desired effect. This evolution of program evaluation is necessary to further shift attention to instructional issues in this field.

Conclusion

In this chapter, we have developed a theoretical framework that can be used to guide future research and practice surrounding the development, design, and use of DLS. Given the lack of existing theory and the inadequacies of current research, the framework provides a foundation for a research agenda that is focused on the development of an elaborated set of scientific principles to guide DLS design and to address important theoretical and pragmatic concerns. Although there is no question that distributed learning holds the potential to enhance training and organizational effectiveness, a theoretically grounded approach to DLS design is needed if this potential is to be realized. We hope that this chapter stimulates efforts to elaborate our approach.

REFERENCES

Anderson, J. R. (1982). The acquisition of cognitive skill. *Psychological Review*, 89, 369–406.

Anderson, J. R. (1983). *The architecture of cognition*. Cambridge, MA: Harvard University Press.

Bell, B. S., & Kozlowski, S. W. J. (2002). Adaptive guidance: Enhancing self-regulation, knowledge, and performance in technology-based training. *Personnel Psychology*, 55, 267–307.

Bell, B. S., & Kozlowski, S. W. J. (2003, April). An examination of the instructional, motivational, and emotional elements of active learning. In B. S. Bell & S. W. J. Kozlowski (Chairs), *Active learning: Critical elements, instructional supports, and learning processes.* Symposium conducted at the 18th annual conference of the Society for Industrial and Organizational Psychology, Orlando, FL.

Bell, B. S., & Kozlowski, S. W. J. (2006). *Distributed learning system design: A new approach and an agenda for future research.* Center for Advanced Human Resource Studies Working Paper Series (CAHRS Working Paper Series, (No. 06-07). Ithaca, NY: CAHRS.

Bouras, C., Philopoulos, A., & Tsiatsos, T. (2001). E-learning through distributed virtual environments. *Journal of Network and Computer Applications, 24,* 175–199.

Cannon-Bowers, J. A., Tannenbaum, S. I., Salas, E., & Volpe, C. E. (1995). Defining team competencies and establishing team training requirements. In R. Guzzo & E. Salas (Eds.), *Team effectiveness and decision making in organizations* (pp. 333–380). San Francisco: Jossey-Bass.

Clark, R. C., & Mayer, R. E. (2002). *E-learning and the science of instruction: Proven guidelines for consumers and designers of multimedia learning.* San Francisco: Jossey-Bass.

Collis, B., & Smith, C. (1997). Desktop multimedia environments to support collaborative distance learning. *Instructional Science, 25,* 433–462.

Faux, T. L., & Black-Hughes, C. (2000). A comparison of the Internet versus lectures to teach social work history. *Research on Social Work Practice, 10,* 454–466.

Fiore, S. M., Cuevas, H. M., Scielzo, S., & Salas, E. (2002). Training individuals for distributed teams: Cognitively diagnostic assessment for distributed mission research. *Computers in Human Behavior, 18,* 729–744.

Flavell, J. H. (1979). Metacognition and cognitive monitoring: A new area of cognitive-developmental inquiry. *American Psychologist, 34,* 906–911.

Ford, J. K., & Kraiger, K. (1995). The application of cognitive constructs and principles to the instructional systems model of training: Implications for needs assessment, design, and transfer. In C. L. Cooper & I. T. Robertson (Eds.), *International review of industrial and organizational psychology* (Vol. 10, pp. 1–48). New York: Wiley.

Glaser, R. (1989). Expertise in learning: How do we think about instructional processes now that we have discovered knowledge structures? In D. Klahr & K. Kotovsky (Eds.), *Complex information processing: The impact of Herbert A. Simon* (pp. 269–282). Hillsdale, NJ: Erlbaum.

Glaser, R. (1994). Learning theory and instruction. In G. d'Ydewalle, P. Eelen, & P. Bertelson (Eds.), *International perspectives on psychological science: Vol. 2, The state of the art* (pp. 341–357). Hove, England: Erlbaum.

Govindasamy, T. (2002). Successful implementation of e-learning: Pedagogical considerations. *The Internet and Higher Education, 4,* 287–299.

Guzley, R. M., Avanzino, S., & Bor, A. (2001). Simulated computer-mediated/ video-interactive distance learning: A test of motivation, interaction satisfaction, delivery, learning & perceived effectiveness. *Journal of Computer-Mediated Communication, 6(3)*. Retrieved December, 5, 2006, from http://jcmc.indiana. edu/vol6/issue3/guzley.html

Hamid, A. A. (2002). e-Learning: Is it the "e" or the learning that matters? *Internet and Higher Education, 4*, 311–316.

Hatano, G., & Inagaki, K. (1986). Two courses of expertise. In H. Stevenson, H. Azuma, & K. Hatuka (Eds.), *Child development and education in Japan* (pp. 262–272). San Francisco: Freeman.

Holyoak, K. J. (1991). Symbolic connectionism: Toward third-generation theories of expertise. In K. A. Ericsson & J. Smith (Eds.), *Toward a general theory of expertise: Prospects and limits* (pp. 301–355). Cambridge, England: Cambridge University Press.

Huff, M. T. (2000). A comparison study of live instruction versus interactive television for teaching MSW students critical thinking skills. *Research on Social Work Practice, 10*, 400–416.

Johnson, M. M., & Huff, M. T. (2000). Students' use of computer-mediated communication in a distance education course. *Research on Social Work Practice, 10*, 519–532.

Kalyuga, S., Chandler, P., & Sweller, J. (1999). Managing split-attention and redundancy in multimedia instruction. *Applied Cognitive Psychology, 13*, 351–371.

Kanfer, R., & Ackerman, P. L. (1989). Motivation and cognitive abilities: An integrative/aptitude-treatment interaction approach to skill acquisition. *Journal of Applied Psychology, 74*, 657–690.

Kiser, K. (2001, October). *State of the industry 2001*. Minneapolis, MN: Online Learning Magazine. Retrieved February 1, 2002, from http://www.online learningmag.com/onlinelearning/images/pdf/2001state_of_industry.pdf

Kozlowski, S. W. J. (1998). Training and developing adaptive teams: Theory, principles, and research. In J. A. Cannon-Bowers & E. Salas (Eds.), *Decision making under stress: Implications for training and simulation* (pp. 115–153). Washington, DC: American Psychological Association.

Kozlowski, S. W. J., & Bell, B. B. (2002). *Enhancing the effectiveness of distance learning and distributed training: A theoretical framework for the design of remote learning systems* (Final Report, Contract No. DAAH04-96-C-0086, TCN: 00156). Research Triangle Park, NC: Battelle Scientific Services.

Kozlowski, S. W. J., & Bell, B. S. (2003). Work groups and teams in organizations. In W. C. Borman, D. R. Ilgen, & R. J. Klimoski (Eds.), *Handbook of psychology: Industrial and organizational psychology* (Vol. 12, pp. 333–375). New York: Wiley.

Kozlowski, S. W. J., & DeShon, R. P. (2004). A psychological fidelity approach to simulation-based training: Theory, research, and principles. In E. Salas, L. R. Elliott, S. G. Schflett, & M. D. Coovert (Eds.), *Scaled worlds: Development, validation, and applications* (pp. 75–99). Burlington, VT: Ashgate.

Kozlowski, S. W. J., Gully, S. M., Brown, K. G., Salas, E., Smith, E. A., & Nason, E. R. (2001). Effects of training goals and goal orientation traits on multi-dimensional training outcomes and performance adaptability. *Organizational Behavior and Human Decision Processes, 85,* 1–31.

Kozlowski, S. W. J., Toney, R. J., Mullins, M. E., Weissbein, D. A., Brown, K. G., & Bell, B. S. (2001). Developing adaptability: A theory for the design of integrated-embedded training systems. In E. Salas (Ed.), *Advances in human performance and cognitive engineering research* (Vol. 1, pp. 59–123). New York: JAI Press.

Kraiger, K., Salas, E., & Cannon-Bowers, J. A. (1995). Cognitively-based measures of learning during training. *Human Factors, 37,* 1–13.

Larkin, J. H. (1983). The role of problem representation in physics. In D. Gentner & A. L. Stevens (Eds.), *Mental models* (pp. 75–98). Hillsdale, NJ: Erlbaum.

Mayer, R. E. (2001). *Multi-media learning.* Cambridge, England: Cambridge University Press.

Mayer, R. E., & Anderson, R. B. (1992). The instructive animation: Helping students build connections between words and pictures in multimedia learning. *Journal of Educational Psychology, 84,* 444–452.

Mayer, R. E., & Moreno, R. (2003). Nine ways to reduce cognitive load in multimedia learning. *Educational Psychologist, 38,* 43–52.

McGrath, J. E., & Hollingshead, A. B. (1994). *Groups interacting with technology.* Thousand Oaks, CA: Sage.

McKenna, K. Y. A., & Green, A. S. (2002). Virtual group dynamics. *Group Dynamics: Theory, Research, and Practice, 6,* 116–127.

Meisel, S., & Marx, B. (1999). Screen to screen versus face to face: Experiencing the difference in management education. *Journal of Management Education, 23,* 719–732.

Noe, R. A. (1999). *Employee training and development.* Burr Ridge, IL: McGraw-Hill.

O'Donnell, A. M. (1996). Effects of explicit incentives on scripted and unscripted cooperation. *Journal of Educational Psychology, 88,* 74–86.

Ohlsson, S. (1987). Truth versus appropriateness: Relating declarative to procedural knowledge. In D. Klahr, P. Langley, & R. Neches (Eds.), *Production system models of learning and development* (pp. 287–327). Cambridge, MA: MIT Press.

Paas, F., Renkl, A., & Sweller, J. (2003). Cognitive load theory and instructional design: Recent developments. *Educational Psychologist, 38,* 1–4.

Paas, F. G. W. C., & Van Merriënboer, J. J. G. (1994). Variability of worked examples and transfer of geometrical problem-solving skills: A cognitive-load approach. *Journal of Educational Psychology, 86,* 122–133.

Parush, A., Hamm, H., & Shtub, A. (2002). Learning histories in simulation-based teaching: The effects on self-learning and transfer. *Computers & Education, 39,* 319–332.

Rosenshine, B., & Meister, C. (1995). Direct instruction. In L. W. Anderson (Ed.), *International encyclopedia of teaching and teacher education* (2nd ed., pp. 143–149). Oxford, England: Pergamon.

Salas, E., & Cannon-Bowers, J. A. (2001). The science of training: A decade of progress. *Annual Review of Psychology, 52,* 471–499.

Salas, E., Kosarzycki, M. P., Burke, C. S., Fiore, S. M., & Stone, D. L. (2002). Emerging themes in distance learning research and practice: Some food for thought. *International Journal of Management Reviews, 4,* 135–153.

Schiflett, S. G., Elliott, L. R., Salas, E., & Coovert, M. D. (Eds.). (2004). *Scaled worlds: Development, validation, and application.* Surrey, England: Ashgate.

Schmidt, A. M., & Ford, J. K. (2003). Learning within a learner control training environment: The interactive effects of goal orientation and metacognitive instruction on learning outcomes. *Personnel Psychology, 56,* 405–429.

Schreiber, D. A. (1998). Organizational technology and its impact on distance training. In D. A. Schreiber & Z. L. Berge (Eds.), *Distance training: How innovative organizations are using technology to maximize learning and meet business objectives* (pp. 37–65). San Francisco: Jossey-Bass.

Smith, E. M., Ford, J. K., & Kozlowski, S. W. J. (1997). Building adaptive expertise: Implications for training design. In M. A. Quinones & A. Dudda (Eds.), *Training for a rapidly changing workplace: Applications of psychological research* (pp. 89–118). Washington, DC: American Psychological Association.

VanLehn, K. (1996). Cognitive skill acquisition. *Annual Review of Psychology, 47,* 513–539.

Welsh, E. T., Wanberg, C. R., Brown, K. G., & Simmering, M. J. (2003). E-learning: Emerging uses, empirical results and future directions. *International Journal of Training and Development, 7,* 245–258.

Wisher, R. A., & Curnow, C. K. (1999). Perceptions and effects of image transmissions during Internet-based training. *The American Journal of Distance Education, 13,* 37–51.

3

APPLYING A SOCIAL CAPITAL PERSPECTIVE TO THE EVALUATION OF DISTANCE TRAINING

KENNETH G. BROWN AND MARK E. VAN BUREN

A number of published reviews have addressed the relative effectiveness of different types of training delivery technology, including comparisons between distance training by means of the Internet (or corporate intranet) and more traditional face-to-face training. These reviews generally conclude that there are no significant differences in reactions and learning across delivery options, provided the training is designed similarly in other respects (Clark, 1994; Kosarzycki, Salas, DeRouin, & Fiore, 2003; Russell, 2001; Welsh, Wanberg, Brown, & Simmering, 2003). Despite this finding, limitations in the research suggest that it would be premature to conclude that it does not matter whether training in organizations is conducted at a distance or face to face.

The research covered by these reviews typically has compared learner reactions and learning outcomes across various delivery technologies; for example, do learners who receive instruction by means of some form of technology indicate the same level of satisfaction and perform as well on knowledge tests as learners who receive instruction from a person in a face-to-face setting? A close examination of this research reveals two important limitations to a full understanding of the effect of distance training (compared with face-to-face training) in work organizations.

The first limitation is that this area of research has primarily focused on individual reactions and learning, thus ignoring a number of other potential outcomes.[1] In particular, training may influence other individual-level outcomes, such as trainees' attitudes toward the organization and relationships with other employees. This possibility has been, at least in part, captured by the concept of affective learning outcomes (Kraiger, Ford, & Salas, 1993). However, affective learning outcomes as described in the existing literature focus on individual-level attitudes and motivation and do not typically consider individual constructs that relate to relationship-building or higher level constructs such as the network of social relationships in an organization. We believe that this is an important oversight and that group- and organizational-level outcomes may be affected by training and, in particular, the choice of delivery technology.

The second limitation is that research in this area is often atheoretical. Many studies about delivery technologies have asked a somewhat simplistic question: Which technology is better? This research often examines differences in learning across different delivery technologies but does little to explain why differences occur, if they occur at all (Clark, 1994; Welsh et al., 2003). We believe that greater use of theory is needed to explain why delivery technology does (or does not) make a difference. As part of this effort, we strive in this chapter to provide a relatively balanced answer to the question of which technology is better by answering with: It depends on what outcome you are hoping to achieve.

In this chapter, we argue that the criteria used to evaluate training, particularly when distance training is being compared with face-to-face training, should be expanded. More specifically, we use social capital theory to suggest that organizational-level outcomes may be influenced by training characteristics, including the choice of delivery medium. Using social capital as a starting point, we develop a conceptual framework for researchers interested in studying the effects of training at the organizational level of analysis. Most relevant to the purpose of this volume, the framework can guide both theoretical and practical research on the possible effects of shifting training from traditional face-to-face instruction to distance training. The propositions that follow from the framework are unique in the training literature in both their focus on relationships and social processes, which are often ignored in this area, and their emphasis on organizational-level outcomes.

---

[1] This criticism is not limited to research on distance training; training research generally focuses on a limited range of individual-level outcomes (Feldman, 1989; Kozlowski, Brown, Weissbein, Cannon-Bowers, & Salas, 2000).

This chapter is organized as follows: First, we review social capital theory to establish the importance of social processes as they relate to learning and performance in organizations. Second, we explore connections between the social capital concept and existing training research and present propositions. Third, we review research on the use of technology for communications along with propositions about the effect of delivering training via distance on the development of social capital. Finally, we offer a discussion that raises a number of issues to consider in future research.

SOCIAL CAPITAL

The fundamental premise of the concept of social capital is that the goodwill others feel toward us has value (Adler & Kwon, 2002). As with physical capital (i.e., manufacturing equipment) and human capital (i.e., skilled workers), social capital facilitates productive activity. Goodwill has value because it facilitates the flow of information and influence among people. Although social capital can be defined at the individual (e.g., Morrison, 2002), organizational (e.g., Adler & Kwon, 2002), and societal levels (e.g., Putnam, 1995), our focus is at the organizational level, where social capital has been demonstrated to provide competitive advantage for organizations (Florin, Lubatkin, & Schulze, 2003; Pennings & Lee, 1998; Tsai & Ghoshal, 1998).

Before we provide a formal definition of *social capital*, it may be useful to illustrate its value. To do so, we offer the following hypothetical example. Because of an established relationship, a senior manager receives a call about an impending new product release from a friend who works for a competitor. This manager immediately calls other managers in the company and because of the quality of their relationships, easily convinces them to cancel their weekend plans and meet to discuss how to react to this news. A sense of solidarity among the managers expedites changes to their organization's product mix and advertising strategy in response to the competitor's product release.

In this example, the organization's response to a change in its competitive environment is expedient because of the goodwill that exists between one of its managers and a person external to the organization, and among the managers as a group. In short, the organization benefits from social relationships that exist within the organization and between its employees and people outside the organization (for additional examples, see Adler & Kwon, 2002; Coleman, 1988). As this example demonstrates, social capital is actually an umbrella concept that integrates benefits of positive social relations discussed in other areas of research, such as social network structure (Burt, 1992), trust (Tyler & Kramer, 1996), organizational citizenship behavior (Podsakoff, MacKenzie, Paine, & Bachrach, 2000), job embed-dedness (Mitchell & Lee, 2001), and cohesion (Beal, Cohen, Burke, & McLendon, 2003). The expansiveness of the concept explains much of its appeal, but it is also the source of confusion. For the purpose of developing propositions about the effects of training and technology on social capital, we define social capital in more detail in the next section.

Forms and Dimensions

Recent treatments of social capital in the management literature have distinguished forms (internal and external; Adler & Kwon, 2002) and dimen-sions of social capital (structural, relational, and cognitive; Nahapiet & Ghoshal, 1998). These distinctions are reviewed next.

Forms

Adler and Kwon (2002) categorized most definitions of social capital into two broad forms: (a) external and (b) internal. These two definitions and approaches are reviewed briefly next. In addition, benefits and drawbacks of each form of social capital are reviewed.

External social capital focuses on social ties that bridge group members with other people external to their immediate social group. Definitions from this perspective include Portes's (1998)—"the ability of actors to secure benefits by virtue of membership in social networks or other social structure" (p. 6)—and Burt's (1992): "friends, colleagues, and more general contacts through whom you receive opportunities to use your financial and human capital" (p. 119). In these cases, social capital refers to information and influence that accrue to people and organizations that have social connec-tions that others do not have. For example, a university whose staff have social ties to staff at an accrediting agency may have an easier time with accreditation than a university that does not have such ties.

External social capital has benefits and drawbacks. The benefits, as previously suggested, include access to information and resources that would otherwise be unavailable. By extension, individuals and groups with these ties gain power and influence relative to other individuals and groups who do not have these ties. A commonly cited drawback of external social capital is the time that it takes to establish and maintain social relationships (Adler & Kwon, 2002). Relationships require maintenance in the form of sustained contact, which takes away time from other tasks and activities (Leana & Van Buren, 1999).

Internal social capital focuses on social ties that bond group members to each other within a social group. Definitions from this perspective include Fukuyama's (1995)—"the ability of people to work together for common purpose in groups and organizations" (p. 10)—and Putnam (1995): "features of social organization such as networks, norms, and social trust that facilitate coordination and cooperation for mutual benefit" (p. 67). In these cases, social capital refers to the solidarity or cohesion that is felt among people within a closely connected group. For example, a university with senior officials in each of its colleges who trust one another may be better able to cooperate in a time of fiscal crisis compared with a university in which such trusting relationships do not exist.

Internal social capital also has benefits and drawbacks. The benefits include information exchange within the organization, cohesion that facilitates compliance with group norms, and collaboration toward accomplishing group goals. In recent research, these benefits are assumed to be the causal mechanisms underlying the positive effects of social capital (Fischer & Pollock, 2004; Tsai & Ghoshal, 1998). The primary drawback of internal social capital is insularity from high levels of cohesion, which may limit constructive conflict and innovation (Adler & Kwon, 2002; Leana & Van Buren, 1999).

Dimensions

Nahapiet and Ghoshal (1998) described social capital along three dimensions: (a) structural, (b) relational, and (c) cognitive. The *structural dimension* refers to the relationships or network ties among actors. It is the most basic dimension, as relationships among people are a necessary precursor to the use of those relationships for information and/or influence. The *relational dimension* refers to the nature of the relationships, most notably the degree to which they are characterized by trust and norms for reciprocity. The *cognitive dimension* refers to shared paradigms that facilitate common understanding and collective action. Along with the relational dimension, the cognitive dimension of social capital addresses what Leana and Van Buren (1999) referred to as *associability*, which is the willingness of employees to subordinate individual goals for the good of the organization. This willingness is important because it helps ensure that an employee's relationships (the structural dimension) will be leveraged to the benefit of the organization (as opposed to solely for the benefit of the employee). From this perspective, the structural dimension of social capital describes relationships that could benefit the organization, and the relational and cognitive dimensions describe conditions under which employees are likely to use those relationships for the organization's benefit.

In a recent empirical study, Tsai and Ghoshal (1998) examined the relationships among these three dimensions of social capital and their effects on resource exchange among business units within a large firm. They focused on social ties as a measure of the structural dimension, trust as a measure of the relational dimension, and shared vision as a measure of the cognitive dimension. Social ties between business units and trust predicted resource exchange, which was operationalized as the provision of valued information, service, and support. Shared vision influenced resource exchange by means of increases in trust. Thus, this study demonstrated that each dimension of social capital is useful to organizations because it facilitates resource exchange.

Summary

The concept of social capital argues that certain relationships have value and can benefit organizations because they facilitate the flow of information and influence. Social capital can be conceptualized at different levels and can be characterized in two distinct forms (internal and external) and as having three distinct dimensions (structural, relational, and cognitive). In the following section, we address the degree to which training can influence the dimensions of social capital in organizations. To keep the number of propositions manageable, we do not formally present propositions for external social capital, although many of the points that follow are applicable to both forms of social capital. This issue is addressed in the Discussion section.

TRAINING AND SOCIAL CAPITAL

Training has historically had as its primary concern the development of human capital. *Human capital* refers to people and their ability to be economically productive (Coleman, 1988). The purpose of training, after all, is to develop employee knowledge and skills so that employees are better able to perform their jobs. Of course, training can have many different objectives, and any particular training program should be evaluated on the basis of those objectives (Goldstein & Ford, 2002; Noe, 2005). For example, some training programs have an objective to improve or otherwise alter employees' attitudes, and in those instances the trainees' attitudes should be evaluated. Even from this perspective, prior training literature does not typically address the degree to which ancillary and perhaps unanticipated outcomes may arise from training (Whiting & Dreher, 2006). In that regard, Coleman's (1988) classic work argues for the importance of considering the impact that any intervention may have on social processes within organizations.

What is currently known about the effect of training on the social processes subsumed under the concept of social capital? The answer is, unfortunately, very little. Discussions of the concept of social capital in the context of human resources practices have ignored the role that training might play (Leana & Van Buren, 1999; Marsden, 2001). The key point we raise in this section is that training can affect the structural, relational, and cognitive dimensions of social capital. The measures Tsai and Ghoshal (1998) used—social ties, trust, and shared vision—are used here, along with reciprocity norms, to develop testable propositions about which training characteristics are most likely to influence these dimensions of social capital. Training characteristics that are considered in this section include the participants (i.e., who is trained?) and the training methods (i.e., what is trained, and how?). We discuss the influence of training technology (in particular, distance training by computer or face-to-face instruction) in the next section. Because of space limitations in this chapter, the propositions we offer are intended to be illustrative rather than exhaustive.

The Structural Dimension: Creating Social Ties

Training offers one means to create relationships that would not exist otherwise. In short, training provides an opportunity for people to meet and interact. Such interaction need not be limited to members of immediate work groups; organizations can invite employees across functional areas of the organization and from various levels of management.[2] Thus, organizations can use training to foster network ties and create a denser social network. The first training characteristic that determines the extent to which training will influence network density is *overall breadth of participation*. Organizations vary in the degree to which they offer training to all employees or select groups of employees, such as front-line employees or managers (Sugrue, 2003). In general, organizations that bring a greater percentage of their workforce through training programs should offer more opportunities for relationship development than organizations that train only a few select employees.

> PROPOSITION 1: Organizations that involve larger percentages of their employees in training will have denser social networks than organizations that involve smaller percentages of their employees in training.

Of course, it is unlikely that all training is created equal with regard to fostering relationships. We believe that the timing of the training matters as well. More specifically, we argue that training that occurs during employee role transitions, when employees are most open to support, is most likely to create new relationships. Once established, habits drive information-

[2]Organizations can also invite suppliers, contractors, and customers to training, but this is related to the creation of external social capital, which we have set aside for now to keep the number of propositions manageable.

seeking and decision making by individuals in work groups (Gersick & Hackman, 1990). When employees are moved into a new role and work group, they are likely to refrain from powerful habits, at least temporarily, that constrain their social interaction and prevent them from interacting with new people and developing new relationships. Once they settle into a position and work group, however, their interaction patterns once again become entrenched and less prone to change. As a result, employees are less open to relationship development when it is offered at other points in their careers.

Prevalent training programs that occur at career transition stages include orientation programs (offered when an employee starts work with a new organization) and introductory supervisory training and leadership development programs (offered with promotion into a new role). At these points in time, employees are undergoing changes in their work-related identities and social networks (see, e.g., Hill, 1992), and they should be more receptive to training that enables them to cultivate new relationships, particularly with peers going through similar transitions.

> PROPOSITION 2: Organizations that provide more training during role transitions (entry and promotions) will have denser social networks than organizations that provide less training during role transitions.

Other training characteristics relevant to network density are the *extent* and *duration of interaction* among trainees. Many theories of relationship formation indicate the importance of repeated interaction for lasting relationships to develop (e.g., Berger & Calabrese, 1975; Kelley, 1979). Of course, training programs vary in the degree to which they encourage trainees to get to know one another, discuss issues, and interact frequently. Some training programs, for example, begin with ice-breakers that encourage social interaction and require trainees to work together. Programs that do not have these activities offer little opportunity for trainees to develop relationships. Similarly, some organizations primarily offer short training programs that do not afford much time for trainees to get to know one another. Other organizations offer longer training programs that allow time for trainees to establish relationships. Both the extent and the duration of interaction should influence the degree to which training programs build relationships among employees.

> PROPOSITION 3: Organizations with training programs that encourage interpersonal interaction among trainees will have denser social networks than organizations that do not encourage interaction among trainees.

> PROPOSITION 4: Organizations with longer training programs will have denser social networks than organizations with shorter training programs.

The Relational Dimension: Building Trust and Reciprocity Norms

The presence of social ties does not ensure that those ties will be used for the benefit of the organization (Leana & Van Buren, 1999). The nature of the relationships formed influences whether the organization will benefit from them. Two elements of the relational dimension that help ensure that relationships will benefit the organization are *institutional trust* and *reciprocity norms*.

As with social capital, *trust* has been defined in many ways, and it occurs simultaneously at different levels of analysis (Tyler & Kramer, 1996). Generally speaking, trust is defined as a "psychological state comprising the intention to accept vulnerability based on positive expectations of the intentions or behavior of another" (Rousseau, Sitkin, Burt, & Camerer, 1998, p. 395). Of interest for organizational social capital, and related positive outcomes of information exchange and collaboration, is trust in the organization and organizational members by nature of their membership in the organization. This type of trust is referred to as *institutional trust* or *category-based trust* (Kramer, 1999; Rousseau et al., 1998). It is important to note that we are not specifically concerned with the creation of trust among trainees (such as what might be accomplished with a team-building exercise) but with building trust toward the organization and its members. It is this latter form of trust that is related to internal social capital.

What characteristics of training programs would facilitate institutional trust? Social identity theory suggests that people who view themselves as similar to others will be more likely to trust them (Brewer, 1981). Thus, organizations that use training to create a shared organizational identity will establish a shared characteristic on the basis of which employees may initially trust one another. Kramer, Brewer, and Hanna (1996) specifically noted that strong socialization toward a common identity will create more trust among employees.

> PROPOSITION 5: Organizations in which training emphasizes a shared organizational identity will have greater levels of institutional trust than organizations in which training does not emphasize such an identity.

Hodson (2004) recently argued that institutional trust is based on two factors: (a) a set of supportive employment practices and (b) coherent and competent management of production. Examining 204 separate organizational ethnographies, Hodson found support for the idea that these factors predicted organizational outcomes related to internal social capital, including organizational citizenship behaviors, coworker infighting, and employee–management conflict. In other words, organizations that use supportive employment practices and manage effectively generally have employees who commit higher levels of discretionary effort to the organization and come into conflict with each other and the organization less often. Training characteristics are relevant to Hodson's work in two ways: (a) providing training is one way organizations can support employees, and (b) offering effectively run training programs helps demonstrate and build managerial competence.

First, organizations that provide greater amounts of training are likely to be viewed as supportive of their employees, and thus employees will be more likely to trust the organization. This hypothesis is reinforced by theory and research on perceived organizational support, which suggests that organizations that are perceived to support their employees (e.g., by providing opportunities to learn) create a sense of obligation in their employees to reciprocate and help the organization succeed (Eisenberger, Armeli, Rexwinkel, Lynch, & Rhoades, 2001).

> PROPOSITION 6: Organizations that provide more opportunities for training will have greater levels of institutional trust than organizations that provide fewer opportunities.

The second way in which Hodson's (2004) work is relevant concerns *managerial competence*. All basic models of trust contain competence as a key factor (e.g., Rousseau et al., 1998), so organizations with competent managers should be more likely to be judged as trustworthy. Training is relevant here as both a symbol of managerial competence and a means to achieve it. First, the effectiveness of the design and administration of training may be interpreted by employees as an indicator of managerial competence. Training that is poorly designed, and poorly administered, may lead employees to question the competence of management in general. For example, the following scenario would likely damage employees' beliefs about managerial competence: A large training initiative frustrates employees because of administrative hassles to sign up and attend a session and because the material presented is not relevant to the employees' jobs. Second, training is relevant as a means to managerial competence. The provision of managerial training can improve the competence with which managers handle their jobs. Thus, the provision of management training by an organization can directly influence managerial competence and, thus, trust by employees in the organization.

> PROPOSITION 7: Organizations in which training is competently administered, designed, and delivered will have greater levels of institutional trust than organizations in which training is not competently administered, designed, and delivered.

> PROPOSITION 8: Organizations that offer more and higher quality management training will have greater levels of institutional trust than organizations that offer less and lower quality management training.

Reciprocity norms are another important relational element of social capital. *Norms* are general expectations about what is and what is not appropriate behavior, and *reciprocity norms* specifically refers to the general expectation that people return assistance they have received from others (Gouldner, 1960). Although there is a general societal norm for reciprocity, organizations can and do vary in the degree to which such norms are present and enforced. That is, organizations may vary in the degree to which employees engage in generous reciprocity. A strong norm for reciprocity should foster trust among employees because employees know that good deeds will be repaid at a later date.

Feldman (1989) argued that training programs are well suited to influence the development of organizational norms because they can provide explicit statements about behavioral expectations, stories about critical events to establish precedents about what is appropriate behavior, and punishment for behavior that deviates from the desired norm. It is easy to see that training programs can influence norms in part by articulating desired (and undesired) behaviors as well as soliciting (and punishing) those behaviors within the training environment. Thus, training programs that emphasize reciprocity with other employees, and embed it within the training, such as with small-group discussion activities in which employees share information and ideas, should help establish and reinforce reciprocity norms.

> PROPOSITION 9: Organizations in which training encourages employees to help one another will have stronger reciprocity norms than organizations in which training does not encourage helping behavior.

Research on reciprocity in organizations suggests that employees are more likely to be committed to and work for the organization when the organization is perceived to have made a *commitment* to the employee (Eisenberger et al., 2001). Thus, when organizations are perceived to be committed to employees and exerting effort to advance employees' interests, employees should be more likely to engage in discretionary behaviors associated with social capital. Related to training programs, training and development opportunities are often seen as an important way that organizations can help employees, by enhancing their human capital. Thus, put more broadly, organizations that provide more opportunities for training should be viewed as giving something of value to the employees, so employees should feel an obligation to return something of value.

> PROPOSITION 10: Organizations that provide more opportunities for training will have stronger reciprocity norms than organizations that provide fewer opportunities.

The Cognitive Dimension: Establishing Shared Vision

Shared vision requires common language and perspectives by employees and entails having similar beliefs about the purpose and future of the organization. Commonality in language, perspectives, and beliefs increases the ease with which employees can communicate with one another and helps ensure that communications do not result in confusion and poor coordination. Developing a shared vision may be especially critical when organizations experience a tremendous influx of new employees, such as when undergoing a merger or an acquisition, having a period of rapid growth, or entering a new territory. During such periods, training programs can have a direct and powerful influence on the degree of commonality. First, and perhaps most obviously, training can be used to teach all employees, new and old, about the organization.

> PROPOSITION 11: Organizations that provide training focused explicitly on their mission, vision, beliefs, and values will have employees who share a common vision to a greater extent than organizations in which such training is not provided.

Learning about the organization is one element of becoming socialized (e.g., Chao, O'Leary-Kelly, Wolf, Klein, & Gardner, 1994), and new employee orientation programs often serve this function. Thus, organizations that provide new employee orientation can create common ground by increasing the degree to which all employees use the same language and possess similar values and beliefs (Klein & Weaver, 2000).

> PROPOSITION 12: Organizations that provide extensive new employee orientations will have employees who share a common vision for the organization to a greater extent than organizations that do not provide new employee orientation.

Not all orientation programs are created equal with regard to forging shared perspectives. One means that organizations can use to develop a widely held set of beliefs is through strong *socialization tactics*, or tactics used to transition outside members to full membership in the organization. Ashforth and Saks (1996) and Bauer, Morrison, and Callister (1998) have argued that many characteristics of socialization programs are sufficiently correlated that programs can be described along a continuum from individualized (where new employees are treated as individuals and activities are informal, random, and variable) to institutionalized (where new employees are processed as a collective and activities are formal, sequential, and fixed). The use of institutionalized socialization practices obviously should lead employees to identify with their organization and share a common view of it.

PROPOSITION 13: Organizations in which the training of new employees is institutionalized will have employees who share a common vision for the organization to a greater extent than organizations in which the training of new employees is individualized.

Summary

We have argued not only that training programs can influence social capital but also that the participants who attend training programs, and the methods trainers use in training programs, will determine the degree to which training influences dimensions of internal social capital. We turn next to research that explains how the use of technology for distance training may affect the development of social capital.

TECHNOLOGY, DISTANCE TRAINING, AND SOCIAL CAPITAL

Research from various disciplines and levels of analysis suggests that technology-mediated interaction used in distance training may not be as useful as traditional face-to-face training in building trust, norms, and shared perspectives (e.g., Olson & Olson, 2000). To translate this research into propositions regarding distance training, we focus on distance training programs that rely solely (or at least primarily) on computer-mediated communication. So, for purposes of this chapter, we define *distance training* as computer-delivered training that occurs without the physical presence of an instructor or other learners.

The Structural Dimension: Creating Social Ties

Putnam (2000) discussed the high hopes that some people place in technology for forging social ties. He challenged these hopes by arguing that the increased use of network technology is unlikely to build social capital. Putnam (2000) argued, first, that there is social inequality in access to network technologies. Thus, only the relatively affluent will use the technology, and this will reinforce existing social networks instead of building new ones. Second, the Internet may turn out to be a passive form of entertainment (like the television) rather than an active form of communication (like the telephone). Putnam (2000) reviewed evidence that television watching is associated with declines in social and civic participation; it eats away at the time available for building and maintaining social relationships.

At this stage, it is unclear whether people will use network technology in ways that produce the same results as television. It is also unclear whether

Putnam's (2000) concerns are equally applicable to communications at work as they are to communications at home and play. However, it seems plausible that not all employees in a company will have ready access to and experience with technology, and thus trainees' social ties after training may reinforce existing communication patterns instead of forging new ones (Orlikowski, 1992).

There is also evidence from communications research that relationships started via distance are slow to develop and hard to maintain. When communicating using computer technology, there is considerable uncertainty because of a relative lack of social and nonverbal cues and the potential for feedback delays (Parks & Floyd, 1996). Uncertainty regarding how to behave, how the other person will behave, or how to explain the other person's behavior are all theorized to prevent or at least slow down the development of relationships (Berger & Calabrese, 1975).

The concerns voiced by Putnam (2000) and others must be balanced against the ease with which communication can occur with communications technology. Electronic mail, in particular, is becoming increasingly prevalent as a means to keep in touch and help maintain social ties. Moreover, Parks and Floyd (1996) found that relationships can develop from online interactions, and people frequently expanded the relationships to include communication by other means (e.g., telephone, postal mail, and face to face). McKenna, Green, and Gleason (2002) found that some people developed rich and long-lasting relationships with people whom they had met only through computer. In a distance training environment, trainees can meet a broad range of people, and they can use network technology to maintain these connections. They may also begin communicating by other means more suitable to relationship development.

Taken as a whole, technology is a mixed blessing when it comes to relationship development: It reduces transactions costs, so it allows for more communication, but it reduces the quality of that communication such that relationship-building and maintenance is more difficult. The net effect with regard to distance training is likely to be that the actual number of social ties in organizations that make heavy use of technology-delivered training (vs. face-to-face training) will not be that different. Rather than propose the null, we do not offer a proposition regarding distance training and social ties.

The Relational Dimension: Building Trust and Reciprocity Norms

Because the information transmitted through computers is less rich than the information transmitted face to face, nonverbal messages that are useful for building trust are not transmitted (Rocco, 1998). To make matters worse, the anonymity of some computer-mediated communication makes cheating, reneging, and extreme language—"flaming"—more common occurrences (Putnam, 2000). Thus, when interacting with others at a distance, behaviors that reduce trust are more likely to occur. Thus, Putnam (2000) concluded that "building trust and goodwill is not easy in cyberspace" (p. 176).

Rocco (1998) found that teams communicating electronically did not build trust, whereas those working face to face did. Aubert and Kelsey (2003) reported that teams working remotely and working face to face experienced differences in changes in trust over time. Trust between members of local groups went up over time as they worked together, but trust between members of a remote team went down over time. So, in addition to initially lower trust for remote teams, they had more difficulty developing trust over time.

These effects suggest that it is less likely that trainees within a single distance training program will develop trusting relationships compared with trainees taking a similar course face to face. However, these results do not speak directly to the issue of institutional trust. Although it is possible that these individual trusting relationships will, over time, aggregate to influence institutional trust, such emergent effects would take considerable time to unfold. From our perspective, it is unclear whether direct effects on institutional trust would occur. Of course, referring back to the issue of managerial competence, it does seem possible that poorly designed distance training would reduce employees' perceptions of managerial competence. In other words, the quality of distance training is likely to have an effect. Because this is simply a restatement of Proposition 7, no formal proposition is offered with regard to distance training.

Can norms be fostered by means of online training the way Feldman (1989) argued they can with traditional, face-to-face training? It seems unlikely. Feldman asserted that training would offer an opportunity for norms to develop because desired behavior could be explicitly described and rewarded, and undesirable behavior could be punished. Training online offers fewer opportunities for the observation of the full range of behaviors that are relevant to reciprocity. In other words, in distance training it may be possible to articulate the importance of sharing and reciprocity, but it is harder to have it demonstrated positively or negatively. In distance training, there are generally fewer opportunities for exchange and discussion. Even when such exchanges are made possible by text exchanges or video, they do not have the same vividness and intensity as face-to-face exchanges (Daft & Lengel, 1984). Consequently, it seems likely that organizations would be more likely to develop reciprocity norms through training when they make heavy use of face-to-face rather than distance training.

PROPOSITION 14: Compared with organizations that make heavier use of face-to-face training, organizations that make heavier use of distance training will have more difficulty establishing and maintaining reciprocity norms.

The Cognitive Dimension: Establishing Shared Vision

Putnam (2000) argued that the Internet allows people to confine their communications to people with whom they share common perspectives, and thus it encourages single-stranded, or tightly focused communication. Because it is relatively easy to walk away from an electronic mail message or a Web posting without attending to the message, ideas that people disagree with or do not understand can simply be ignored. The end result is that "local heterogeneity may give way to more focused virtual homogeneity as communities coalesce across space" (Putnam, 2000, p. 178).

Where this limitation of communication technology is most relevant is in the socialization of new employees. Orientation programs can help people understand the language, values, and goals of the company (Klein & Weaver, 1998; Wesson & Gogus, 2005); however, Wesson et al. (in press) found that when orientations were conducted via computer, employees were less effectively socialized to the organization's vision and values. In other words, by shifting to computer delivery, the company was less effective at establishing shared values and vision.

PROPOSITION 15: Organizations that orient new employees by means of distance training will have fewer employees who share a common vision for the organization than organizations who orient new employees face to face.

Summary

The results of this review suggest that the increasing use of technology to deliver training programs may reduce the degree to which training builds trust, reciprocity norms, and shared vision and thus may hinder the development of internal social capital. By extension, organizations that shift much of their training to technology delivery may, over time, reduce the internal social capital that would otherwise have been created by face-to-face interactions.

DISCUSSION

Training has been primarily conceived as a means to improve human capital, or the capabilities of the workforce. The social capital perspective suggests that human capital is insufficient for understanding how organizations gain competitive advantage. In addition to individual capability, the nature of the relationships both within the organization and between members of the organization and external stakeholders plays an important role. The importance of relationships for people and organizations, and the fact that training and technology influence them, is not entirely new. There is a rich, historic tradition regarding the importance of social relationships in organizations (Blau, 1964; Homans, 1950) and, more specifically, how technology influences those relationships (Trist & Bamforth, 1951). In addition, the concept of affective learning outcomes (Kraiger et al., 1993), research on team training (Salas & Cannon-Bowers, 2001), and theory and practice in organizational development (French & Bell, 1998), all acknowledge that training can change participant attitudes and relationships. Nevertheless, the net influence of training, at a distance or in the classroom, on relationships has gone essentially unexplored. For example, a recent theoretical treatment of the relationship between human resources practices and social capital addressed the role of selection and placement, but not the role of training and development (Leana & Van Buren, 1999). Similarly, glossaries and indexes of popular training and development textbooks (Blanchard & Thacker, 2004; Desimone, Werner, & Harris, 2002; Goldstein & Ford, 2002; Noe, 2005) reveal no reference to the term *social capital* or related social processes. Even recent treatments of the relationship of training to types of capital beyond human and financial capital often focus on intellectual capital rather than social capital (Ardichvili, 2002; Van Buren, 2002). As a consequence, very little is known about how training influences the development of social capital.

The theory and propositions presented in this chapter offer suggestions for future research and practice. The remainder of this discussion covers the research and suggestions for practice, with as great a focus on remaining questions as on implications.

Research Implications

The model offered here suggests a new set of training evaluation criteria. In addition to reactions and learning, researchers should examine changes in attitudes and beliefs related to social capital, such as institutional trust, reciprocity norms, and so on. Moreover, the effects of training programs on organizational, rather than just individual, outcomes should be considered. The theory and propositions raise a few more specific questions that bear further research.

First, by focusing solely on social capital, we have assumed that an organization's choices about training characteristics (including delivery technology) do not differentially affect learning and thus the development of human capital over time. Although research supports the conclusion that well-designed training can stimulate learning with any delivery technology (Clark, 1994), it is possible that organizations systematically vary in how well they use particular technologies. Some organizations, for example, may have excellent classroom trainers. If the same organization hires novices with little instructional design experience to build online training, then it is unlikely that learning outcomes will be the same. The opposite may also hold true. Consider an organization that has considerable competence in building online systems and employees with experience using them; such an organization may obtain better learning with distance training. So, an interesting avenue for future research is to examine trade-offs between human and social capital development depending on firm competency, or previous experience, with various training design and delivery technologies.

Second, we recognize that there may be moderators in the relationship between training characteristics and social capital. For instance, high levels of employee turnover may make it difficult to develop social capital regardless of training efforts. Likewise, training may be insufficient when social capital is very low, or redundant when social capital is very high. Thus, organizational characteristics such as high turnover rate and very high (or low levels) of social capital may diminish the effects that training has on the dimensions of social capital.

Third, we did not address external social capital. Propositions could be developed about how organizations can use training to develop external social capital. In particular, involving customers, suppliers, and other stakeholders in training may prove to be one useful way for training to build relationships that connect employees to other organizations.

Practice Implications

In regard to practice, the theory suggests that organizations consider more than costs, reactions, and learning when designing training, in particular when changing delivery technology. To the degree that training has historically provided useful opportunities to develop trust, norms, and shared vision, large-scale transitions to distance training may have subtle but far-reaching effects on the organization. Careful consideration of the effect of training on social processes is warranted in any deliberation of face-to-face versus distance training. By demonstrating the scope and scale of such effects, particularly to the organization's financial performance, a more thorough business case could be constructed to guide investments in distance training.

This chapter raises one immediate practical question: How often do organizations convert courses that may be useful in developing social capital from collaborative, face-to-face formats to technology delivery that involves no collaboration? We not only believe this occurs but also have specific examples: one from the literature and one from personal experience. First, in the literature, organizations have reported shifting orientation and socialization programs to the Web (e.g., Wesson & Gogus, 2005). Early orientation affords the foundation for creating social ties and building trust and norms. Thus, shifting orientation and socialization efforts to the Internet has the potential to hinder the development of internal social capital. Second, in our experience, we have witnessed a course high in collaboration shifted to a distance version that required no peer interaction. The course was a popular one taken by employees around the world. However, it often had a waiting list, and the costs of flying people to a common location to go through the training and complete the group exercises were seen as too high. The course was redesigned as a stand-alone one with no opportunities to meet and collaborate (Brown & Gerhardt, 2002). It was, in short, the desire to increase "throughput" and decrease costs that led the organization to make this shift. In the absence of any theory or data suggesting this practice is problematic, organizations are unlikely to understand the full consequences of such decisions.

CONCLUSION

The historical focus of research comparing training outcomes across delivery media leaves unanswered questions about the effect of wholesale transitions of training from the classroom to distance delivery. Prior research does suggest that distance training can reduce administration costs and, as long it is well designed, will otherwise be "not significantly" different from face-to-face training (Welsh et al., 2003). However, cost and individual-level learning do not fully capture the outcomes related to training practices. In this chapter, we have built a theoretical framework for studying the effect of training on social capital as one important and generally overlooked outcome. Drawing on prior theory and research, we suggest that social capital can be influenced by training practices, including the choice of distance versus classroom training. We hope that the model and propositions we have offered will not only inform research on distance training but also broaden the focus of training research and evaluation to social as well as human capital.

REFERENCES

Adler, P. S., & Kwon, S. (2002). Social capital: Prospects for a new concept. *Academy of Management Review, 27,* 17–40

Ardichvili, A. (2002). The role of human resource development in transitioning from technology-focused to people-centered knowledge management. In C. M. Sleezer, T. L. Wentling, & R. L. Cude (Eds.), *Human resource development and information technology* (pp. 89–104). Norwell, MA: Kluwer Academic.

Ashforth, B. E., & Saks, A. M. (1996). Socialization tactics: Longitudinal effects of newcomer adjustment. *Academy of Management Journal, 39,* 149–178.

Aubert, B. A., & Kelsey, B. A. (2003). Further understanding trust and performance in virtual teams. *Small Group Research, 34,* 575–618.

Bauer, T. N., Morrison, E. W., & Callister, R. R. (1998). Organizational socialization: A review and directions for future research. *Research in Personnel and Human Resource Management, 16,* 149–214.

Beal, D. J., Cohen, R. R., Burke, M. J., & McLendon, C. L. (2003). Cohesion and performance in groups: A meta-analytic clarification on construct relations. *Journal of Applied Psychology, 88,* 989–1004.

Berger, C. R., & Calabrese, R. J. (1975). Some explorations in initial interaction and beyond: Toward a developmental theory of interpersonal communication. *Human Communication Research, 1,* 99–112.

Blanchard, N. P., & Thacker, J. (2004). *Effective training: Systems, strategies, and practices* (2nd ed.). Upper Saddle River, NJ: Prentice Hall.

Blau, P. M. (1964). *Exchange and power in social life.* New York: Wiley.

Brewer, M. B. (1981). Ethnocentrism and its role in interpersonal trust. In M. B. Brewer & B. Collins (Eds.), *Scientific inquiry and the social sciences* (pp. 345–360). San Francisco: Jossey-Bass.

Brown, K. G., & Gerhardt, M. W. (2002). Formative evaluation: An integrated practice model and case study. *Personnel Psychology, 55,* 951–983.

Burt, R. S. (1992). *Structural holes.* Cambridge, MA: Harvard University Press.

Chao, G. T., O'Leary-Kelly, A. M., Wolf, S., Klein, H. J., & Gardner, P. D. (1994). Organizational socialization: Its content and consequences. *Journal of Applied Psychology, 79,* 730–743.

Clark, R. E. (1994). Media will never influence learning. *Educational Technology Research and Development, 42,* 21–29.

Coleman, J. S. (1988). Social capital in the creation of human capital. *American Journal of Sociology, 94,* 95–120.

Daft, R. L., & Lengel, R. H. (1984). Information richness: A new approach to managerial behavior and organizational design. In L. L. Cummings & B. M. Staw (Eds.), *Research in organizational behavior* (Vol. 6, pp. 191–233). Homewood, IL: JAI Press.

Desimone, R. L., Werner, J. M., & Harris, D. M. (2002). *Human resource development* (3rd ed.). Fort Worth, TX: Harcourt College Publishers.

Eisenberger, R., Armeli, S., Rexwinkel, B., Lynch, P. D., & Rhoades, L. (2001). Reciprocation of perceived organizational support. *Journal of Applied Psychology, 86,* 42–51.

Feldman, D. C. (1989). Socialization, resocialization, and training: Reframing the research agenda. In I. Goldstein (Ed.), *Training and development in organizations* (pp. 376–416). San Francisco: Jossey-Bass.

Fischer, H. M., & Pollock, T. G. (2004). Effects of social capital and power on surviving transformational change: The case of initial public offerings. *Academy of Management Journal, 47,* 463–481.

Florin, J., Lubatkin, M., & Schulze, W. (2003). A social capital model of high-growth ventures. *Academy of Management Journal, 46,* 374–384.

French, W. L., & Bell, C. H. (1998). *Organization development: Behavioral science interventions for organization improvement* (6th ed.). Upper Saddle River, NJ: Prentice Hall.

Fukuyama, F. (1995). *Trust: The social virtues and the creation of prosperity.* New York: Free Press.

Gersick, C. J., & Hackman, J. R. (1990). Habitual routines in task-performing groups. *Organizational Behavior and Human Decision Processes, 47,* 65–97.

Goldstein, I., & Ford, K. (2002). *Training in work organizations: Needs assessment, development, and evaluation* (4th ed.). Belmont, CA: Wadsworth.

Gouldner, A. W. (1960). The norm of reciprocity. *American Sociological Review, 25,* 165–167.

Hill, L. A. (1992). *Becoming a manager: Mastery of a new identity.* New York: Penguin Books.

Hodson, R. (2004). Organizational trustworthiness: Findings from the population of organizational ethnographies. *Organization Science, 15,* 432–445.

Homans, G. C. (1950). *The human group.* New York: Harcourt, Brace.

Kelley, H. H. (1979). *Personal relationships: Their structure and processes.* New York: Wiley.

Klein, H. J., & Weaver, N. A. (2000). The effectiveness of an organizational–level orientation training program in the socialization of new hires. *Personnel Psychology, 53,* 47–66.

Kosarzycki, M. P., Salas, E., DeRouin, R. E., & Fiore, S. M. (2003). Distance learning in organizations: A review and assessment of future needs. In D. L. Stone (Ed.), *Advances in human performance and cognitive engineering research* (Vol. 3, pp. 69–98). Oxford, England: Elsevier Science.

Kozlowski, S. W. J., Brown, K. G., Weissbein, D. A., Cannon-Bowers, J., & Salas, E. (2000). A multi-level perspective on training effectiveness: Enhancing horizontal and vertical transfer. In K. J. Klein & S. W. J. Kozlowski (Eds.), *Multilevel theory, research, and methods in organizations* (pp. 157–210). San Francisco: Jossey-Bass.

Kraiger, K., Ford, J. K., & Salas, E. (1993). Application of cognitive, skill-based, and affective theories of learning outcomes to new methods of training evaluation. *Journal of Applied Psychology, 78,* 311–328.

Kramer, R. M. (1999). Trust and distrust in organizations: Emerging perspectives, enduring questions. *Annual Review of Psychology, 50,* 569–598.

Kramer, R. M., Brewer, M. B., & Hanna, B. (1996). Collective trust and collective action in organizations: The decision to trust as a social decision. In R. M. Kramer & T. R. Tyler (Eds.), *Trust in organizations: Frontiers of theory and research* (pp. 357–389). Thousand Oaks, CA: Sage.

Leana, C. R., & Van Buren, H. J., III. (1999). Organizational social capital and employment practices. *Academy of Management Review, 24,* 538–555.

Marsden, P. V. (2001). Interpersonal ties, social capital, and employer staffing practices. In N. Lin, K. Cook, & R. S. Burt (Eds.), *Social capital: Theory and research* (pp. 105–126). New York: Walter de Gruyter.

McKenna, K. Y. A., Green, A. S., & Gleason, M. E. J. (2002). Relationship formation on the Internet: What's the big attraction? *Journal of Social Issues, 58,* 9–31.

Mitchell, T. R., & Lee, T. W. (2001). The unfolding model of voluntary turnover and job embeddedness: Foundations for a comprehensive theory of attachment. In B. M. Staw & R. I. Sutton (Eds.), *Research in organizational behavior* (Vol. 23, pp. 189–246). London: JAI Press.

Morrison, E. W. (2002). Newcomers' relationships: The role of social network ties during socialization. *Academy of Management Journal, 45,* 1149–1160.

Nahapiet, J., & Ghoshal, S. (1998). Social capital, intellectual capital, and the organizational advantage. *Academy of Management Review, 23,* 242–266.

Noe, R. A. (2005). *Employee training and development* (3rd ed.). New York: McGraw Hill.

Olson, G. M., & Olson, J. S. (2000). Distance matters. *Human–Computer Interaction, 15,* 139–178.

Orlikowski, W. J. (1992). Learning from notes: Organizational issues in groupware implementation. *Proceedings of the ACM conference on computer-supported cooperative work* (pp. 362–369). New York: ACM Press.

Parks, M. R., & Floyd, K. (1996). Making friends in cyberspace. *Journal of computer-mediated Communication, 1*(4). Retrieved December 11, 2006, from http://jcmc.indiana.edu/vol1/issue4/parks.html

Pennings, J. M., & Lee, K. (1998). Human capital, social, and firm dissolution. *Academy of Management Journal, 41,* 425–441.

Podsakoff, P. M., MacKenzie, S. B., Paine, J. B., & Bachrach, D. G. (2000). Organizational citizenship behaviors: A critical review of the theoretical and empirical literature and suggestions for future research. *Journal of Management, 26,* 513–563.

Portes, A. (1998). Social capital: Its origins and applications in modern sociology. *Annual Review of Sociology, 24,* 1–24.

Putnam, R. D. (1995). Bowling alone: America's declining social capital. *Journal of Democracy, 6,* 65–78.

Putnam, R. D. (2000). *Bowling alone: The collapse and revival of American community.* New York: Simon & Schuster.

Rocco, E. (1998). Trust breaks down in electronic contexts but can be repaired by some initial face-to-face contact. *CHI 1998 conference proceedings* (pp. 496–502). New York: ACM Press.

Rousseau, D. M., Sitkin, S. B., Burt, R. S., & Camerer, C. (1998). Not so different after all: A cross-discipline view of trust. *Academy of Management Review, 23*, 393–404.

Russell, T. L. (2001). *The no significant difference phenomenon: A comparative research annotated bibliography on technology for distance education* (5th ed.). Montgomery, AL: International Distance Education Certification Center.

Salas, E., & Cannon-Bowers, J. A. (2001). The science of training: A decade of progress. *Annual Review of Psychology, 52*, 471–499.

Sugrue, B. (2003). *State of the industry: ASTD's annual review of U.S. and international trends in workplace learning and performance*. Alexandria, VA: American Society for Training & Development.

Trist, E. L., & Bamforth, K. W. (1951). Some social and psychological consequences of the longwall method of coal-getting. *Human Relations, 4*, 3–38.

Tsai, W., & Ghoshal, S. (1998). Social capital and value creation: The role of intrafirm networks. *Academy of Management Journal, 41*, 454–476.

Tyler, T. R., & Kramer, R. M. (1996). Whither trust? In R. M. Kramer & T. R. Tyler (Eds.), *Trust in organizations: Frontiers of theory and research* (pp. 1–15). Thousand Oaks, CA: Sage.

Van Buren, M. E. (2002). Making knowledge count: Knowledge management systems and the human element. In C. M. Sleezer, T. L. Wentling, & R. L. Cude (Eds.), *Human resource development and information technology* (pp. 105–130). Norwell, MA: Kluwer.

Welsh, E. T., Wanberg, C. R., Brown, K. G., & Simmering, M. J. (2003). E-learning: Emerging uses, empirical results, and future directions. *International Journal of Training and Development, 7*, 245–258.

Wesson, M. J., & Gogus, C. I. (2005). Shaking hands with a computer: An examination of two methods of organizational newcomer orientation. *Journal of Applied Psychology, 90*, 1018–1026.

Whiting, S. W., & Dreher, G. F. (2006). *Employee education and development programs: A framework for understanding unintended consequences*. Unpublished manuscript, Indiana University, Bloomington.

4

A META-ANALYTIC INVESTIGATION OF LEARNER CONTROL: OLD FINDINGS AND NEW DIRECTIONS

KURT KRAIGER AND EDDIE JERDEN

This chapter addresses the role of learner control in distributed learning environments (DLEs). DLEs are those that use some form of technology (e.g., computers or videodiscs) to deliver training to individuals who may be separated from the instructional source by space or time. Common formats include computer-based instruction, computer-aided instruction, multimedia learning environments, intranet- and Internet-based instruction, Web-based instruction, and e-learning. In particular, we focus on learner-centered formats in which the software functions as a learning portal, exposing the learner to choices in both what and how to learn. For example, account managers may choose to read or listen to descriptions of new products, new sales techniques, or problems encountered by peers. Many modern forms of Internet-based training (or e-learning) follow this format. In this chapter, we address issues related to choices made by learners in such a flexible learning environment. We provide an updated meta-analysis of the learner control literature, derive a new model of learner control processes and outcomes, and suggest new avenues for research and application in the form of propositions.

UNDERSTANDING LEARNER CONTROL

Learner control refers to the extent to which a learner can affect his or her own learning experience through control over features in his or her learning environment, such as the path, pace, or contingencies of instruction (Friend & Cole, 1990). In DLE contexts, learner control is thus distinguished from *program control*, in which the instructional software controls most or all of the decisions about what and how the trainee interacts with the training content (Hannafin, 1984). Program features that may or may not be under the control of the learner include topic choice, sequencing of information, pacing of information, on-demand assessment (i.e., testing at any time on a particular topic), capacity to modify screen design and text density, and opportunities for program advisement (Sims & Hedberg, 1995). Thus, learner control is intended to provide both customization of the content and the ability to accommodate learners' preferences for the amount or type of instruction (e.g., Freitag & Sullivan, 1995).

For example, suppose that an employee is promoted to a team leader position and must take on project management responsibilities. She identifies an online project management training course. Her employer agrees to pay the fee for the course, but she must pay another important cost: her own time. As she begins to work through the online course late at night from home, she realizes that she already knows much of the fundamentals of project management and would like to skip ahead to specific knowledge and skills she needs for her job. Does the program allow her to do this? Is she correct in her assessment that she understands the basics? One of the useful features of the course she chose was the availability of streaming videos that use professional actors to illustrate principles covered in text. However, on some nights the new supervisor is tired and would like to skip the videos. On other nights, she wants to go back and review videos seen earlier in the training. Does the program allow her to do this? Does the program track where she is in the training so that if she backtracks, she is able to return exactly to where she departed? Can she modify how information is presented to her, for example, choosing to either read text online or listen to a narrator as she prepares herself for the next day? What type of feedback is available to her, and can she choose when she gets that feedback? Will she understand how to modify her approach to training if the feedback is negative, and will the program offer suggestions to help her with that decision?

As illustrated in this example, it is important to understand that there are many ways in which learners may affect the instructional context. For the sake of brevity, it is useful to organize these characteristics into four broad categories (see Milheim & Martin, 1991; Tennyson, Park, & Christensen, 1985): (a) pace control, (b) sequence control, (c) content control, and (d) advisory control. *Pace control* allows learners to select the pace of work, for example, skipping easier material and dwelling on more difficult content. *Sequence control* allows learners choice in how to navigate course topics, for example, skipping topics or completing topics out of order. *Content control* allows learners to choose topics or assessments. Finally, *advisory control* refers to program-generated advice that informs learners of their progress or suggests a course of action. It is important to note that learner control may be provided in either DLEs or traditional classroom environments; much of the original learner control research was conducted in classroom settings (see Steinberg, 1977, 1989). However, because classroom instruction is typically tailored to the average learner and DLEs seek to provide individualized instruction (DeRouin, Fritzsche, & Salas, 2004), for the present purposes we restrict our investigation to DLEs.

The previous example also highlights many of the proposed benefits of high learner control: principally, the opportunity to customize training content and training methods and the anticipated gains in trainee motivation and learning that result from that customization (Kinzie & Sullivan, 1989; Lepper, 1985). Here, *trainee motivation* refers simply to the desire to engage the learning software. Other proposed benefits of learner control include learning how to learn (Merrill, 1975) and opportunities for serendipitous learning (Staninger, 1994).

Outcomes of Learner Control

As noted previously, there are a number of hypothesized outcomes of learner control of interest to educational institutions or work organizations. These include effects on trainee learning (e.g., Gray, 1987) and trainees' reactions to instruction (Milheim, 1989) as well as other motivational, attitudinal, and cognitive outcomes, such as intrinsic interest in the training content (Becker & Dwyer, 1994), intrinsic interest in the learning process (Reigeluth & Stein, 1983), development of effective learning tactics and strategies (e.g., Merrill, 1975), and a willingness to explore the trained topic or other topics in greater detail (Kinzie & Sullivan, 1989). However, as we later show, research evidence supporting the impact of learner control on any of these outcomes is mixed (Hannafin, 1984; Milheim & Martin, 1991; Niemiec, Sikorski, & Walberg, 1996; Steinberg, 1977, 1989).

With respect to specific outcomes, a number of studies have found evidence for more learning in learner control environments (e.g., Avner, Moore, & Smith, 1980; Gray, 1987; Kinzie, Sullivan, & Berdel, 1988), whereas other studies have reported greater learning in program control conditions (e.g., S. S. Lee & Wong, 1989; MacGregor, 1988; Morrison,

Ross, & Baldwin, 1992; Steinberg, 1977). Still, other studies have reported no significant differences between learner control and program control conditions (Arnone & Grabowski, 1992; Gray, 1987; Kinzie & Sullivan, 1989).

Several studies have found evidence that providing learner control has positive influences on trainees' attitudes. For example, Becker and Dwyer (1994) found that learners reported greater intrinsic motivation when working on a computer-aided instruction (CAI) program with learner control compared with students working on a paper-based task. Although a few studies have found negative effects (Gray, 1987) or no effects (Arnone & Grabowski, 1992), most have reported that providing learner control resulted in more positive affective reactions to the learning experience (e.g., Hintze, Mohr, & Wenzel, 1988; Milheim, 1989; Morrison et al., 1992). In general, most of these studies used between-group designs, so evidence of positive attitudes may be more properly interpreted as "participants receiving learner control responded more positively than participants receiving program control," rather than "participants preferred learner control to program control." In contrast, Hintze et al. (1988) used a within-subject design by exposing Danish dental students to complete learner-controlled, partial learner-controlled, and computer-controlled instructional situations. The researchers found that most of these students preferred partial or complete learner control.

Finally, a number of studies have examined the effects of learner control on time on task, or how long learners choose to engage in learning tasks. Various studies have found that learner control lessons take more time to complete (e.g., Dalton, 1990; MacGregor, 1988; Shyu & Brown, 1992), less time to complete (e.g., Murphy & Davidson, 1991; Tennyson & Buttrey, 1980), or about the same amount of time to complete (e.g., Kinzie & Sullivan, 1989; Lahey et al., 1973). On reflection, it is difficult to be certain what the intended effect should be. If the benefit of providing learner control is greater efficiency, then learners should be expected to spend less time on task than with high learner control. If the intended benefit is greater interest in the learning task or instructional material (Kinzie & Sullivan, 1989), then learners given control may spend more time on task because they choose to explore the material in detail.

Meta-Analyses of Learner Control Studies

Partly in response to the variability in study outcomes, several meta-analyses and reviews have been conducted on the effectiveness of learner control over the past decade. A meta-analysis provides a quantitative review of prior published and unpublished studies; each study outcome is treated as a data point, and outcomes can be averaged over studies to determine an overall effect. An unpublished meta-analysis on the efficacy of learner control in CAI by Parsons (1992) found a decrease in achievement of 0.04 standard deviations for students using computer-based programs that provided more learner control than alternative programs. A subsequent meta-analysis by Niemiec et al. (1996) concluded that although the learner control construct is theoretically appealing, the overall effects of learner control in CAI seem "neither powerful nor consistent."

Although Niemiec et al.'s (1996) review is relatively recent, we elected to conduct an updated meta-analysis on learner control for four reasons. First, we anticipated that there may have been a substantial number of additional studies published since their review. In fact, although Niemiec et al. reported a total of 24 usable studies, we found an additional 11 published or unpublished studies dated 1996 or later. Second, Niemiec et al. included samples of all ages, and we wanted to focus exclusively on adult populations to be able to address learner control issues in work-related situations. Third, the nature of CAI is continually changing, and the impact of learner control on learning may vary depending on emerging training systems. In particular, hypertext and hypermedia systems popularized around 1990 (Ayersman, 1996; Borsook & Higginbotham-Wheat, 1992), and Web-based instruction introduced around 2000 (Rosenberg, 2001), offer interactive formats that seem to lend themselves better to exploration and customization by learners. *Hypertext learning systems* are ones in which users operate in an open and exploratory space in which information is structured using nodes and links (Conklin, 1987). Hypermedia systems include links that use multimodal methods of learning, including visual, auditory, and text-based information (Jonassen, 1989). Regarding the relationship of hypermedia systems to learner control, Marchionini (1988) wrote the following: "such a fluid environment requires learners to constantly make decisions and evaluate progress, thus forcing students to apply higher order thinking skills" (p. 9). We were curious as to whether learner control might be more effective given the growing popularity of flexible CAI systems (as well as learners' increasing familiarity with link-based navigation systems). Fourth, although Niemiec et al. investigated some moderators such as study source or sample characteristics, they did not investigate all moderators of interest to us; neither did they use state-of-the-art methods for evaluating the efficacy of moderators (Hedges & Olkin, 1985; Hunter & Schmidt, 2004).

Accordingly, we conducted an updated meta-analysis on the effectiveness of learner control in computer-based training. Our primary research questions were how learner control affects learning outcomes and attitudes toward instruction. In addition, we were interested in the potential moderating effects of several research and training design variables as well.

An attempt was made to locate, summarize, and analyze the results of all published studies, unpublished doctoral dissertations, and conference presentations reporting the effects of learner control on training outcomes using computer-based training. Only studies that included a direct comparison of CAI with learner control to CAI without learner control were considered for inclusion in the analysis. Studies needed to use adult (18 years or older) participants to be included. The indexes used in the search were PsycINFO, ERIC, ABI/INFORM, and the Social Sciences Index for studies dated from 1989 through the present. The start date of 1989 was selected to coincide with the publication of Steinberg's (1989) review of the cognition and learner control literature.

Key words used in the literature search were *learner control and computer-based instruction*, *learner control and computer-assisted instruction*, *learner control and computer-based training*, and *learner control and computer-based learning*. Reference checks from popular review articles and previous learner control meta-analyses were conducted as well. Forty-nine published studies, 9 unpublished dissertations, and 9 conference papers were identified as usable through a review of abstracts. Of the 67 studies, only 30 were suitable for inclusion in the analysis.[1] Of those excluded, 20 did not report information necessary to calculate an effect size, 2 were redundant with samples from other studies, and 15 did not directly compare the effects of learner control with the effects of no learner control.

Data Coding

The following variables were coded for each study: year published, group means and standard deviations, zero-order correlations for the relationships between group membership and training outcomes, sample size, sample demographics, and a variety of study quality variables (e.g., study design, threats to validity, sampling strategy). Moderator variables coded were source (published vs. nonpublished), type of training task (applied vs. educational), learner experience with the training task (none vs. at least some), computer experience (not reported vs. reported), sample (work vs. university), type of learning outcome (cognitive, skill based, or affective), type of learner control (pace, navigation, or instructional style), and length of training.

---

[1] Studies included in the meta-analysis can be found in the references section of this chapter as asterisked entries.

Analytic Methods

The studies included in this analysis contrasted two or more groups on learning and affective outcome measures. The effect sizes reported were a mixture of d- and r-type indexes. The most common d-type scenario was an evaluation of the mean difference between the group that received CAI with learner control and a group that received either no training or some alternative (e.g., program control). Studies reporting r-type effects provided findings in the form of a relationship between the dichotomous variable learner control versus program or alternative to learner control and a continuous outcome variable. For our analysis, d statistics were converted to point-biserial correlations and then corrected for dichotomization prior to being included in the meta-analysis. In all cases, learner control was the treatment group. Thus a positive effect size reflects the positive effect of learner control on training outcomes.

A total of 54 effect sizes were obtained from the 30 studies retained for the analysis. All outcome variables were coded in two ways. First, they were coded as either learning outcomes or affective outcomes. For the purpose of this analysis, *affective outcomes* refer to emotionally based reactions to the training (e.g., satisfaction, amount of anxiety during training). Second, measures of learning outcomes were categorized into four subcategories based on the goals of training and measure content. The four subcategories were (a) procedural knowledge, (b) declarative learning, (c) transfer, and (d) retention (see Kraiger, 2002). *Procedural knowledge* refers to learning information about "how," and *declarative knowledge* refers to learning information about "what." *Transfer* refers to a change in on-the-job behavior as intended by training. The final subcategory, *retention*, can be defined as the extent to which the application or frequency of the new behaviors learned during training is maintained over time.

Huffcutt and Arthur's (1995) sample-adjusted meta-analytic deviance outlier analysis was computed on the uncorrected effect size estimates. The criteria used for the cutoff point were a sample-adjusted meta-analytic deviance statistic at least 1.5 standard deviations above the mean and the value at which the first break in the scree plot analysis of the statistics occurred.[2] Results are presented with both outliers removed and included for each analysis.

We corrected for sampling error and error of measurement in the dependent variable at the individual study level using procedures described

---

[2] When this cutoff was used, four studies were identified as outliers for the learning outcomes meta-analysis (Gist, Schwoerer, & Rosen, 1989; Jeffries, 2001; Pridemore & Klein, 1993; Simon &

by Hunter and Schmidt (2004). A sample weighted average correlation was computed and then corrected for unreliability in the dependent variable. Overall, reliability estimates were available for 22 of the 30 studies. For studies that did not report outcome reliabilities, the average of all reported reliabilities for that outcome variable was used. For the learning category, the average reliabilities were .70 for the overall analysis, .70 for declarative learning, .67 for procedural learning, .77 for transfer, and .69 for retention. For the affective category, the mean reliability was .91.

Two indexes were used to assess the degree to which variation in the corrected correlations was due to statistical artifacts. The first is the *75% rule*. According to this rule, if 75% or more of the variance is due to artifacts, then one can conclude that all of it is, on the grounds that the remaining 25% is likely to be due to artifacts not corrected for (Hunter & Schmidt, 1990). The percentage of variance accounted for by the artifacts corrected for—sampling error and error of measurement in the dependent variables in this case—is represented in the tables as V_{art}. The other test index was the credibility interval, also provided in the tables.[3]

RESULTS

The results of the analyses both with and without outliers are shown in Table 4.1. On the basis of the size of the confidence intervals, the effect statistics show more stability without the outliers. With the outliers removed, the omnibus (or overall) results for the learning category go from a corrected r of .09 to .11, with an interval supporting significance. The affective outcome results increase from .00 to .11.

A one-way analysis of variance was used to determine whether effect sizes differed by the type of learning outcome. We conducted this procedure using all 54 observed effects and the type of learning outcome as the independent variable. To address variability in sample sizes and error variance, we weighted the effects by the inverse of the sampling error variance for the analysis (Hedges & Olkin, 1985). Overall, learning type did have a significant effect on the results of the training programs for both the full analysis, $F(3, 41) = 4.64$, $p < .05$, and the analysis with outliers removed,

---

Werner, 1996), and three studies were identified for the affective outcomes meta-analysis (Gist et al., 1989; Maki, Maki, Patterson, & Whittaker, 2000; Simon & Werner, 1996).

[3] Whereas confidence intervals can be used to assess the accuracy of the sample size weighted mean effect size by constructing intervals around the standard error of the uncorrected mean effect size, credibility intervals should be used to determine whether moderators are operating using the corrected standard deviation around the mean corrected correlation to create intervals (Whitener, 1990). In general, if the credibility interval is sufficiently large or does include zero, then one can infer that the mean corrected effect size is probably the mean of several subpopulations determined by the influence of moderators (Whitener, 1990).

TABLE 4.1
Relationships Between Learner Control and Learning Outcomes (With and Without Outliers Omitted)

Studies	k	N	r	95% Confidence interval		r_c	d_c	$V(r_c)$	$V(ve_c)$	V_{art}	95% Credibility interval	
All studies												
Omnibus learning[a]	30	2,655	.08	-.02,	.19	.09	.19	.1209	.0156	12.92	-.45,	.64
Declarative learning	16	1,699	.04	-.07,	.16	.05	.10	.0764	.0134	17.5	-.37,	.47
Procedural learning	11	864	.18	.00,	.36	.19	.39	.1354	.0175	12.96	-.36,	.75
Transfer	5	334	.03	-.31,	.36	.03	.06	.1380	.0197	14.2	-.68,	.74
Retention	9	651	-.10	-.24,	.04	-.13	-.26	.0684	.0205	30.0	-.49,	.23
Affective	13	1,490	.00	-.17,	.16	.00	.00	.0992	.0097	9.8	-.57,	.56
Outliers omitted												
Omnibus learning[a]	26	2,272	.10	.02,	.18	.11	.23	.0558	.0154	27.6	-.23,	.46
Procedural learning	9	735	.06	-.02,	.15	.08	.16	.0194	.0167	85.9	-.04,	.20
Transfer	4	206	.26	.03,	.48	.29	.61	.0472	.0224	47.3	-.07,	.65
Retention	8	525	-.01	-.10,	.08	-.02	-.03	.0243	.0233	95.9	-.07,	.03
Affective	10	977	.10	.00,	.21	.11	.22	.0295	.0112	38.0	-.15,	.37

Note. The 95% confidence intervals were set around the uncorrected correlation using the standard error formula for heterogeneous studies, and the 95% credibility intervals were set around the corrected correlation using the standard error formula for heterogeneous studies. k = number of samples; N = total sample size; r = sample weighted average correlation; r_c = corrected weighted average correlation; d_c = corrected weighted average d statistic; $V(r_c)$ = weighted variance of the corrected correlation; $V(ve_c)$ = weighted sampling error variance; V_{art} = percentage of variance in r_c explained by study artifacts.
[a]Omnibus learning consists of a combination of the four learning subcategories designed to maximize equal representation in the overall analysis; affective outcomes were calculated separately.

$F(3, 38) = 3.81$, p < .05. Post hoc tests revealed significant differences between procedural learning (mean $r = .34$) and declarative learning (mean $r = -.05$), and procedural learning and retention (mean $r = -.15$) for the full analysis. In the outliers-removed analysis, significant differences were found between procedural learning (mean $r = .32$) and declarative learning (mean $r = -.05$).

The moderator indexes both suggested the presence of moderators based on the omnibus learning and affective results. Artifacts explained only 12.92% and 27.6% of variance in the corrected correlations for the full and outliers-removed analyses, respectively. In addition, the credibility intervals in each case were large and included zero. On the basis of these results, the effects of the coded moderator variables were examined.

Subgroup analyses were conducted within each level of the eight dichotomous moderators for the no-outlier samples. These analyses were broken down into two categories based on the type of moderator represented. The first category, *methodological*, refers to research design and procedural features. The second category, *pedagogical*, consists of theoretical variables related to the instruction process and design of the training program. Tables 4.2 and 4.3 show the meta-analytic results of the analyses along with the results of independent-samples t tests conducted between the levels of the individual variables. Of these tests, a significant difference was found for the task experience variable. A review of the mean effects shows that learner control was more effective for participants with no experience on the training task.

Finally, because we expected that learner control might be more effective as DLEs become more technologically sophisticated and flexible, we calculated the correlation between the coded effect size and the year of the study. Note that the year of the study is an imperfect proxy for sophistication of technology as it may be contaminated by factors such as journal lag times. We calculated separate correlations (with and without the outlier studies included) for all learning measures and for affective measures. Effect sizes for learner control were positively correlated with study date. For the learning measures, the correlation was .41 ($k = 30$, $p < .05$) for all studies and .27 ($k = 26$, ns) without outliers. For affective outcomes, the correlation was .40 ($k = 13$, ns) for all studies and .64 ($k = 10$, $p < .05$) without outliers.

DISCUSSION AND FUTURE DIRECTIONS

Consistent with prior reviews, our meta-analysis provides mild support for the use of learner control. The overall effect size suggested that learner control is better than no learner control, although the impact is small. Analyses of specific outcomes and moderator variables also indicated the

TABLE 4.2
Subgroup Analyses Between Learning Outcome Moderator Variables

Subgroup	k	N	r	95% Confidence interval		r_c	d_c	$V(r_c)$	$V(ve_c)$	V_{art} (%)	t^a
Methodological											
Nonpublished	13	1,034	.01	−.09,	.11	.01	.02	.0456	.0171	37.6	−1.46
Published	13	1,238	.17	.07,	.27	.20	.41	.0480	.0136	28.4	
Work sample	4	256	.30	−.04,	.63	.34	.73	.1388	.0165	11.9	−0.21
School sample	22	2,055	.10	.01,	.18	.11	.23	.0586	.0146	24.9	
Computer experience not reported	15	1,274	.13	.03,	.24	.15	.31	.0566	.0149	26.3	1.42
Computer experience reported	11	998	.05	−.06,	.16	.06	.13	.0508	.0164	32.2	
Pedagogical											
No task experience	11	853	.17	.04,	.29	.19	.39	.0484	.0160	33.2	2.06*
Some task experience	15	1,419	.06	−.04,	.16	.07	.13	.0526	.0144	27.4	
Work task	12	734	.18	.03,	.32	.22	.45	.0908	.0223	24.6	0.34
Educational task	14	1,538	.06	−.03,	.15	.07	.14	.0337	.0120	35.6	
Cognitive outcomes	21	1,892	.07	−.02,	.15	.08	.16	.0494	.0155	31.5	−0.82
Skill-based outcomes	5	380	.25	.07,	.44	.27	.56	.0478	.0133	27.7	
Control over pace/navigation	19	1,661	.14	.04,	.23	.17	.34	.0602	.0154	25.7	0.78
Control over content	7	611	−.02	−.13,	.09	−.01	−.03	.0222	.0148	66.9	

Note. The 95% confidence intervals were set around the uncorrected correlation using the standard error formula for heterogeneous studies. k = number of samples; N = total sample size; r = sample weighted average correlation; r_c = corrected weighted average correlation; d_c = corrected weighted average d statistic; $V(r_c)$ = weighted variance of the corrected correlation; $V(ve_c)$ = weighted sampling error variance; V_{art} = percentage of variance in r_c explained by study artifacts.
[a] t tests were conducted on the observed effect sizes.
*$p \leq .05$

TABLE 4.3
Subgroup Analyses Between Affective Outcome and Moderator Variables

Subgroup	k	N	r	95% Confidence interval		r_c	d_c	$V(r_c)$	$V(ve_c)$	V_{art} (%)	t^a
Methodological											
Nonpublished	5	540	.04	-.05,	.13	.04	.08	.0107	.0102	95.7	-1.33
Published	5	437	.19	.01,	.36	.20	.40	.0399	.0121	30.3	
Computer experience not reported	4	490	.14	.05,	.23	.15	.30	.0078	.0089	–	0.59
Computer experience reported	6	487	.07	-.10,	.24	.07	.14	.0474	.0134	28.3	
Pedagogical											
Work task	6	452	.06	-.04,	.16	.06	.12	.0159	.0150	94.0	-0.81
Educational task	4	525	.14	-.04,	.33	.15	.30	.0371	.0080	21.7	
No task experience	2	126	.02	-.04,	.08	.02	.04	.0019	.0177	–	-0.46
Some task experience	8	851	.12	.00,	.24	.12	.25	.0323	.0102	31.7	
Cognitive outcomes	7	707	.11	-.02,	.24	.11	.23	.0321	.0107	33.2	0.07
Skill-based outcomes	3	270	.10	-.06,	.26	.10	.20	.0217	.0126	57.8	

Note. The 95% confidence intervals were set around the uncorrected correlation using the standard error formula for heterogeneous studies. k = number of samples; N = total sample size; r = sample weighted average correlation; r_c = corrected weighted average correlation; d_c = corrected weighted average d statistic; $V(r_c)$ = weighted variance of the corrected correlation; $V(ve_c)$ = weighted sampling error variance; V_{art} = percentage of variance in r_c explained by study artifacts.
[a] t tests were conducted on the observed effect sizes.

following: Learner control has a larger effect on measures of procedural learning than declarative learning, or for skill-based outcomes than for cognitive outcomes; learner control is more effective in the learning of work-related tasks (than educational tasks) and when trainees have no prior task experience; learner control over pace and navigation results in better results than control over content; and the overall effectiveness of learner control is greater in more recent studies than in older studies.

On the one hand, the results suggest that the benefit of learner control lies in its ability to allow motivated learners to customize the learning environment to accomplish specific goals with respect to mastery of the content domain. On the other hand, there is little evidence in our meta-analysis that learner control led to more positive attitudes about training or the training content.

A New Model of Learner Control

Given a history of strong advocacy for learner control, it is surprising that cumulative research has failed to find strong support for the effects of learner control either on learning or on learner satisfaction. Our analyses indicate that although these effects are either small (on learning) or negligible (on attitudes), there remains considerable unexplained variance in effect sizes. Accordingly, there may be as-yet-unidentified variables that moderate the relationship between learner control and learner control outcomes. The model presented in the second half of this chapter proposes potential moderator variables for both learning and learner attitudes. Specifically, we propose that training characteristics and learner characteristics moderate the relationship between learner control (as classically defined) and learning, whereas learner preferences for control moderate the relationship between learner control and learner affect. In the next section, we discuss these relationships and distinguish among three newly defined variables: (a) objective learner control, (b) perceived learner control, and (c) preferred learner control. The proposed model is intended to apply to situations in which adult learners are acquiring work-related knowledge and skills.

Our proposed model is shown in Figure 4.1. In the center of the figure is *objective learner control*, which refers to the actual level and type of control afforded to learners in an instructional environment. This variable corresponds closely to traditional conceptualizations of learner control. We distinguish objective learner control from perceived learner control, which has received little prior attention (cf. Perlmuter & Monty, 1977). *Perceived learner control* refers to the extent to which learners believe or report that they can affect the pace, sequence, content, or advisement of training. As shown in the model, objective control leads to perceived learner control, but they are different constructs and not perfectly related.

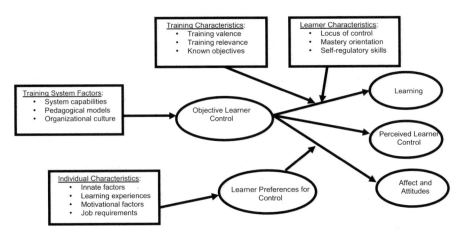

Figure 4.1. A proposed model of objective and perceived learner control.

The distinction between perceived and objective learner control suggests that in some situations learners may believe they have more or less control than they actually do. Little is known about the relationship between specific dimensions of objective learner control and perceived control. Thus, it is not known whether some dimensions of objective control are more salient to trainees than others. For example, would trainees who are given pace and advisement control perceive that they have more learner control than trainees who are given content and sequencing control? In one recent study, Park and Kraiger (2005) found that compared with participants in a low learner control condition, participants in a high learner control condition perceived that they had more control on the dimensions of sequence and advisement, but not on pace and content. The relationship between objective attributes of learner control and learner perceptions of control represent one fruitful area for future research. It also leads to the following proposition:

> PROPOSITION 1: There is not a perfect correspondence between objective and perceived learner control. In some situations, learners will perceive more or less control intended by the design of the learning system.

Figure 4.1 also includes learner preferences for control as a moderator of the relationship between objective and affect toward and attitudes about training. *Learner preference for control* refers to the extent to which learners desire control over the pace, sequence, content, or advisement of training (cf. Hannafin & Sullivan, 1996). Previous researchers have recognized that certain learners may prefer more control than others, particularly if they are older (Belbin, 1970; Hannafin, 1984) or more intelligent (Campbell,

1964; Snow, 1980). We suggest that this is a general preference across learners; each trainee enters a DLE with a conscious or unconscious preference for the level of control he or she will exert over that environment. Specifically, we propose the following:

> PROPOSITION 2: There is variability among learners in their preferences for learner control.

Antecedents of Learner Control

As shown in Figure 4.1, different factors influence objective and preferred learner control. Objective learner control occurs as a result of decision making or habit during the instructional design process. It is primarily affected by DLE capabilities, pedagogical models, and organizational culture. Specifically, the level of learner control will be influenced in part by the bandwidth available to learners or training system capabilities (e.g., Forcheri, Molfino, & Quarati, 1998).

How much learner control is given to trainees will also be influenced by the pedagogical models underlying design processes. High levels of learner control are likely to be implemented by instructional designers who favor cognitive (e.g., Merrill, 1983; Reigeluth & Stein, 1983), situated cognition (e.g., J. S. Brown, Collins, & Duguid, 1989) or constructivist instructional models (e.g., Spiro, Feltovich, Jacobson, & Coulson, 1991). Similarly, efforts to plan for aptitude–treatment interactions (Cronbach & Snow, 1981) may lead to decisions for greater customization of the learning environment through high learner control.

Finally, decisions about learner control may be shaped by the organizational culture in which training is embedded. For example, the U.S. military culture is mechanistic in nature, emphasizing hierarchical decision making and high structure. Most military training uses intelligent tutoring systems that limit learner choices (e.g., Burns & Capps, 1988; Ong & Ramachandran, 2000). In contrast, companies that value individual autonomy may tend to develop more open training systems that provide employees opportunities to decide what and how to learn.

Whereas objective learner control is determined largely by system factors, trainees' preferences for learner control are determined entirely by individual-difference variables, including innate individual factors, prior experiences in learning environments, motivational factors, and their perceptions of relevant job requirements. By *innate factors* we mean variables such as cognitive ability (Ackerman, 1988; Campbell, 1964; Hannafin, 1984), psychomotor ability (Kanfer & Ackerman, 1989) or perceptual speed and accuracy. Learners high in cognitive ability may impose constraints on learning tasks and prefer learning spaces that allow them to focus only on gaps in their knowledge.

Preferences will also be influenced by a number of beliefs and expectancies shaped by prior instructional experiences, the valence of learning new knowledge and skills, maturation with respect to individualized strategies and tactics for self-regulated learning (Winne, 1996), and motivational or attitudinal variables such as self-efficacy or locus of control (Keller, Goldman, & Sutterer, 1978). In short, learners will seek more control when they believe it is advantageous for learning. Our model predicts that trainees who perceive training as relevant, believe they can be successful in training, and are motivated to do well in training are more likely to be active learners and prefer greater control over the learning environment. In work settings, trainees who perceive the need for specific information to meet job requirements will also desire more control than trainees who are unfamiliar with work requirements or who do not need specific job-related information. In sum, we propose the following:

> PROPOSITION 3: Individuals' preferences for learner control can be predicted from other individual-level factors, including innate abilities, prior experience in DLEs, motivation to learn, and perceptions of work requirements.

Consequences of Learner Control: Learning

The model in Figure 4.1 proposes that objective learner control will have a direct influence on both trainee learning and trainees' affect and attitudes but that each relationship will be moderated by other variables. Learning outcomes are defined broadly (Kraiger, 2002) and include variables such as knowledge acquisition, long-term transfer and retention, and acquisition/enhancement of self-regulatory processes such as learning to learn (i.e., the development of learning strategies and tactics). The proposed relationship is consistent with our meta-analytic results that show both a main effect of learner control and unexplained variance due to possible moderators.

Although the model proposes that training characteristics will moderate the relationship between objective learner control and learning, there is little research on which to draw to support hypothesized relationships because most prior research has been done in educational psychology, where learning is not discretionary. However, in work settings employees may find learner control more or less advantageous to learning. In these situations, we propose the following:

> PROPOSITION 4: Learner control will have a greater impact on individual learning when: training has a high valence, training is linked to specific job requirements (as opposed to general trainee development), and training objectives are known to trainees.

We predict that under these conditions trainees will be motivated to seek the specific information necessary to do their jobs and will use learner control to improve the efficiency and quality of their learning.

The relationship between objective learner control and trainee learning will also be moderated by learner characteristics: learners' locus of control, mastery orientation, and self-regulatory learning skills. *Locus of control* refers to a generalized expectancy of the extent to which a person perceives that life events are a consequence of one's behavior (Rotter, 1966). Individuals with an internal locus of control may be more likely to benefit from learner control given a personal history that has reinforced such control in the past. Past research has shown that locus of control moderates learning in learner control and program control studies (G. J. Allen, Giat, & Cherney, 1974; Sandler, Reese, Spencer, & Harpin, 1983).

Goal orientation refers to the goals typically set by individuals in achievement situations (including instructional settings). Trainees with a performance orientation are concerned with demonstrating competence or achieving positive evaluations. Trainees with a mastery orientation seek to learn new skills and knowledge through training (Dweck, 1986). Trainees with a mastery orientation are more likely to try new behaviors or persist in the learning of difficult tasks (e.g., S. L. Fisher & Ford, 1998). Accordingly, goal orientation should moderate the objective learner control–learning relationship. Specifically, trainees with a mastery orientation will be more likely to learn given learner control because they will demonstrate more exploratory behaviors, persist in the event of initial learning difficulty, and better monitor and self-correct learning performance.

The third individually based moderator is trainees' self-regulatory learning skills. *Self-regulated learning skills* refers to the set of metacognitive, motivational, and behavioral techniques used by a learner to control his or her own learning process (Zimmerman, 1990). *Metacognitive skills* refers to both learners' awareness of their learning process and progress and their ability to control such processes (Winne, 1996). For example, a trainee may or may not sense that listening to training content is an effective method for learning, and he or she may or may not choose an alternative instructional method given this awareness. Self-regulatory learning skills may also involve motivational goal-setting or affect regulation, such as dealing with frustration (Winne, 1995). Self-regulated learners also may engage in behaviors that facilitate learning, such as self-generating or seeking external feedback (Winne, 1996), setting goals and controlling their behavior to attain that goal (Pintrich, 1995), and actively connecting new information with existing knowledge (Corno & Mandinach, 1983). There has been only limited research on self-regulated learning skills as a moderator of the learner control–learning relationship (see Eom & Reiser, 2000), although other studies have shown that the impact of learner control on learning outcomes is moderated by the component variables of self-regulated learning, such as use of available resources (Ross & Rakow, 1981) and meta-cognitive skills (see Goforth, 1994, for a review). Accordingly, learners who are characterized as having high self-regulatory learning skills should be more likely to learn in environments with high learner control. In summary, we propose the following with respect to individual characteristics as moderators:

> PROPOSITION 5: The relationship between objective learner control and learning in DLEs will be moderated by the extent to which learners exhibit an internal locus of control, a mastery orientation, and components of self-regulated learning skills.

Consequences of Learner Control: Affect and Attitudes

Figure 4.1 also shows that affective and attitudinal variables are hypothesized to result from the relationship between objective and preferred learner control. Affective and attitudinal outcomes include affective reactions to training, intrinsic motivation, willingness to attend additional training, and time on task (see Kraiger, 2002).

Specifically, the more the actual level of learner control matches preferred control, the more positive will be the affect or attitudes of trainees. K. G. Brown (2005) recently presented a model suggesting that trainees' reactions to training include both specific dimensions and an underlying general affective component. Thus, when asked to rate a DLE experience, learners may report specific reactions linked to training events. However, the level of these evaluations (and the intercorrelations among ratings) may be influenced by an overall mood-enhancing or -debilitating effect. In our model, that effect would be the extent to which objective learner control matches preferred learner control. Trainees who experience a level of control that corresponds with their preferred level will enjoy training more, engage in training longer, and be more likely to take more training than trainees who receive too much or too little control.

Because few others have examined preferences for learner control as an individual-difference variable, there has been little research on its role as a moderator. Hannafin and Sullivan (1996) found no evidence of more positive relationships when objective and preferred control matched, but positive support was found in studies by Domino (1971) and Freitag and Sullivan (1995). Although more research is needed to understand the effects of correspondence on specific outcome variables, K. G. Brown's (2005) model of general affect and aforementioned research are sufficient to propose the following:

PROPOSITION 6: Learner preferences for control will moderate the relationship between objective control and learners' affect toward or attitudes about instruction.

SUMMARY AND CONCLUSION

In this chapter, we have summarized past research on learner control through a meta-analysis that shows that learner control works for certain learning outcomes under certain conditions. However, study outcomes in general have not been as positive as might be predicted by learner control advocates, for either learning or affective reactions to training. It is possible that prior research has failed in part because prior studies have not adequately distinguished between actual learner control and perceived control and prior studies have not adequately considered potential moderators between objective learner control and learning in and reactions toward instruction. Accordingly, we proposed a model of learner control for adult learners that distinguished objective learner control and perceived learner control. We also consider learner preferences for control an important moderator between objective control and affect toward and attitudes about instruction: Learner control will be positively perceived only when it matches learner preferences for control. Finally, we suggest that objective learner control will not always lead to greater learning, only when certain training and trainee characteristics are present. The model is accompanied by a number of general propositions in the hope that these will generate additional productive research on the important topic of learner control.

REFERENCES

References marked with an asterisk indicate studies included in the meta-analysis.

Ackerman, P. L. (1988). Determinants of individual differences during skill acquisition: Cognitive abilities and information processing. *Journal of Experimental Psychology: General, 117,* 288–318.

Allen, G. J., Giat, L., & Cherney, R. J. (1974). Locus of control, test anxiety, and student performance in a PSI course. *Journal of Educational Psychology, 66,* 968–973.

*Allen, G. W. (1990, February). *Learner control of review in computer assisted instruction within a military training environment.* Paper presented at the annual convention of the Association for Educational Communications and Technology, Anaheim, CA.

Arnone, M. P., & Grabowski, B. L. (1992). Effects on children's achievement and curiosity of variations in learner control over an interactive video lesson. *Educational Technology Research and Development, 40*, 15–27.

Avner, A., Moore, C., & Smith, S. (1980). Active external control: A basis for superiority of CBI. *Journal of Computer-Based Instruction, 6*, 115–118.

Ayersman, D. J. (1996). Reviewing the research on hypermedia-based learning. *Journal of Research on Computing in Education, 28*, 500–525.

Becker, D. A., & Dwyer, M. M. (1994). Using hypermedia to provide learner control. *Journal of Educational Multimedia and Hypermedia, 3*, 155–172.

Belbin, R. M. (1970). The discovery method in training older workers. In H. L. Sheppard (Ed.), *Towards an industrial gerontology* (pp. 56–60). Cambridge, MA: Schenkman.

*Bill, R. L. (1990). The role of advance organizers, learner control, and student's locus-of-control on acquisition of pharmacokinetic concepts and attitudes towards computer-assisted instruction (Doctoral dissertation, Purdue University, 1990). *Dissertation Abstracts International, 51*, 1885.

*Boling, N. C., & Robinson, D. H. (1999). Individual study, interactive multimedia, or cooperative learning: Which activity best supplements lecture-based distance education? *Journal of Educational Psychology, 91*, 169–174.

Borsook, T. K., & Higginbotham-Wheat, N. (1992, February). *A psychology of hypermedia: A conceptual framework for research and development.* Paper presented at the annual meeting of the Association for Educational Communications and Technology, Washington, DC.

Brown, J. S., Collins, A., & Duguid, P. (1989). Situated cognition and the culture of learning. *Education Researcher, 18*, 32–42.

Brown, K. G. (2005). An examination of the structure and nomological network of trainee reactions: A closer look at "smile sheets." *Journal of Applied Psychology, 90*, 991–1001.

Burns, H., & Capps, C. (1988). Foundations of intelligent tutoring systems: An introduction. In M. C. Polson & J. J. Richardson (Eds.), *Foundations of intelligent tutoring systems* (pp. 1–19). Hillsdale, NJ: Erlbaum.

*Burwell, L. B. (1989). The interaction of learning styles with learner control treatments in an interactive videodisk lesson on astronomy (Doctoral dissertation, University of North Carolina at Greensboro, 1989). *Dissertation Abstracts International, 50*, 3458.

Campbell, V. N. (1964). Self-direction and programmed instruction for five different types of learning objectives. *Psychology in the Schools, 1*, 348–359.

*Cho, Y. (1995, June). *Learner control, cognitive processes, and hypertext learning environments.* Paper presented at the Annual National Educational Computing Conference and Technology, Baltimore.

Conklin, J. (1987). Hypertext: An introduction and survey. *IEEE Computer, 20*, 17–41.

*Coorough, R. P. (1990). The effects of program control, learner control and learner control with advisement lesson control strategies on anxiety and learning from computer-assisted instruction (Doctoral dissertation, University of Florida, 1990). *Dissertation Abstracts International, 51*, 3391.

Corno, L., & Mandinach, E. B. (1983). The role of cognitive engagement in classroom learning and motivation. *Educational Psychologist, 18*, 88–108.

Cronbach, L. J., & Snow, R. E. (1981). *Aptitudes and instructional methods: A handbook for research on interactions.* New York: Irvington.

*Crooks, S. M., & Klein, J. D. (1996). Effects of cooperative learning and learner-control modes in computer-based instruction. *Journal of Research on Computing in Education, 29*, 109–121.

Dalton, D. W. (1990). The effects of cooperative learning strategies on achievement and attitudes during interactive video. *Journal of Computer-Based Instruction, 17*, 8–16.

DeRouin, R. E., Fritzsche, B. A., & Salas, E. (2004). Optimizing e-learning: Research-based guidelines for learner-controlled training. *Human Resource Management, 43*, 147–162.

*Diaz, V. M. (1994). The effects of cognitive style and locus of instructional control strategies on learner achievement and anxiety in an interactive videodisk lesson on the structure and function of the human brain (Doctoral dissertation, University of Florida, 1994). *Dissertation Abstracts International, 54*, 6772.

Domino, G. (1971). Interactive effects of achievement orientation and teaching style on academic achievement. *Journal of Educational Psychology, 62*, 427–431.

Dweck, C. S. (1986). Motivational processes affecting learning. *American Psychologist, 41*, 1040–1048.

*Eom, W., & Reiser, R. A. (2000). The effects of self-regulation and instructional control on performance and motivation in computer-based instruction. *International Journal of Instructional Media, 27*, 247–260.

*Fisher, J. B., Deshler, D. D., & Schumaker, J. B. (1999). The effects of an interactive multimedia program on teachers' understanding and implementation of an inclusive practice. *Learning Disability Quarterly, 22*, 127–142.

Fisher, S. L., & Ford, J. K. (1998). Differential effects of learner effort and goal orientation on two learner outcomes. *Personnel Psychology, 51*, 397–420.

Forcheri, P., Molfino, M. T., & Quarati, A. (1998). Design of learner-centered tools for continuous training in SMEs. *Education & Information Technology, 3*, 1–16.

Freitag, E. T., & Sullivan, H. J. (1995). Matching learner preference to amount of instruction: An alternative form of learner control. *Educational Technology Research and Development, 43*(2), 5–14.

Friend, C. L., & Cole, C. L. (1990). Learner control in computer-based instruction: A current literature review. *Educational Technology, 20*, 47–49.

Gist, M. E., Schwoerer, C., & Rosen, B. (1989). Effects of alternative training methods on self-efficacy and performance in computer software training. *Journal of Applied Psychology, 74*, 884–891.

Goforth, D. J. (1994). Learner control = decision making + information: A model and meta-analysis. *Journal of Educational Computing Research, 11*, 1–26.

Gray, S. H. (1987). The effect of sequence control on computer assisted learning. *Journal of Computer-Based Instruction 14*, 54–56.

Hannafin, M. J. (1984). Guidelines for using locus of instructional control in the design of computer-assisted instruction. *Journal of Instructional Development, 7*, 6–10.

Hannafin, M. J., & Sullivan, H. J. (1996). Preferences and learner control over amount of instruction. *Journal of Educational Psychology, 88*, 162–173.

*Hassett, M. R. (1990). Differences in attitude toward computer-based video instruction and learner control choices made by baccalaureate nursing students of sensing and intuitive psychological type (Doctoral dissertation, University of Texas, 1990). *Dissertation Abstracts International, 51*, 4277.

Hedges, L. V., & Olkin, I. (1985). *Statistical methods for meta-analysis*. Orlando, FL: Academic Press.

Hintze, H., Mohr, H., & Wenzel, A. (1988). Students' attitudes towards control methods in computer-assisted instruction. *Journal of Computer Assisted Learning, 4*, 3–10.

*Howell, A. W. (2002). A process model of learner behavior and engagement during Web-based training (Doctoral dissertation, Michigan State University, 2002). *Dissertation Abstracts International, 62*, 3834.

*Hsin-Yih, S., & Brown, S. W. (1992). Learner control versus program in interactive videodisc instruction: What are the effects in procedural learning? *International Journal of Instructional Media, 19*, 85–96.

*Hsin-Yih, S., & Brown, S. W. (1995). Learner-control: The effects of learning a procedural task during computer-based videodisc instruction. *International Journal of Instructional Media, 22*, 217–229.

Huffcutt, A. I., & Arthur, W. (1995). Development of a new outlier statistic for meta-analytic data. *Journal of Applied Psychology, 80*, 327–334.

Hunter, J. E., & Schmidt, F. L. (1990). *Methods of meta-analysis: Correcting error and bias in research findings*. Newbury Park, CA: Sage.

Hunter, J. E., & Schmidt, F. L. (2004). *Methods of meta-analysis: Correcting for bias in research findings* (2nd ed.). Thousand Oaks, CA: Sage.

Jeffries, P. R. (2001). Computer versus lecture: A comparison of two methods of teaching oral medication administration in a nursing skills laboratory. *Journal of Nursing Education, 40*, 323–329.

Jonassen, D. H. (1989). *Hypertext/hypermedia*. Englewood Cliffs, NJ: Educational Technology Publications.

Kanfer, R., & Ackerman, P. L. (1989). Motivation and cognitive abilities: An integrative/aptitude–treatment interaction approach to skill acquisition [Monograph]. *Journal of Applied Psychology, 74*, 657–690.

Keller, J. M., Goldman, J. A., & Sutterer, J. R. (1978). Locus of control in relation to academic attitudes and performance in a personalized system of instruction course. *Journal of Educational Psychology, 70*, 414–421.

Kinzie, M. B., & Sullivan, H. J. (1989). Continuing motivation, learner control, and CAI. *Educational Technology Research and Development, 37(2)*, 5–14.

Kinzie, M. B., Sullivan, H. J., & Berdel, R. L. (1988). Learner control and achievement in science computer-assisted instruction. *Journal of Educational Psychology, 80*, 299–303.

Kraiger, K. (2002). Decision-based evaluation. In K. Kraiger (Ed.), *Creating, implementing, and maintaining effective training and development: State-of-the-art lessons for practice* (pp. 331–375). San Francisco: Jossey-Bass.

Lahey, G. F., Hurlock, R. E., & McCann, P. H. (1973). *Post-lesson remediation and learner control of branching in computer-based learning.* (ERIC Document Reproduction Service No. ED083797)

*Lee, J. (1999). The effects of students' choice of instructional control in computer-based instruction (Doctoral dissertation, University of Wyoming, 1999). *Dissertation Abstracts International, 60*, 0105.

Lee, S. S., & Wong, S. C. H. (1989). Adaptive program vs. learner control strategy on computer-aided learning of gravimetric stoichiometry problems. *Journal of Research on Computing in Education, 21*, 367–379.

Lepper, M. R. (1985). Microcomputers in education: Motivational and social issues. *American Psychologist, 40*, 1–18.

MacGregor, S. K. (1988). Instructional design for computer-mediated text systems: Effects of motivation, learner control, and collaboration on reading performance. *Journal of Experimental Education, 56*, 142–147.

*Maier, D. J. (2002). *The impact of learner control over sequencing on retention and transfer in time-controlled Web-based instruction.* Unpublished doctoral dissertation, Wayne State University.

Maki, R. H., Maki, W. S., Patterson, M., & Whittaker, P. D. (2000). Evaluation of a Web-based introductory psychology course: I. learning and satisfaction in on-line versus lecture courses. *Behavior Research Methods, Instruments, & Computers, 32*, 230–239.

Marchionini, G. (1988). Hypermedia and learning: Freedom and chaos. *Educational Technology, 28*, 8–12.

*Mattoon, J. S. (1991, January). *Learner control versus computer control in instructional simulation.* Paper presented at the convention of the Association for Educational Communications and Technology, Orlando, FL.

*Mayer, R. E., & Chandler, P. (2001). When learning is just a click away: Does simple user interaction foster deeper understanding of multimedia messages. *Journal of Educational Psychology, 93*, 390–397.

*McGrath, D. (1992). Hypertext, CAI, paper, or program control: Do learners benefit from choices? *Journal of Research on Computing in Education, 24*, 513–531.

Merrill, M. D. (1975). Learner control: Beyond aptitude–treatment interactions. *AV Communication Review, 23*, 217–226.

Merrill, M. D. (1983). Component display theory. In C. M. Reigeluth (Ed.), *Instructional design theories and models* (pp. 279–327). Hillsdale, NJ: Erlbaum.

Milheim, W. D. (1989, February). *Perceived attitudinal effects of various types of learner control in an interactive video lesson.* Paper presented at the annual meetings of the Association for Educational Communications and Technology, Dallas, TX. (ERIC Document Reproduction Service No. ED308828)

Milheim, W. D., & Martin, B. L. (1991). Theoretical basis for the use of learner control: Three different perspectives. *Journal of Computer-Based Instruction, 18*, 99–105.

Morrison, G. R., Ross, S. M., & Baldwin, W. (1992). Learner control of context and instructional support in learning elementary school mathematics. *Educational Technology Research and Development, 40(1)*, 5–13.

Murphy, M. A., & Davidson, G. V. (1991). Computer-based adaptive instruction: Effects of learner control on concept learning. *Journal of Computer-Based Instruction, 18*, 51–56.

Niemiec, R. P., Sikorski, C., & Walberg, H. J. (1996). Learner-control effects: A review of reviews and a meta-analysis. *Journal of Educational Computing Research, 15*, 157–174.

Ong, J., & Ramachandran, S. (2000, February). Intelligent tutoring systems: The what and how. *ASTD Learning Circuits.* Retrieved July 6, 2006, from http://www.learningcircuits.org/feb2000/ong.html

Park, S., & Kraiger, K. (2005, August). *The relationship between actual and perceived learner control.* Paper presented at the annual meeting of the Academy of Management, Honolulu, HI.

Parsons, J. A. (1992). A meta-analysis of learner control in computer-based learning environments (Doctoral dissertation, Nova University, 1991). *Dissertation Abstracts International, 53*, 4290.

*Penland, P. (1979). Self-initiated learning. *Adult Education, 39*, 170–179.

Perlmuter, L. C., & Monty, R. A. (1977). The importance of perceived control: Fact or fantasy? *American Scientist, 65*, 759–765.

Pintrich, P. R. (1995). Understanding self-regulated learning. *New Directions for Teaching and Learning, 63*, 3–12.

*Pridemore, D. R., & Klein, J. D. (1991). Control of feedback in computer-assisted instruction. *Educational Technology Research and Development, 39(4)*, 27–32.

*Pridemore, D. R., & Klein, J. D. (1992, February). *Effects of learner control over feedback in computer-based instruction.* Paper presented at the convention of the Association for Educational Communications and Technology, Washington, DC.

Pridemore, D. R., & Klein, J. D. (1993, January). *Learner control of feedback in a computer lesson.* Paper presented at the convention of the Association for Educational Communications and Technology, New Orleans, LA.

*Reeves, T. C. (1993). Pseudoscience in computer-based instruction: The case of learner control research. *Journal of Computer-Based Instruction, 20*, 39–46.

Reigeluth, C. M., & Stein, F. S. (1983). The elaboration theory of instruction. In C. M. Reigeluth (Ed.), *Instructional design theories and models: An overview of their current status* (pp. 335–381). Hillsdale, NJ: Erlbaum.

Rosenberg, M. J. (2001). *E-learning: Strategies for delivering knowledge in the digital age.* New York: McGraw-Hill.

*Ross, S. M., & Rakow, E. A. (1981). Learner control versus program control as adaptive strategies for selection of instruction support on math rules. *Journal of Educational Psychology, 73*, 745–753.

Rotter, J. B. (1966). Generalized expectancies for internal locus of control of reinforcement. *Psychological Monographs, 80*(1, Whole No. 60).

Sandler, I., Reese, F., Spencer, L., & Harpin, P. (1983). Person × Environment interaction and locus of control: Laboratory therapy, and classroom studies. In H. M. Lefcourt (Ed.), *Research with the locus of control construct: Vol. 2. Developments and social problems* (pp. 187–251). Hillsdale, NJ: Erlbaum.

*Schnackenberg, H. L., & Sullivan, H. J. (2000). Learner control over full and lean computer-based instruction under differing ability levels. *Educational Technology Research and Development, 48*(2), 19–35.

Shyu, H. Y., & Brown, S. W. (1992). Learner control versus program control in interactive videodisc instruction: What are the effects in procedural learning? *International Journal of Instructional Media, 19*, 85–96.

*Silverstein, N. E. (1989). Computer-based training: The effects of graphics and learner control on retention (Doctoral dissertation, Hofstra University, 1989). *Dissertation Abstracts International, 50*, 1996.

Simon, S. J., & Werner, J. M. (1996). Computer training through behavior modeling, self-paced, and instructional approaches: A field experiment. *Journal of Applied Psychology, 81*, 648–659.

Sims, R., & Hedberg, J. (1995). Dimensions of learner control: A reappraisal for interactive multimedia instruction. In J. M. Pearce & A. Ellis (Eds.), *Learning with technology: Proceedings of the Twelfth Annual Conference of the Australian Society for Computers in Learning in Tertiary Education* (pp. 468–475). Melbourne, Australia: University of Melbourne.

Snow, R. E. (1980). Aptitude, learner control, and adaptive instruction. *Educational Psychologist, 15*, 151–158.

Spiro, R. J., Feltovich, P. L., Jacobson, M. J., & Coulson, R. L. (1991). Cognitive flexibility, constructivism, and hypertext: Random access instruction for advanced knowledge acquisition in ill-structured domains. *Educational Technology, 31*(5), 24–33.

Staninger, S. W. (1994). Hypertext technology: Educational consequences. *Educational Technology, 6*, 51–53.

Steinberg, E. R. (1977). Review of student control in computer-assisted instruction. *Journal of Computer-Based Instruction, 3*, 84–90.

Steinberg, E. R. (1989). Cognition and learner control: A literature review, 1977–1988. *Journal of Computer-Based Instruction, 16,* 117–121.

*Swaak, J., & De Jong, T. (2001). Learner vs. system control in using online support for simulation-based discovery learning. *Learning Environments Research, 4,* 217–241.

Tennyson, R. D., & Buttrey, T. (1980). Advisement and management strategies as design variables in computer-assisted instruction. *Educational Communications and Technology Journal, 28,* 169–176.

Tennyson, R. D., Park, O. C., & Christensen, D. L. (1985). Adaptive control of learning time and content sequence in concept learning using computer-based instruction. *Journal of Educational Psychology, 77,* 481–491.

*Timmons, P. L., Oehlert, M. E., Summerall, S. W., Timmons, C. W., & Borgers, S. B. (1997). Stress inoculation training for maladaptive anger: Comparison of group counseling versus computer guidance. *Computers in Human Behavior, 13,* 51–64.

Whitener, E. M. (1990). Confusion of confidence intervals and credibility intervals in meta-analysis. *Journal of Applied Psychology, 75,* 315–321.

Winne, P. H. (1995). Inherent details in self-regulated learning. *Educational Psychologist, 30,* 173–187.

Winne, P. H. (1996). A metacognitive view of individual differences in self-regulatory learning. *Learning and Individual Differences, 8,* 327–353.

Zimmerman, B. J. (1990). Self-regulated learning and academic achievement: An overview. *Educational Psychologist, 2,* 3–17.

II

DISTRIBUTED TEAMS AND DISTRIBUTED TEAM TRAINING

5

ADVANCED DISTRIBUTED LEARNING FOR TEAM TRAINING IN COMMAND AND CONTROL APPLICATIONS

BARRY P. GOETTL, ALAN R. S. ASHWORTH III, AND SCOTT R. CHAIKEN

Today's technological advances in weaponry and communications systems, along with military drawbacks, leaner budgets, and the changing nature of modern warfare, combine to place serious demands on Department of Defense (DOD) training programs. One consequence of this interaction is a push within the DOD for distributed learning and training (DLT) systems. In this chapter, we discuss the unique training needs of the DOD and how DLT can be exploited to address the increased training demands. We also discuss the important distinction between *physical* and *cognitive* fidelity and how these dimensions relate to the efficiency and effectiveness of training. We define *fidelity* as the degree to which a training system accurately reflects a particular characteristic of the domain to be learned. The distinction between physical and cognitive fidelity is critical, because many training developers try to maximize physical fidelity in the hopes of maximizing transfer. Often, this leads to poor training because the critical cognitive elements are not apparent to learners and must be divined through repetition. We argue that cognitive fidelity is critical early in training, whereas physical fidelity is important later in training. We discuss an important challenge that cognitive fidelity poses for validation of training and present a validation method, called *backward transfer* that is ideally suited for systems that have high cognitive fidelity and low physical fidelity. Finally, we demonstrate the utility of backward transfer by applying it to a simulated Airborne Warning and Control Systems (AWACS) task. Although our discussion focuses on Air Force training, much of what we argue and demonstrate applies to any training system, distributed or not, military or not.

DEPARTMENT OF DEFENSE POLICY ON ADVANCED DISTRIBUTED LEARNING

To meet increased training needs of the DOD, the Office of the Secretary of Defense has created the *Advanced Distributed Learning initiative* (ADL), whose mission is "to provide the highest quality education and training that can be tailored to individual needs and delivered cost effectively, anywhere and anytime" (DOD, 1999, p. 37). As noted in the DOD implementation plan for ADL, one of the primary objectives of the DOD ADL initiative is to develop guidelines for large-scale development and implementation of efficient and effective distributed learning. In short, the ADL initiative is the DOD's program for pursuing DLT systems. The ADL mission of the DOD to deliver courseware and training "anywhere, anytime" has important implications not only for how courseware elements can be readily shared across platforms but also for the pedagogical principles underlying the content, structure, and validation of training. Our goal in writing this chapter is to advocate that these pedagogical principles be given adequate consideration in the design and development of distributed training within the DOD.

One example of a DLT approach to training is the Air Force's Distributed Mission Training (DMT) program (Andrews, 2000). In DMT, high-fidelity simulators located at various bases around the world and connected through a high-speed network are used to create a simulated battlefield in which teams of Air Force, Army, and Navy personnel can execute a simulated battle plan, rehearse missions, and engage synthetic enemies. DMT is an amazing demonstration of technological advances in training. It also illustrates a strong tendency in the DOD to develop training systems of high physical fidelity that are captured in the popular phrase "train the way we fight and fight the way we train" (Rumsfeld, 2001). This training policy is strongly emphasized in the DOD because of the necessity of combat training to maximize transfer.

PHYSICAL FIDELITY AND TRANSFER

The ultimate goal of military training is to prepare soldiers for all aspects of war. In this context, the consequence of inadequate or improper training is mission failure. Moreover, combat induces extreme levels of stress that hinders performance of trained soldiers. For example, after the battle of Gettysburg, more than 200 rifles were found to have been muzzle-loaded five or more times without being fired (Walker & Burkhardt, 1965, as cited in Idzikowski & Baddeley, 1983). Thus, training to achieve war-fighting capability demands the highest levels of skill possible, and these skills must be insulated from the deleterious effects of stress. History suggests that combat experience reduces the detrimental effects of stress on performance. It is often the first battle in a war that incurs the most casualties (Druckman & Bjork, 1994). These findings, along with the inputs from soldiers with combat experience, have initiated and maintained the view that to maximize transfer of combat training, you must "train the way you fight."

Learning theory also provides some support for the train-the-way-you-fight principle. Thorndike and Woodworth's (1901) *theory of identical elements* (as cited in Druckman & Bjork, 1994) states that the amount of transfer depends on the extent to which the training and transfer environments contain identical features. Singley and Anderson (1989) updated this theory and suggested that production rules are the identical elements necessary for transfer. Similar instantiations of the identical-elements notion are evident in Rajaram, Srinivas, and Roediger's (1998) transfer-appropriate-processing account of implicit memory; Healy and Bourne's work on arithmetic skills (e.g., Rickard, Healy, & Bourne, 1994) and Morse Code reception (Clawson, Healy, Ericsson, & Bourne, 2001); and Baldwin and Ford's (1988) work on transfer in the work environment. These theories argue the notion that as the number of features shared between the training and transfer environment increases, so does the amount of transfer. These theories differ, of course, in the extent to which those identical elements are physical features, abstract representations, or specific procedures.

Limitations of Physical Fidelity

Training Efficiency

Training efficiency is defined as the cost of training relative to transfer. High physical fidelity has a negative impact on training efficiency. Roscoe (1980) described the relationships between transfer and fidelity and cost and fidelity. Figure 5.1 is adapted from his book. The upper curve in this figure shows the relationship between the transfer and fidelity. This is a negatively accelerating function indicating that increased fidelity leads to

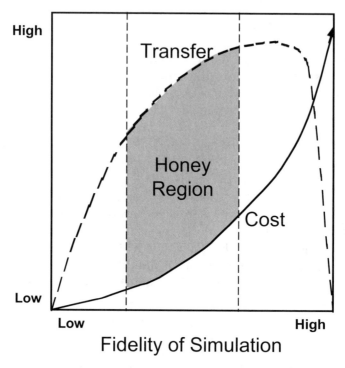

Figure 5.1. Roscoe's (1980) honey region, showing the relationship among fidelity, cost, and transfer of training. From *Aviation Psychology* (p. 197), by S. N. Roscoe, 1980, Ames: Iowa State University Press. Copyright 1980 by Iowa State University Press. Adapted with permission.

smaller and smaller gains in transfer as fidelity increases. At the same time, the cost of fidelity, the bottom curve in Figure 5.1, increases exponentially as fidelity increases. Together, these curves illustrate the point that as fidelity increases, the cost per unit of transfer increases dramatically; training becomes less efficient. The region in between these curves is what Roscoe referred to as the *honey region*, the area where a large amount of transfer can be achieved through relatively low-fidelity, low-cost training systems.

Training Effectiveness

Training effectiveness relates to the overall quality of the training. High physical fidelity does not always result in effective training systems. The emphasis on physical fidelity embodied in the train-the-way-you-fight principle tends to assume that the world is ideally designed for learning. It also assumes that the training environment should be as similar to the operational environment as possible and that whole-task training is the most effective approach. Schneider (1985) enumerated six questionable assumptions of the train-the-way-you-fight principle: (a) the real world optimally presents learners the information they need to learn a task, (b) the real world optimally sequences training events, (c) it is best to train when attentional capacities are overloaded, (d) it is acceptable to be confused about how errors influence performance, (e) frustration due to errors and poor performance does not reduce effort, and (f) there is little transfer from component task training to total performance.

The reality is that the world does not always present the information in a format that is optimal for learning. For example, the learning literature demonstrates that large and enduring training effects can be gained by manipulating the order and spacing of items during learning (Baddeley & Longman, 1978); training the most difficult aspects to criterion first (Bailey, Hughes, & Jones, 1980; Wightman & Sistrunk, 1987); training attentional allocation to avoid focusing on task elements that improve immediate performance, but not long-term performance (Yechiam, Erev, Yehene, & Gopher, 2003); and presenting information in ways that encourage the development of pattern recognition skill (Biederman & Shiffrar, 1987; Vidulich, Yeh, & Schneider, 1983). Similarly, Renkl and Atkinson (2003) recommended starting with worked examples and gradually integrating problem-solving elements until learners are finally capable of solving problems on their own. Space limitations do not permit a detailed discussion of all these effects, but two examples will illustrate the point.

Biederman and Shiffrar (1987) examined the training of chicken plant workers whose task is to sex the chicks (i.e., determine the sex of chicks) so that they may be sorted shortly after birth. This task is traditionally trained through apprenticeship, wherein novices are placed in front of trays of live chicks and must sort them by gender. Experts check and grade the apprentices' performance. It is estimated that visual discrimination skill acquisition with this approach takes 2.4 months to reach 90% accuracy and up to 6 years to reach maximum performance. Moreover, experts trained with this approach are unable to specify what physical characteristics are essential for successfully performing the task. After a single afternoon of studying professional chicken sorters, Biederman and his colleagues identified one isolated physical characteristic that allowed novices to improve from 60% on a pretest to 90% on a posttest after a 1-minute training session. Novices who did not receive the training performed at 65% on the posttest. Experts with an average of 24 years of experience performed at 84% on the posttest. It is clear that "training like you sex" was not the optimal pedagogy for acquiring the skill of identifying the gender of day-old chicks. By identifying and stressing one physical feature, 1 min of theory-driven training led to pattern recognition skill equivalent to that of 24 years of experience.

Vidulich et al. (1983) provided another illustration. Here the task was training air traffic controllers on air intercept of two aircraft for refueling. The train-the-way-you-fight approach would prescribe putting controllers in front of an air traffic controller display and require that they perform the air intercept task in real time. With that training approach, students observe dots on the screen that are moving so slowly that they cannot perceive the movement. Additionally, they observe only eight trials in 1 hour. Vidulich et al. increased the frame rate to present hundreds of intercept trials in an hour. As a result of this simple modification, students integrated the perceptual information and saw the paths that the aircraft followed instead of dots on a screen (enhanced perceptual cues), received many more training trials in the same amount of time (training efficiency), received better feedback from the training, developed a richer cognitive representation of the air intercept task domain, and could visualize multiple-intercept pathways on request. These gains were made by reducing the physical fidelity of the training environment and focusing on the critical components of the task.

We are not suggesting that the train-as-you-fight principle is always inappropriate. Instead, we are suggesting that one must consider the phase of skill acquisition as well as other dimensions of fidelity. The train-as-you-fight principle may be most appropriate for maximizing transfer of an already well-learned task.

Phases of Skill Acquisition

Fitts (1964) and Anderson (1982) have characterized *skill acquisition* as consisting of three phases: (a) cognitive, (b) associative, and (c) autonomous. In the *cognitive phase*, all learning is, in essence, represented verbally. Learning may best be characterized as a problem-solving task. Verbalization is required for learners to rehearse new rules and to learn the conditions in which they apply. In the *associative phase*, the skill becomes procedural. Condition and action sequences are learned and stored, and learning can be described as associative because specific stimuli are associated to specific responses: "If Condition A, then Response B." In the *automation phase*, skill continues to become smoother and faster, allowing for appropriate responses to previously unseen situations. Performance requires less and less attentional resources; task sequences begin to merge into a continuous action sequence or motor program. Evidence of the increasing task compilation is reflected by people's inability to stop a response sequence once it is initiated. Ackerman's work has been instrumental in empirically validating the shift in processing requirements as skill advances through these phases (Ackerman, 1994; Ackerman & Kanfer, 1993). Taatgen (2005) presented a model of how the compilation of cognitive skills leads to both parallel processing and increased response flexibility.

It is our position that training that uses extremely high physical fidelity is most appropriate and effective for later phases of skill acquisition, such as when highly skilled learners need to fine-tune skills, maintain skill readiness, and prepare for unique missions. For example, in the *procedural phase* some physical fidelity is needed so that perceptual patterns and specific responses can become associated. Learners must acquire the ability to recognize the critical elements in the environment and associate appropriate responses to them. Later, in the automation phase of learning, physical fidelity is even more important because the learner's skill is leaving volitional control and moving toward environmental control. The training environment should closely match the operational environment.

However, high physical fidelity is overly expensive and rather ineffective for initial skill development. In the declarative phase of learning, highly accurate physical representations of the task are not critical because learners are focusing at the level of verbal knowledge. Most critical at these early stages of skill acquisition is the fundamental nature (i.e., the deep structure) of the task (Clawson et al., 2001; Rickard et al., 1994). Training in the early stage should maximize cognitive fidelity.

COGNITIVE FIDELITY

Cognitive fidelity is defined as high conceptual similarity between training and performance environments. Whereas high physical fidelity mediates procedural transfer, high cognitive fidelity mediates conceptual transfer. An illustration of cognitive fidelity is provided in Figure 5.2. There are numerous examples of training environments with low physical fidelity but very high cognitive fidelity. Examples from the educational community include Voltaville (Glaser, Raghavan, & Schauble, 1988), which teaches circuits; Smithtown (Shute & Glaser, 1990), which teaches economics; Fundamental Skills Tutor (Meyer, Miller, Steuck, & Kretschmer, 1999; Steuck & Miller, 1997; Wheeler & Regian, 1999), which teaches science, algebra, and writing; and SHERLOCK, which teaches electronics troubleshooting (Lesgold, Lajoie, Bunzo, & Eggan, 1992). Another example is the Space Fortress task (see Gopher, Weil, & Bareket, 1994, for a full description). This task runs on a low-end PC and looks similar to a first-generation video game, such as Asteroids. Nevertheless, cognitive task analysis suggests that Space Fortress has a hierarchical structure (Frederiksen & White, 1989) that requires coordinated use of perceptual and motor skills as well as conceptual and strategic knowledge (Donchin, 1989; Mané & Donchin, 1989). Space Fortress represents some of the information-processing demands that are present in aviation, such as short- and long-term memory loading, high workload demands, dynamic attention allocation, decision making, prioritization, resource management, continuous motor control, and discrete motor responses (Gopher, Weil, & Siegel, 1989). Because of its high cognitive fidelity, Space Fortress has shown positive transfer to flight training for U.S. Army

Conceptual Analogy Between
Physical and Synthetic

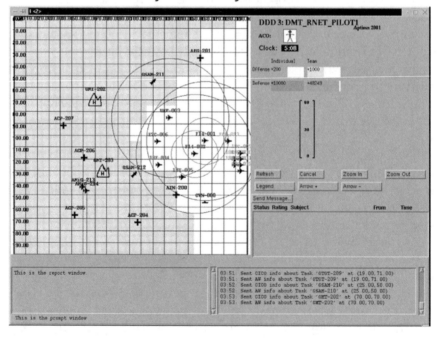

Figure 5.2. Although different in appearance (physical fidelity), the synthetic task (bottom) incorporates the same basic cognitive processes as the Airborne Warning and Control System (AWACS) weapons director task (top).

helicopter pilots (Hart & Battiste, 1992) and Israeli Air Force pilots (Gopher et al., 1994).

The problem-solving research of Holyoak and colleagues (e.g., Gick & Holyoak, 1980; Holyoak, 1985; Holyoak & Thagard, 1997) further demonstrates the power of conceptual transfer through cognitive analogy. They have shown strong transfer of problem-solving ability between problems with high concept structural overlap and virtually no physical resemblance. For example, Gick and Holyoak (1980) gave participants a problem-solving task taken from Duncker (1945). The problem concerned destroying a tumor using radiation. The amount of radiation needed to destroy the tumor would also damage healthy tissue. Participants had to devise a procedure for using the radiation to destroy the tumor but leave healthy tissue intact. The solution to the radiation problem is to divide the ray into several low-intensity rays all focused on the tumor from different angles. The effect of the combined rays would destroy the tumor without harming the tissue along any single ray pathway. This is an extremely difficult problem for which typically only 8% of respondents offer viable answers.

To test transfer of problem solving by means of shared cognitive concepts, Gick and Holyoak (1980) gave an analogous problem and solution to some participants before giving them the radiation problem. This problem concerned a general trying to attack a castle with a large army. The numerous roads leading to the castle contained mines that would be detonated by the vast army and prevent a successful attack on the castle. The general solved the problem by dividing his army into several small groups, each marching down a different road so that they all arrived at the castle at the same time. Notice that this problem and solution has a similar deep structure to the radiation problem but a completely different surface structure. About 76% of respondents given the general-attacking-the-castle problem offered the correct solution for the radiation problem. This is a tremendous increase in transfer from one problem to another, and it is mediated almost solely by the shared higher order construct of decomposing wholes into parts and then reassembling them somewhere else.

The notion of cognitive fidelity can also be framed in terms of surface structure versus deep structure. *Surface structure* is defined as the details of a task or problem that are readily apparent but not necessarily conceptually or functionally relevant. *Deep structure* is the underlying conceptual or functional representation of the task or problem, independent of physical features. Cognitive fidelity captures deep structure but not necessarily surface structure; physical fidelity captures both. Moreover, there is an asymmetrical relationship between deep structure and surface structure. Deep structure will readily facilitate the learning of surface structure; however, surface structure will not readily facilitate the learning of deep structure. It is only through prolonged experience that learners induce the deep structure from the surface structure.

Our earlier discussion of the work of Holyoak and colleagues (e.g., Gick & Holyoak, 1980; Holyoak, 1985; Holyoak & Thagard, 1997) clarifies how deep structure facilitates the learning of surface structure. Research comparing experts and novices provides additional support for this claim. Much of this research shows that experts can focus on deep structure, whereas novices tend to focus on surface structure. For example, Chi, Feltovich, and Glaser (1981) found that novices tend to categorize physics problems on the basis of surface features, such as key words and visual similarity between drawings, whereas experts classify the same problems on the basis of the underlying physical principles. Classic work by Chase and Simon (1973) demonstrated that chess experts view chessboards as a conglomeration of meaningful multipiece configurations, whereas novices tend to perceive and remember individual chess pieces. In the domains of arithmetic and algebra, Novick (1988) found that novices are more likely than experts to inappropriately transfer surface details from learning to test. (For an overview of differences between knowledge representation in experts and novices, see Chi, Glaser, & Farr, 1988.) Thus, for initial training, cognitive fidelity, which captures the deep structure of the target task, is essential. This, however, raises the issue of training validation.

VALIDATION OF TRAINING

How can one validate training systems based on cognitive fidelity? For training systems with high physical fidelity, validation may come in the form of physical measurements to determine whether the system accurately represents the physical measurements in the environment. Validation may also come from subjective evaluations by experts. Here, experts interact with the training system and rate it on how accurately it represents the operational task. Validation of training systems focusing on cognitive fidelity is more complex. Given that these systems may not have high physical fidelity, training must be validated through performance metrics designed to determine how much savings can be realized with the training system.

Transfer of Training

The most common approach is the *transfer of training* (TOT) paradigm. In this approach, during the training phase, a control group receives training on the whole or criterion task while the experimental group receives training on one or more part tasks. During transfer, both groups are given an appropriate test on the criterion task. Transfer is measured by comparing the performance of the experimental group in the transfer phase with that of the control group during initial training. This comparison reveals how much skill is transferred from the part task to the criterion task. Differential transfer is measured by comparing the performance of the experimental group with that of the control group during the transfer phase. This comparison shows the relative benefits of part-task versus whole-task training. The obvious problem with a TOT approach for many military systems is that the criterion task is live combat. A more effective, efficient, and safer validation method is needed.

Backward Transfer

One alternative validation technique, suggested by Wightman and Lintern (1985), is referred to as *backward transfer*. The general experimental design in backward transfer is similar to a TOT design, but the goal is to measure transfer from the criterion task to the training tasks. During training, one group is trained on the criterion task; the other group receives no training. During the transfer phase, both groups are tested on the training tasks rather than the criterion task. Backward transfer to the training tasks can be estimated by comparing the performance of the trained group (e.g., experts) on the training tasks with that of the untrained group (e.g., novices). Training tasks on which the experts outperform the novices tap skills related to the deep structure of the criterion task acquisition and indicate elements critical for training.

Goettl and Shute (1996) demonstrated the utility of the backward-transfer technique for developing effective part-task training regimens. They used the backward-transfer method to identify component tasks critical to a complex flight task and then developed a part-task training regimen composed of those critical component tasks. They found that the validated part-task training paradigm produced greater transfer than whole-task training.

We recently developed and validated a tutor for training C-130 aircrews to visually discriminate ground-based threats such as Anti Aircraft Artillery and Surface-to-Air Missiles. The system was validated by demonstrating that crew members with combat experience performed better than novices on the training task (Ashworth, Anthony, Derek, & Goettl, 2001; Goettl, Ashworth, McCormick, & Anthony, 2004). This example also illustrates the advantage of the backward-transfer technique in situations where a normal transfer study might simply be too hazardous, costly, impractical, or unethical. In the remainder of this chapter, we demonstrate the application of the backward-transfer approach for validating a simulation of an AWACS weapons director task.

VALIDATION STUDY

The purpose of the experiment reported here is to demonstrate the cognitive fidelity of two synthetic tasks using the backward-transfer procedure. The basic theoretical issue is one of knowledge representation in three entities: (a) experts in the domain of question, (b) novices in the domain of question, and (c) synthetic tasks that purport to be cognitive analogs of the domain of question. The underlying logic of the procedure is straightforward: If the synthetic tasks accurately represent and exercise the knowledge representations necessary to perform the real world task, then experts who already have these knowledge representations will excel at the synthetic tasks because of the match between their prior knowledge and that embedded in the synthetic tasks. By the same logic, novices should perform poorly because of the lack of match between their task representations (they have none) and those embedded in the synthetic tasks. The hypotheses for the experiment reported here were driven by these representational concepts of deep structure and surface structure. Previous knowledge of deep structure will enable experts to outperform novices during training and during traditional transfer tests mediated by deep structure.

We proposed the following two hypotheses:

Hypothesis 1: Experts will outperform novices during training. Experts' prior knowledge of deep structure would enable them to learn the surface structure of the synthetic task faster than novices. Thus, experts would outperform novices on all training sessions. To test this hypothesis, we put both novices and experts through the same training regimen.

Hypothesis 2: There will be a performance interaction between participant populations when surface structure is manipulated. Specifically, novices would perform poorly when surface structure is changed, whereas experts' performance would be relatively unaffected. To test this hypothesis, after training, we measured the performance of experts and novices in two transfer conditions. In the *control transfer condition* the synthetic task environment remained constant, and a new scenario that was similar in difficulty to the training scenario was introduced. Because there was no substantive conceptual difference in the scenario from training to transfer, the control transfer condition closely resembled a fifth training block, and performance for both participant populations was predicted to continue the trends observed during training. In the *deep-to-surface transfer condition* the synthetic task platform differed from that used during training, while the scenario was the same as that used in the control transfer condition. This manipulation measured the participants' ability to apply their conceptual knowledge of the task (deep structure) to a new interface (surface structure). The literature unambiguously demonstrates that experts will outperform novices.

Method

Participants

A total of 88 participants were organized into teams of 4. Teams were categorized as either experts or novices. There were seven expert teams composed of Modular Control Equipment operators who had been recruited from the 133rd Test Squadron, Iowa Air National Guard, Fort Dodge; the 107th Air Control Squadron, Arizona Air National Guard, Phoenix; and the 607th Air Control Squadron, Luke Air Force Base, Arizona. Modular Control Equipment operators conduct the same functions as AWACS weapons directors, except from ground-based stations. There were 15 teams of novices who were recruited through temporary employment agencies and met the following criteria: 18 to 35 years old, high school degree or GED, and no physical handicaps.

Hardware

Data were collected on two testbeds. A mobile testbed composed of four networked Dell Inspiron 7500 laptop computers (500 MHz, Pentium III) was used to collect the expert data. The novice data were collected on four networked Gateway desktop computers (600 MHz, Pentium III). All computers were configured to dual boot using Windows 98 and Red Hat Linux.

Synthetic Tasks

All eight computers were equipped with two software training simulations: (a) DDD (Distributed Dynamic Decision-Making) and (b) AWACS-AEDGE (Agent Enabled Decision Guide Environment) team aircrew tasks. The interfaces for these two tasks are shown in Figure 5.3. The DDD team

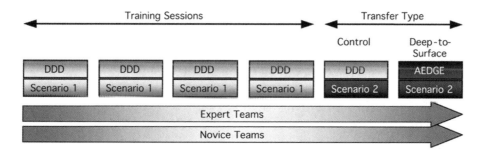

Figure 5.3. Two synthetic tasks for representing AWACS weapons directors. Panel A: the Distributed Dynamic Decision-Making (DDD) environment, developed by Aptima Incorporated, and Panel B: the Agent Enabled Decision Guide Environment (AEDGE), developed by 21st Century Incorporated.

simulation (see Figure 5.3A) is a distributed multiperson simulation and software tool used to simulate how high-performance teams operate in complex environments. The DDD captures the main elements of various aircrew team tasks and permits the experimenter to change team structure, control of resources, and access to information.

Like the DDD, the AWACS-AEDGE (see Figure 5.3B) task is a real-time team decision support environment permitting simulation of various AWACS weapons director tasks. Students control various friendly air, sea, and ground assets against enemy assets in a simulated combat scenario. Although AEDGE also includes intelligent agents that assist in decision making, this feature was turned off during all training and testing sessions.

The DDD and AEDGE simulations are conceptually the same task. In this experiment, both were configured to simulate the duties and responsibilities of a team of AWACS weapons directors. These duties and responsibilities include controlling friendly fighter aircraft, monitoring friendly fuel consumption, refueling friendly assets, monitoring hostile aircraft, protecting ground assets, deploying fighters against hostiles when necessary, collaborating with other operators, and passing control of aircraft back and forth between sectors of the airspace.

Although conceptually identical, the DDD and AEDGE are physically different in appearance. In both tasks, the duties and responsibilities are the same, but the ways in which those duties are executed are different. The differences include physical appearance of switches, buttons, commands, pulldown menus, iconographic representation of aircraft and assets, and visual representation of land mass. In addition, the tasks differ in procedural knowledge. Because of differences in the interface, such as where and how asset information is displayed, menu options, and button functionality, the mechanics of performing similar operations vary greatly across platforms.

Scenarios

Two different scenarios were created for the purpose of this experiment. The scenarios were created by a subject-matter expert, Matt Dalrymple, who has 12 years of experience in various command, control, and communications systems and 14 years of experience developing AWACS training scenarios for synthetic tasks such as DDD and AEDGE.

The first scenario was built only for the DDD task. The airspace to be defended consisted of four quadrants, each controlled by a different team member. The team consisted of three weapons directors and a senior director who supervised and coordinated the activities of the other team members. Each of the three weapons directors controlled four fighter aircraft. The senior director controlled the AWACS aircraft and two tankers. Additionally, the senior director had access to two additional aircraft at each of two bases that could be released and handed off to other team members. The goals were to defend the friendly area from hostile penetration, protect airbases, cities, and surface-to-air missile sites, identify and intercept targets, and destroy hostile aircraft but not friendly aircraft or unknown aircraft. There were a total of 26 hostile aircraft and 12 unknown aircraft in the scenario. Hostile aircraft entered the scenario in groups of four (four-ship formation). Hostile aircraft entered the scenario from three directions, through either the northeast, southeast, or southwest quadrant. A different weapons director controlled each quadrant. Interdependencies between team members were limited to refueling operations, hand-offs, and replacing friendly aircraft lost from the scenario. The scenario lasted approximately 30 minutes.

The second scenario was created for both DDD and the AEDGE. Thus, both versions of Scenario 2 are analogs of each other, just represented on different platforms. All features of this scenario replicated features of the first scenario, with two exceptions. First, the terrain to be protected was different. Second, instead of attacking in groups of four from each of three directions, hostile aircraft attacked one at a time and from any one of the 12 clock positions in the airspace. Compared with Scenario 1, the four roles in the scenario had the same goals and responsibilities, the same number and composition of friendly assets, the same number of hostile and unknown aircraft, and the same fuel load and weapons capabilities.

Procedure

The experiment consisted of a training phase followed by a transfer phase. This procedure is depicted in Figure 5.4. Participants performed four training sessions of the same scenario in the same synthetic task. In the *control transfer condition* the scenario changed while the environment remained the same, whereas in the *deep-to-surface transfer condition* the environment changed while the scenario remained the same. Participation was identical for experts and novices in both phases.

Training Phase. As mentioned previously, participants performed in teams of 4, consisting of a senior director and three weapons directors. Each team completed four replications of Scenario 1 on the DDD platform. Each scenario lasted 30 minutes. Participants had a 15-minute rest-break between each scenario. Participants rotated roles in each replication of the scenario so that each participant performed each role once.

Transfer Phase. Two types of transfers were evaluated. In the control transfer condition, the platform remained the same as in the training sessions, but the scenario was changed from Scenario 1 to Scenario 2. In this transfer the interface remains the same but the characteristics of the scenario change. Also, team members do not rotate positions. They perform the same roles they performed in Training Session 4. In the second transfer phase, deep-

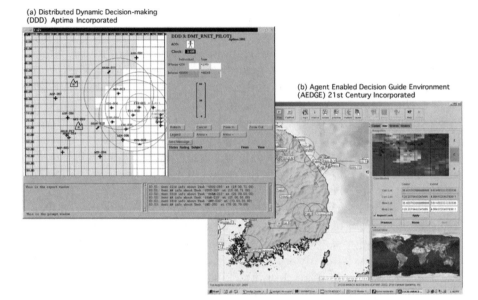

(a) Distributed Dynamic Decision-making
(DDD) Aptima Incorporated

(b) Agent Enabled Decision Guide Environment
(AEDGE) 21st Century Incorporated

Figure 5.4. Schematic of the experimental design. Four training sessions of the same scenario in the same synthetic task environment preceded two transfer conditions.

to-surface transfer, teams performed Scenario 2 on the AEDGE platform. Thus, in this situation the conceptual knowledge is the same as in the first transfer phase, but the interface is different.

Design

The dependent measures were identical for training and transfer phases of the experiment. The first measure, capturing the offensive successes of the team, was the number of enemy aircraft destroyed in air combat. This was a simple count of the number of hostile aircraft killed by friendly aircraft. The second measure, assessing defensive performance, was the number of friendly aircraft lost. Friendly aircraft could be lost as a result of either enemy fire or lack of fuel. Both represent poor management of assets and were combined into a single score.

The independent variables examined in the study included experience, training session, and transfer type. Experience was a between-subjects factor. Seven teams of modular control equipment operators were compared with 15 teams of novices having no weapons director experience. Training session was a repeated-measures factor for assessing skill learning. Participants completed four training sessions using Scenario 1 on the DDD platform. *Transfer type* was a repeated-measure variable consisting of two levels: (a) surface structure and (b) deep structure.

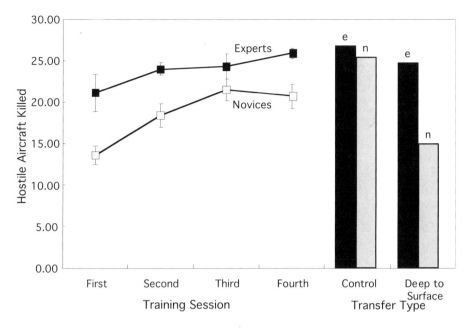

Figure 5.5. Training and transfer data on number of hostile aircraft killed during four training sessions and two transfer sessions.

Results

Training

Enemy Aircraft Killed. The mean numbers of enemy aircraft killed during training and transfer conditions for novice and expert teams are shown in Figure 5.5. The line graph portion of this figure represents performance during the four training sessions. These data were submitted to a 2 (expertise: novice vs. expert) × 4 (session) mixed-factors analysis of variance (ANOVA). As indicated in the figure, expert teams shot down more enemy planes than did the novices. This observation is supported by a significant main effect of expertise, $F(1, 20) = 8.23$, $p < .01$, $MSE = 64.05$. Overall, expert and novice teams averaged 23.83 and 18.57 kills, respectively. Separate t tests showed that the differences between experts and novices were significant for each session except Session 3.

In addition to the main effect of expertise, enemy aircraft killed also showed a main effect of training session, $F(3, 60) = 15.37$, $p < .01$, $MSE = 139.81$. Mean kills increased across the four training sessions with average kills of 16.00, 20.18, 22.41, and 22.36 for Sessions 1 to 4, respectively. The interaction between expertise and training session was not significant $(p > .10)$.

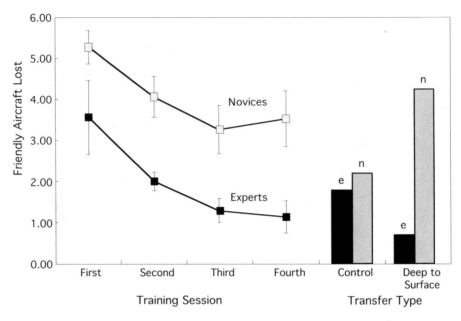

Figure 5.6. Training and transfer data on number of friendly aircraft lost. The pattern of results is identical to that seen for number of hostile aircraft killed in Figure 5.5.

Friendly Aircraft Lost. The mean number of friendly aircraft lost during training and transfer sessions for novice and expert teams are shown in Figure 5.6. The line graph portion of this figure represents performance during the four training sessions. These data were submitted to a 2 (expertise) × 4 (session) mixed-factors ANOVA. As indicated in Figure 5.6, expert teams suffered fewer friendly losses than did novice teams. This observation is supported by a main effect of expertise, $F(1, 20) = 12.44$, $p < .01$, MSE = 6.35. Overall, expert and novice teams averaged 2.00 and 4.03 friendly losses per session, respectively. As with kills, separate t tests showed that experts suffered significantly fewer friendly losses in all sessions except Session 1 where the difference was marginally significant.

Also indicated in Figure 5.6 is that teams improved across session. Mean losses reduced across the four sessions with average losses of 4.73, 3.41, 2.64, and 2.77 for Sessions 1 through 4, respectively. This observation is supported by a significant main effect of session, $F(3, 60) = 6.70$, $p < .01$, MSE = 18.94. Finally, there was no interaction between expertise and training session ($F < 1.0$).

Transfer

Enemy Aircraft Killed. The bar graphs in Figure 5.5 show the mean enemy aircraft killed by expert and novice teams in the two transfer sessions.

These data were submitted to a 2 (expertise) × 2 (transfer) mixed-factors ANOVA. Overall mean kills were higher for expert than novice teams, with means of 26.0 and 21.0, respectively. This observation is supported by a main effect of expertise, $F(1, 10) = 6.98$, $p < .05$, $MSE = 21.50$.

However, the main effect of expertise must be interpreted within context of a significant interaction between expertise and transfer, $F(1, 10) = 6.30$, $p < .05$, $MSE = 15.23$. Expert teams showed mean kills of 27.17 and 24.83 for the control and surface-to-deep transfer sessions, respectively. Novice teams showed mean kills of 26.17 and 15.83 for the control and surface-to-deep transfer sessions, respectively. Thus, there appears to be an effect of expertise in the surface-to-deep transfer session but not in the control transfer session. This observation is supported by t tests comparing novice and expert teams separately for control and deep-to-surface transfer. In the control transfer session the difference between expert and novice teams was not significant, $t(10) < 1.0$, $p > .10$. In the surface-to-deep transfer session the difference between expert and novice teams was significant, $t(10) = 2.77$, $p < .05$, $SE = 3.244$.

Friendly Aircraft Lost. The bar graphs in Figure 5.6 show the mean friendly aircraft loss means for expert and novice teams in the two transfer sessions. As with the enemy kill data, expert teams show better performance. Overall, expert teams showed fewer losses, as did novice teams, with mean losses of 1.25 and 3.42 for experts and novices, respectively. This observation is supported by a significant main effect of expertise, $F(1, 10) = 9.66$, $p < .01$, $MSE = 2.92$.

The data for friendly aircraft lost also showed a significant interaction between expertise and transfer, $F(1, 10) = 4.65$, $p < .05$, $MSE = 3.58$. Expert teams showed average friendly losses of 1.83 and 0.67 for control and surface-to-deep transfer, respectively. Novice teams showed average losses of 2.33 and 4.50 for surface transfer and deep transfer, respectively. As with enemy kills, this pattern suggests an effect of expertise in surface-to-deep transfer but not in control transfer. This observation is supported by t tests that showed a significant difference between expert and novice teams in the surface-to-deep transfer condition, $t(10) = 3.78$, $p < .01$, $SE = 1.014$, but not in the control transfer condition, $t(10) < 1.0$, $p > .10$.

Discussion

The hypotheses were derived on the basis of theoretically rigorous and empirically valid assumptions about knowledge representation in experts and novices and its effect on learning and transfer of learning. That deep structure facilitates learning performance and transfer is not in question. The goal was to determine whether the two synthetic task environments were sufficiently accurate cognitive analogs of the AWACS weapons director task to allow the known differential effects of expertise on learning to manifest in a controlled experimental setting. The results indicate that both the DDD environment and the AEDGE are cognitive analogs of the operational tasks performed by AWACS weapons directors. Both of the hypotheses were solidly supported.

Hypothesis 1 predicted that experts would outperform novices in all training sessions. Analyses of the performance per training session support this hypothesis, with experts outperforming novices as a main effect and also in six of the eight tests of simple means. Of the two simple means where no statistical difference was found, the experts' means were nonetheless in the direction indicative of better performance. Also, these two comparisons were in different training sessions: the third training session for enemy aircraft killed and the first training session for friendly aircraft lost, suggesting no systematic effect. Finally, there was no Expertise × Training Session interaction for either enemy aircraft killed or friendly aircraft lost, suggesting a consistent difference between experts and novices across training sessions.

Hypothesis 2 predicted that there would be a performance interaction between participant populations when surface structure was manipulated. Specifically, novices would perform poorly, but experts' performance would be relatively unaffected. Analyses of the performance per transfer condition support this hypothesis. The interaction between expertise and transfer condition for both enemy aircraft killed and friendly aircraft lost suggests that experts and novices performed differently. Tests of simple means elucidate the nature of the difference. When surface structure was not manipulated (control transfer condition), there was no significant difference between expert and novice performance for either enemy aircraft killed or friendly aircraft lost. However, when surface structure was manipulated (deep-to-surface transfer condition), experts maintained their level of performance, whereas that of novices diminished significantly for both enemy aircraft killed and friendly aircraft lost.

GENERAL DISCUSSION

In this chapter, we have discussed the unique training challenges faced by the DOD and the promise of DLT to address those challenges. On the one hand, declining size of forces, new mission needs, emerging new foes, and increased reliance on an expeditionary concept of military training have necessitated advanced distributed training solutions. On the other hand, the nature of combat training requires the highest level of skill to maximize transfer and insulate skill from the negative effects of stress. Thus, in today's military much of the focus of DLT is DMT. There is some validity to this approach, considering the obvious fact that the training environment must be analogous to the performance environment for transfer to occur. However, this approach disregards fundamental distinctions between the surface and deep structures of a task and assumes that high physical fidelity is the only appropriate method of accomplishing analogy between training and performing environments. We described a theoretical approach, supported by human performance data, that demonstrates the effectiveness and efficiency of capturing the deep structure of a task using cognitive fidelity rather than physical fidelity.

Our theory suggests that, early in training and throughout the bulk of skill acquisition, emphasis on training systems having cognitive fidelity, and not physical fidelity, will lead to training that is very efficient and effective. Although he did not make the distinction between cognitive and physical fidelity, Roscoe (1980) described the trade-off among cost, fidelity, and training effectiveness. Over 20 years ago, he urged training developers to exploit the honey region to develop effective and efficient training simulators. In essence, he was arguing that training that captures the deep structure of the task can be an effective and efficient training solution. What we hope to stimulate through this chapter is a rediscovery of basic cognitive and learning principles and more widespread application of those principles to training system development. Only in doing this can we take full advantage of distributed training technology.

Incorporating cognitive and learning principles into training system development is not easy. Cognitive fidelity requires extensive work early in the development process to capture the critical cognitive elements of the task. It also requires a more formal validation process to ensure that the training system has captured the cognitive fidelity and will lead to positive transfer. The data presented in this chapter demonstrate how cognitive fidelity and training effectiveness can be validated through backward transfer. Although our approach is more challenging, it can lead to training systems that are available anywhere and at any time, as well as being more effective and efficient.

Research in this area should continue to explore the relationship between cognitive fidelity and transfer. The backward-transfer technique is helpful for validating whether training has captured the deep structure of the task. In addition, the technique is consistent with Sohn, Douglass, Chen, and Anderson's (2005) recent recommendation that training programs should identify and emphasize component skills with which individual learners have the least experience.

Although in this chapter we have focused on applying the backward-transfer technique to military tasks, it can be applied to any complex task composed of hierarchy of component tasks or skills. Examples include driving, air traffic control, process control, and fault detection and diagnosis. Research should explore expanding the application of this technique to these domains as well as domains in which normal transfer of training procedures are neither practical nor ethical. Research is also needed to further test our proposition that emphasis on deep structure by means of cognitive fidelity early in training leads to more rapid skill acquisition. Our proposition implies that an ideal training program would start with cognitive fidelity and switch to physical fidelity as skill improves. This has implications for advanced distributed learning applications because it suggests that distributed learning environments need not capture physical fidelity early in training. The DLT concept for this is *blended training*. In blended training, the on-site portion of training programs can be significantly reduced by presenting cognitive portions through DLT programs and focusing the on-site portion on physical fidelity applications and maximizing transfer. By focusing research toward these propositions, we can advance the incorporation of learning theory into advance distributed learning.

REFERENCES

Ackerman, P. L. (1994). Intelligence, attention, and learning: Maximal and typical performance. In D. K. Detterman (Ed.), *Current topics in human intelligence: Vol. 4. Theories of intelligence* (pp. 1–27). Norwood, NJ: Ablex.

Ackerman, P. L., & Kanfer, R. (1993). Integrating laboratory and field study for improving selection: Development of a battery for predicting air traffic controller success. *Journal of Applied Psychology, 78*, 413–432.

Anderson, J. R. (1982). Acquisition of cognitive skill. *Psychological Review, 89*, 369–406.

Andrews, D. H. (2000). Distributed mission training. In W. Karwowski (Ed.), *International encyclopedia of ergonomics and human factors* (pp. 1214–1217). Philadelphia: Taylor & Francis.

Ashworth, A. R. S. III, Anthony, M. K., Derek, K., & Goettl, B. P. (2001). Validation of training efficacy through analogical transfer between expert knowledge representations and training environment representations. In *Proceedings of the 45th Annual Meeting of the Human Factors and Ergonomics Society* (pp. 1848–1852). Santa Monica, CA: Human Factors and Ergonomics Society.

Baddeley, A. D., & Longman, D. J. A. (1978). The influence of length and frequency of training session on rate of learning to type. *Ergonomics, 21*, 627–635.

Bailey, J. S., Hughes, R. G., & Jones, W. E. (1980). *Application of backward chaining to air-to-surface weapons delivery training* (AFHRL-TR-79-63). Williams Air Force Base, AZ: Operations Training Division, Human Resources Laboratory.

Baldwin, T. T., & Ford, J. K. (1988). Transfer of training: A review and directions for future research. *Personnel Psychology, 41*, 65–105.

Biederman, I., & Shiffrar, M. M. (1987). Sexing day-old chicks: A case study and expert systems analysis of a difficult perceptual-learning task. *Journal of Experimental Psychology: Learning, Memory, and Cognition, 13*, 640–645.

Chase, W. G., & Simon, H. A., (1973). Perception in chess. *Cognitive Psychology, 4*, 55–81.

Chi, M. T. H., Feltovich, P. J., & Glaser, R. (1981). Categorization and representation of physics problems by experts and novices. *Cognitive Science, 5*, 121–152.

Chi, M. T. H., Glaser, R., & Farr, M. J. (Eds.). (1988). *The nature of expertise.* Hillsdale, NJ: Erlbaum.

Clawson, D. M., Healy, A. F., Ericsson, K. A., & Bourne, L. E. (2001). Retention and transfer of Morse Code reception skill by novices part–whole learning. *Journal of Experimental Psychology: Applied, 2*, 129–142.

Department of Defense. (1999, April 30). *Department of Defense strategic plan for advanced distributed learning.* Retrieved November 29, 2006, from http://www.adlnet.gov/downloads/156.cfm

Donchin, E. (1989). The learning strategies project: Introductory remarks. *Acta Psychologica, 71*, 1–15.

Druckman, D., & Bjork, R. A. (Eds.). (1994). *Learning, remembering, believing: Enhancing human performance.* Washington, DC: National Academy Press.

Duncker, K. (1945). On problem solving. *Psychological Monographs, 58*(270).

Fitts, P. M. (1964). Perceptual-motor skill learning. In A. W. Melton (Ed.), *Categories of human learning* (pp. 245–285). New York: Academic Press.

Frederiksen, J. R., & White, B. Y. (1989). An approach to training based on principled task decomposition. *Acta Psychologica, 71*, 89–146.

Gick, M. L., & Holyoak, K. J. (1980). Analogical problem solving. *Cognitive Psychology, 12*, 306–355.

Glaser, R., Raghavan, K., & Schauble, L. (1988). Voltaville, a discovery environment to explore the laws of DC circuits. In *Proceedings of the 1988 International Conference on Intelligent Tutoring Systems* (pp. 61–66). Montreal, Quebec, Canada: University of Montreal.

Goettl, B. P., Ashworth, A. R. S. III, McCormick, E., & Anthony, M. K. (2004). Validation of visual threat recognition and avoidance training through analogical transfer. In *Proceedings of the North Atlantic Treaty Organization Research and Technology Agency Human Factors and Medicine Panel symposium on advanced technologies for military training* (pp. 113–121). Neuilly-sur-Seine, France: RTO/NATO.

Goettl, B. P., & Shute, V. J. (1996). An analysis of part task training using the backward-transfer technique. *Journal of Experimental Psychology: Applied, 2*, 227–249.

Gopher, D., Weil, M., & Bareket, T. (1994). Transfer of skill from a computer game trainer to flight. *Human Factors, 36*, 387–405.

Gopher, D., Weil, M., & Siegel, D. (1989). Practice under changing priorities: An interactionist perspective. *Acta Psychologica, 71*, 146–178.

Hart, S. G., & Battiste, V. (1992). Field test of video game trainer. In *Proceedings of the Human Factors Society 36th annual meeting* (pp. 1291–1295). Santa Monica, CA: The Human Factors Society.

Holyoak, K. J. (1985). The pragmatics of analogical transfer. In G. H. Bower (Ed.), *The psychology of learning and motivation* (Vol. 19, pp. 59–87). Orlando, FL: Academic Press.

Holyoak, K. J., & Thagard, P. (1997). The analogical mind. *American Psychologist, 52,* 35–44.

Idzikowski, C., & Baddeley, A. D. (1983). Fear and dangerous environments. In G. R. J. Hockey (Ed.), *Stress and fatigue in human performance* (pp. 123–144). New York: Wiley.

Lesgold, A., Lajoie, S., Bunzo, M., & Eggan, G. (1992). SHERLOCK: A coached practice environment for an electronics troubleshooting job. In J. H. Larkin & R. W. Chabay (Eds.), *Computer assisted instruction and intelligent tutoring systems* (pp. 201–238). Hillsdale, NJ: Erlbaum.

Mané, A. M., & Donchin, E. (1989). The space fortress game. *Acta Psychologica, 71,* 17–22.

Meyer, T. N., Miller, T. M., Steuck, K., & Kretschmer, M. (1999). A multi-year large-scale field study of a learner controlled intelligent tutoring system. In S. P. LaJoie & M. Vivek (Eds.), *Proceedings of the 9th International Conference on Artificial Intelligence in Education* (pp. 191–198). Amsterdam, The Netherlands: IOS Press.

Novick, L. R. (1988). Analogical transfer, problem solving, and expertise. *Journal of Experimental Psychology: Learning, Memory, and Cognition, 14,* 510–520.

Rajaram, S., Srinivas, K., & Roediger, H. L., III. (1998). A transfer-appropriate processing account of context effects in word-fragment completion. *Journal of Experimental Psychology: Learning Memory, and Cognition, 24,* 993–1004.

Renkl, A., & Atkinson, R. K. (2003). Structuring the transition from example study to problem solving in cognitive skill acquisition: A cognitive load perspective. *Educational Psychologist, 38,* 15–22.

Rickard, T. C., Healy, A. F., & Bourne, L. E. (1994). On the cognitive structure of basic arithmetic skills operation, order, and symbol transfer effects. *Journal of Experimental Psychology: Learning, Memory, and Cognition, 20,* 1139–1153.

Roscoe, S. N. (1980). *Aviation psychology.* Ames: Iowa State University Press.

Rumsfeld, D. H. (2001, August 22). Secretary Rumsfeld meets with *Washington Post* editorial board. *DefenseLINK.* Retrieved May 7, 2003, from http://www.defenselink.mil/transcripts/2001/t08232001_t0822wp.html

Schneider, W. (1985). Training high-performance skills: Fallacies and guidelines. *Human Factors, 27,* 285–300.

Shute, V. J., & Glaser, R. (1990). A large-scale evaluation of an intelligent discovery world, Smithtown. *Interactive Learning Environments, 1,* 51–77.

Singley, M. K., & Anderson, J. R. (1989). *The transfer of cognitive skill.* Cambridge, MA: Harvard University Press.

Sohn, M.-H., Douglass, S. A., Chen, M.-C, & Anderson, J. R. (2005). Characteristics of fluent skills in a complex, dynamic problem-solving task. *Human Factors, 47,* 742–752.

Steuck, K., & Miller, T. M. (1997, March). *An evaluation of an authentic learning environment for teaching scientific inquiry skills*. Paper presented at the annual meeting of the American Educational Research Association, Chicago.

Taatgen, N. (2005). Modeling parallelization and flexibility improvements in skill acquisition: From dual tasks to complex dynamic tasks. *Cognitive Science: A Multidisciplinary Journal, 29,* 421–455.

Thorndike, E. L., & Woodworth, R. S. (1901). The influence of improvement in one mental function upon the efficiency of other functions. *Psychological Review, 8,* 247–261.

Vidulich, M., Yeh, Y., & Schneider, W. (1983). Time compressed components for air intercept control skills. In *Proceedings of the Human Factors Society 26th annual meeting* (pp. 10–14). Santa Monica, CA: Human Factors Society.

Wheeler, J. L., & Regian, J. W. (1999). The use of a cognitive tutoring system in the improvement of the abstract reasoning component of word problem solving. *Computers in Human Behavior, 15,* 243–254.

Wightman, D. C., & Lintern, G. (1985). Part-task training for tracking and manual control. *Human Factors, 27,* 267–283.

Wightman, D. C., & Sistrunk, F. (1987). Part-task training strategies in simulated carrier landing final-approach training. *Human Factors, 29,* 245–254.

Yechiam, E., Erev, I., Yehene, V., & Gopher, D. (2003). Melioration and the transition from touch-typing training to everyday use. *Human Factors, 45,* 671–684.

6

NARRATIVE THEORY AND DISTRIBUTED TRAINING: USING THE NARRATIVE FORM FOR DEBRIEFING DISTRIBUTED SIMULATION-BASED EXERCISES

STEPHEN M. FIORE, JOAN JOHNSTON, AND RUDY McDANIEL

In this chapter, we suggest that the narrative form represents a cogent means with which to describe and help comprehend complex training events. We discuss the value of narrative within distributed training environments and how it represents an important and little-understood research issue that can support a science of learning for complex organizational entities interacting at a distance. As our focus, we describe narratives in the context of distributed simulation-based exercises, the means through which teams

Work on this chapter was partially supported by funding to Stephen M. Fiore by Grant N000140610118 from the Office of Naval Research. The opinions expressed in this chapter are those of the authors only and do not necessarily represent the official position of the Office of Naval Research, the U.S. Navy, the U.S. Department of Defense, or the University of Central Florida. There is no government express or implied endorsement of any product discussed herein. We thank Clint A. Bowers, Janis A. Cannon-Bowers, Haydee M. Cuevas, Adams Greenwood-Ericksen, Atsusi Hirumi, Charles Hughes, Alicia Sanchez, Eileen Smith, and Christopher Stapleton for their helpful discussions on this topic.

of teams in the military practice complex tactics serving some strategic goal. Our overall theme is predicated on the notion that through the use of the narrative form, learning content can be both more effectively conveyed and more memorable.

This chapter is a continuation of prior work that attempts to rely on sound psychological theory to develop techniques and technologies that can be used to provide an organizing structure for distributed training environments (Fiore, Salas, Cuevas, & Bowers, 2003). This line of inquiry argues that for complex training content to be appropriately processed, and lead to knowledge acquisition and integration, its presentation needs to be more effectively managed. Furthermore, it recognizes that content can be processed not only during actual training execution but also at other stages of learning (see Cannon-Bowers, Rhodenizer, Salas, & Bowers, 1998; Smith-Jentsch, Zeisig, Acton, & McPherson, 1998). Fiore and colleagues have built on these ideas to argue for a firmer understanding of how to develop training by means of approaches that integrate preprocess, in-process, and postprocess factors (Fiore et al., 2003). Their approach illustrates the potential for improvements in knowledge construction based on a principled approach to distributed training design across time. These labels of pre-, in-, and postprocess factors correspond to notions of preparation, execution, and reflection, respectively (see Fiore, Jentsch, Becerra-Fernandez, Salas, & Finkelstein, 2005). Specifically, whereas in-process action (i.e., execution) occurs during actual training, preprocess actions (i.e., preparation) involve preparatory pretask behaviors. These include preparatory behaviors, such as planning sessions (e.g., Cannon-Bowers et al., 1998), or the use of mobile learning technologies to ground upcoming content in some pertinent context (cf. Metcalf, 2006), or pretask briefings where initial expectations are created in anticipation of the interaction (cf. Fiore, Salas, & Cannon-Bowers, 2001). Similarly, postprocess actions (i.e., reflection) include posttask feedback delivery and rumination on performance (e.g., debriefing) where task feedback is administered to individuals and groups by means of after-action review technologies (e.g., Fiore, Johnston, & McDaniel, 2005; Knerr, Lampton, Martin, Washburn, & Cope, 2002). Such antecedent (e.g., Cannon-Bowers et al., 1998; Wittenbaum, Vaughan, & Stasser, 1998) and consequent (e.g., Smith-Jentsch et al., 1998) behaviors can be critical to successful knowledge acquisition when conceptualized within a training paradigm that views learning across time.

Within the context of distributed debriefing, Fiore, Johnston, and Van Duyne (2004) presented a conceptualization of a training space to argue that events within such a space need to be woven together to enable the learner to experientially and cognitively link training concepts (see also Fiore et al., 2005). By integrating memory theory and organizational processes in human memory with techniques to diagnose and debrief performance, Fiore et al. (2004) illustrated how events within the training space can be monitored, filtered, and potentially structured such that they become interconnected across pre-, in-, and postprocess interaction. In this way, performance feedback could be idiosyncratically tailored and integrated within a larger conceptual organization of the overall training mission.

In this prior work, endogenous processes associated with the learner (e.g., organization in memory) were integrated with the exogenous factors associated with the learning environment (e.g., training requirements). Specifically, Fiore et al. (2004) discussed how theories originating in cognitive psychology provide an effective means by which to conceptualize the organization and the presentation of feedback to maximize the implementation of team feedback. This theory was based on a long line of research in human memory documenting the natural tendency for categorization to benefit memory (e.g., Bousfield, 1953; Bower, Clark, Lesgold, & Winzenz, 1969; Mandler, 1967). Fiore et al. (2004) argued that findings on memory hierarchies can be used to develop principled methods for automating the diagnosis of performance and the presentation of feedback during distributed mission training. By deriving hierarchies from the training requirements, a particular form of representation could be developed such that it presented a representation of team members and their actions at a given point in time (e.g., good and poor performance). This representation is necessarily hierarchical in nature, and this inherent organization in distributed teams of teams was leveraged to provide a strong mnemonic that would be robust in the face of competing content.

In short, our prior efforts in this area suggest that an appropriate blend of learning and system factors can assist in developing targeted feedback methods and mechanisms during postprocess interaction (see also Fiore et al., 2003, 2005). In this chapter, we build on this approach to additionally consider how the sequentiality inherent in distributed training can be leveraged. Specifically, our hierarchical consideration of the training space (Fiore et al., 2004) was developed to allow presentation of performance at a given point in time, that is, a "slice in time" of a complex mission, rather than across a time period. Here we continue with the development of theoretical concepts to enable an understanding of how distributed training environments can be efficaciously parsed and presented to maximize learning and retention. We do this from the perspective of narratology, building on our recent discussions of the use of narrative as a learning and performance support tool (see Fiore & McDaniel, 2006; Fiore et al., 2005; Fiore, Metcalf, & McDaniel, 2007). We next provide a brief overview of the different disciplines that have used the narrative form as a means of information conveyance. After this, we discuss some of the primary features of narrative that have been identified as being integral to the narrative form. Finally, we discuss these theoretical approaches in the context of using them for debriefing distributed simulation-based exercises.

THE NARRATIVE FORM IN COGNITION AND LEARNING

In his influential work on narrative, Bruner (1991) described how we come to know our world and construct our representation of reality through the use of narrative. Bruner argued that "we organize our experience and our memory of human happenings mainly in the form of narrative—stories, excuses, myths, reasons for doing or not doing, and so on" (p. 4). Storytelling and the narrative format are argued to be some of the earliest means with which knowledge was retained and passed from generation to generation (e.g., Bal, 1997; Denning, 2001; Snowden, 2001). The utility of story to encompass a number of not only cognitive factors but also attitudinal issues is perhaps one of its strongest points. Indeed, Donald Norman (1993) wrote that "stories are important cognitive events, for they encapsulate, into one compact package, information, knowledge, context, and emotion" (p. 129).

At this more finely grained level of analysis from the viewpoint of cognitive psychology, a long line of research suggests that humans are predisposed to follow scriptlike or schematic structures (e.g., Bartlett, 1932; Bower & Morrow, 1990; Bransford & Franks, 1971; Gagne & Glaser, 1987; Mandler, 1984; Rumelhart, 1980; Schank & Abelson, 1977; Trabasso & Sperry, 1985). Indeed, a number of complex cognitive processes are engaged when one comprehends a story in that "the enabling events and causes form a web of connections among other events and conditions" (Bower & Morrow, 1990, p. 45). Furthermore, a substantial body of research has examined how brain injury hinders one's understanding of narrative. Importantly, illustrating how this ability is strongly linked to cognition, these studies have shown how this deficit can be related to a number of other higher cognitive functions, such as planning and social interaction (Body & Perkins, 1998; Bond-Chapman, Levin, Matejka, Harward, & Kufera, 1995; Chapman et al., 1992; Coelho, Liles, & Duffy, 1995; Togher & Handoe, 1999). Others have used studies of patients with closed-head injuries to illustrate how examination of narrative skills (e.g., discourse generation) can be clinically diagnostic. For example, patients with closed-head injuries are less able to produce cohesive ties across their utterances (Hartley & Jensen, 1991). Such techniques have also been used in developmental studies comparing young children with perinatal brain injury and healthy age-matched control children. Across these groups, the children with brain injuries were less able to integrate their play narrative and were less able to distinguish across types of narratives. Finally, there were significant developmental changes in the normal control children, illustrating how narrative skills develop with maturation (see Hemphill et al., 1994, for a full discussion). As this brief review suggests, a substantial foundation of research exists linking narrative to essential information processing, and this comes from both behaviorally and neurologically based studies. These studies provide a strong body of evidence indicating that the narrative form is a fundamental subcomponent of human cognition.

Some researchers, leveraging off this strong body of extant literature on narrative, have expanded on it to illustrate how to use story as a tool for learning. For example, Schank (1998) argued that human interaction can be better managed through the use of narrative and that the more effective means of reaching someone (whether a customer or a peer) is through stories. Schank argued from a cognitive perspective, suggesting that stories are able to scaffold another's understanding through the conveyance of context, that is, contextual elements facilitating relational thinking involving the incoming information and what one already knows. It is interesting that this same system may allow for temporary suspension of one's normal script or framelike patterns of thinking to allow for a more unconscious type of learning and engagement. Specifically, some researchers have noted that while engaged in listening to, or even telling a story, "our habitual mental sets, common everyday frames of reference, and belief systems are more or less interrupted and suspended" (Abrahamson, 1998, p. 442). Thus, curiously, it is the power of story that lets us suspend our own personal narratives to be engaged by, and potentially learn from, a story.

In a more qualitative analysis of storytelling, Sturm (1999) similarly noted this suspension of our everyday belief systems. Relying on interviewing techniques administered during professional storytelling events, Sturm examined the relationship between storytellers and story-listeners and found that participants in these events experienced "qualitatively different" states of consciousness while listening to various narratives as delivered by seasoned storytellers (p. 6). On the basis of analyses of the interview transcripts, Sturm outlined six categories that described this suspension of normal alertness. These categories included (a) feelings of realism for the story and story characters; (b) a lack of awareness for current surroundings or the current environment; (c) engaged receptive channels (visual, auditory, kinesthetic, and emotional); (d) feelings of control as either being in control of the direction of the story or being helpless; (e) a sense of "placeness," or the feeling as though they were being transported into another space; and (f) time distortion (p. 7). When received in this purely visceral or semi-hypnotic mental state, stories may have the means to elicit affective responses that make conceptual information more meaningful and, perhaps by extension, more transferable from long-term to short-term working memory. From this more visceral or base level, some have researched how storytelling can be used to elicit emotional responses in simulated and mixed-reality environments (Stapleton & Hughes, 2003). This line of inquiry has been built on a collaboration between the computational sciences and digital media, with the goal being an integration of story and entertainment with simulation technologies (Hughes, Konttinen, & Pattanaik, 2004; Stapleton, Hughes, Moshell, Micikevicius, & Altman, 2002). From this theoretical and technological integration, these researchers are exploring how story-driven simulations may enable learning for a variety of domains. For example, Stapleton and colleagues are investigating techniques to teach language skills to children with communicative disorders.

Stories often leave certain connections or causal relationships ambiguous; it is up to the reader to make definitive connections between particular events and characters. The characteristics of uncertainty and incompleteness are also useful components of story for narratives used in learning environments. This responsibility on the part of the reader is often precisely what is needed to give educational material a degree of importance, or even novelty. In particular, some suggest that when stories incorporate uncertainties, readers or listeners engage in imaginative gap-filling by drawing on personal experiences. This in turn may produce a sense of emotional or intellectual attachment to the story (see Gershon & Page, 2001). Gerrig and Egidi (2003) mirrored this sentiment: "Narratives refer to a small selection of details and let readers complete their work by imagining the rest. The resulting discontinuity that characterizes narrative requires an active role on the part of the reader" (p. 36). If one views this concept through cognitive theory, one can see that this process essentially increases the requirements for elaboration and is analogous to memory research showing that manipulations that force the elaboration of the to-be-learned material (e.g., semantic judgments) increase retention. This is also similar to work in self-explanation, which shows how the learner benefits from elaborating on the to-be-learned material (e.g., Anderson & Schunn, 2000; Chi, 2000). In this research, when the learner is encouraged or prompted to self-generate conceptual elaborations, monitoring and comprehension are facilitated, as is knowledge acquisition (e.g., Chi, Bassok, Lewis, Reimann, & Glaser, 1989; Chi, de Leeuw, Chiu, & Lavancher, 1994; King, 1992; Rosenshine, Meister, & Chapman, 1996). On the basis of this theorizing, we suggest that the active information processing on the part of readers as they engage in their personal gap-filling may increase the memorability of the read material. Furthermore, this personalization and contextualization of material may help to build the type of critical thinking skills that are essential for intellectual development.

In terms of specific pedagogical applications, storytelling has long been suggested as a valuable tool for classroom learning. Many of the advantages of story are well suited to teaching and teaching strategies. For instance, narrative has been theorized as being advantageous for memory recall and accessibility (Abbott, 2003), domain-independent types of thinking and the understanding of spatiotemporal relationships (Herman, 2003), and emergent types of learning (Turner, 2003). The power of stories, when used as potential teaching tools, has not gone unnoticed. Mathison and Gallego (2002) wrote that many educators routinely take advantage of stories in various forms (e.g., anecdotes, folk tales, oral histories, or biographies) to help their students understand concepts and ideas from their teaching. Crafting and delivering a good story can often move a student from a state of passive listening and boredom to an active state of engagement with the subject matter. This process can actually contribute to an improvement in the teacher's knowledge of subject matter as well. As Mathison and Gallego explained,

> The creator of a good story has had to reflect on the order, meaning, priority, and usefulness of the events she or he weaves together. So, by its very nature, the process of good story formation involves critical and reflective thinking. (p. 2)

This reciprocal generosity of narrative pedagogy is a definite advantage that comes from the process of incorporating stories into normal classroom activities. Along these lines, research has linked story, technology, and live performance in educational and training environments (Hirumi, Knowland, & Pounds, 2004). These studies have examined how the blending of disciplines can be used to educate teachers in complex content areas, such as computer operations (Mckenna, Pounds, & Hirumi, 2004).

Storytelling practices have also proven beneficial when used as tools for literacy learning for young children. For example, research with intelligent-agent technology has shown how stories can aid in the development of more complex reading skills. Ryokai, Vaucelle, and Cassell (2003) developed an embodied storytelling agent, named Sam, who was projected onto a screen behind a toy castle and figurine. Sam would then tell one or two children stories about the castle and figurine that were designed to model complex linguistic elements such as decontextualized language, quoted speech, spatial expressions, and relative clauses. One important facet of this project was that after a certain amount of time had passed, Sam's stories would become less interesting to the children, and these children would then be compelled to correct Sam by reciting appropriately exciting stories back to the agent. By doing so, Ryokai et al. found that "children practiced ways of clearly presenting narrative ideas for an audience, which is one of the keys to literacy learning" (p. 206).

As this brief review suggests, narrative is an important component of cognition, and its use cuts across the educational spectrum that has been explored with children and adults. Indeed, as Herman (2003) described it, the narrative form is a

> powerful and basic tool for thinking, enabling users of stories to produce and interpret literary texts, carry out spontaneous conversations, make sense of news reports in a variety of media, create and assess medical case histories, and provide testimony in court. (p. 163)

The power of story to express complicated or multifarious ideas is thus revealed in its track record in genres ranging from entertainment to law to politics. Complex thought as expressed in stories is manifested in everything from normal day-to-day conversations to complex descriptions of technical processes or procedures. We turn next to a discussion of how these ideas have been incorporated into technologies that leverage this concept to enable a host of complex automated processes.

COMPUTATIONAL STRUCTURES FOR NARRATIVE

Interesting dynamics are found when storytelling is combined with technology. In particular, narrative has influenced certain areas of research and development in computer science. For example, in areas such as interface design, researchers in human–computer interaction have argued that a metaphor of oral storytelling can be used to organize knowledge bases by incorporating concepts such as storylines and events unfolding over time (Berg, 2000; Don, 1990). Others have viewed narrative in computational systems, not metaphorically but almost literally. Specifically, a *narrative system* is a computer-based technology that is designed according to the way the cognitive sciences suggest we mentally store and categorize information. Both Minsky (1985) and Schank (1998) have developed the concepts—frames and scripts, respectively—to leverage narrative to help explain comprehension processes.

In computer science research, the concept of narrative has been adopted to make computer systems more understandable by developing techniques that facilitate communication in ways that mimic narrative (Mateas & Sengers, 1999). For example, narrative has been pursued within the emerging discipline of texts and technology to examine story and the narrative form in the context of knowledge management within organizations. The goal is to develop artificial intelligence applications using concepts such as narrative information exchange to support organizational memory and learning by capturing experiences in ways that people actually use to make sense of complex events, that is, as experiences conveyed through stories (see McDaniel, 2004).

An additional technique for integrating narrative communication into computers is to adapt the frame model to work within a digitized environment. Minsky (1985) explained that frames can be construed as experience-based structures of knowledge (p. 244). Specifically, he argued that each person acquired a tremendous number of frames, with each differently representing a type of stereotypical situation (e.g., meeting a certain kind of person). He described the structure of the frame as "a sort of skeleton, somewhat like an application form with many blanks or slots to be filled" (p. 245). These blanks inside a person's frame are "terminals" that are used "as connection points to which we can attach other types of information" (Minsky, 1985, p. 245). A frame can therefore be thought of as a template for creating specialized instances of a general idea, or a template for mnemonic abstraction. Story frames, then, are general templates for creating specialized instantiations of stories (Minsky, 1985). For example, from a general story frame it is possible to model a fairy tale, an adventure story, a historical narrative, or a tragic romance.

Just as Minsky's (1985) frames construct can be used to encapsulate digital stories after they have been created, Schank's (1998) ideas about scripts can be used to elicit appropriate stories and shape them into their final forms. Schank defined a *script* as "a set of expectations about what will happen next in a well-understood situation" (1990, p. 7). Scripts are useful in that they map a set of social or cultural conventions into a particular setting, so that when a new setting of that type is encountered the conventions for interacting within that setting are already known. When using scripts to design or control narrative systems, the computer can be programmed to understand normal or abnormal developments that occur within a story situated in a particular environment.

From this perspective of developing computationally robust narrative systems, frames are readily adaptable to technology-based approaches because they are very similar to a computational methodology already in widespread use: the object-oriented programming (OOP) paradigm. In most OOP models a class is first created to specify how objects should be assembled. The class thus acts as a template for one or more objects to be created from, much like a set of blueprints describing how a building should be constructed. From a single class, multiple objects can be produced that contain properties (internal data reflecting the current state of each object) and methods (internal procedures that describe the current allowable behaviors for each object). When dealing with narrative objects, these state properties will be composed of critical story elements, such as times, locations, characters, and events. Behaviors will then be composed of procedures that allow entry into various points in the narrative or that otherwise return meaningful data related to a particular occurrence in a given story.

For a computer language to be considered object oriented, that language must support four properties: (a) abstraction, (b) encapsulation, (c) polymorphism, and (d) inheritance. Like objects used in OOP languages, narrative frames seem to support these same OOP features on a cognitive level. For instance, both the OOP paradigm and the story frame construct support *abstraction*, or the ability to represent complex world data and relationships using abstract constructs (objects or frames). Additionally, frames and objects both encapsulate this abstract material within the boundaries of the frame or the object. Although a story can be blended or combined with another story to create an emergent narrative, the original features of the reactant stories remain encapsulated within their original frameworks.

The next property of OOP languages, although slightly more difficult to define, is still relevant to narrative systems. Polymorphism in OOP is allowing the same code to be used to process different types of data. Another way to think of polymorphism is as the "customized interpretation of a message" and the resulting use of that interpretation by different types of objects (Brookshear, 2000, p. 267). For instance, there might be a Turn_Page method that works with both Book and Newspaper types of objects. The particular implementation of the Turn_Page method needs to be different depending on the type of object that is using that function; the mechanics for each operation are slightly different, which is of course due to the differences in composition of each object.[1] In other words, finding the next page in a newspaper article is often much more convoluted than finding the next page in a cover-bound novel. In a newspaper, this process often involves rotating and folding the newspaper to situate the appropriate continued section into a readable arrangement. With a book, though, turning a page is accomplished simply by moving one's eyes to the next adjacent page or by flipping over the adjacent page to read the back of a page and open up the next two-page segment. The procedure for accessing this functionality, however, remains the same for each object: Book.Turn_Page or Magazine.Turn_Page. Dot notation, or providing a period after each object's name, allows a programmer to fully qualify a method using an object's name and the particular method encapsulated within that object. Although both methods to turn to a new page are named exactly the same in both the book and the magazine objects, the use of dot notation removes ambiguity from any given request to access an object's Turn_Page method.

Thus, polymorphism ensures that although the deep structure of the functionality—that is, its underlying purpose—is similar, its surface structure may vary depending on the nature of the content (object). In a narrative

---

[1] Virtual "objects" discussed in this section are capitalized for clarity, as is often the convention in programming.

frame, the same polymorphic requirements can and should be met. For instance, it might be useful to have instant access to the complicating section of a given narrative, or that point in the narrative in which dramatic action is at its peak. Although the events leading up to this section and the outcomes after these complicating events would likely be very different, one can still access the complication part of a story in the same fashion for two very different types of stories (assuming they both contained complicating events). Dot notation can then be used to call forth these complicating events in a consistent and programmatic fashion by an analyst (i.e., Story1. Get_Complication, Story2.Get_Complication, etc.).

The last property of OOP, *inheritance*, also relates to the narrative frame construct. In programmed inheritance, child objects can inherit property data and functionality from parent objects that exist somewhere higher in the object hierarchy, much like inherited traits found in human genetics. The term property describes an object's data structures and the values assigned to those data structures. Functionality is defined in terms of encapsulated object methods that can provide access to internal data structures or otherwise modify these structures in a meaningful fashion.

For example, in a given simulation it might be useful to model the weather for an environment. In this environment there would be several types of clouds that would have associated probabilities for outcomes, such as rain or extreme temperatures occurring within the simulation. These clouds would be instantiated from a base Cloud object that would have properties defining its characteristics with properties for size, density, rain probability, and location, and perhaps a method Rain for creating virtual rain. In this base object, then, a programmer would assign a number representing the probability that rain will fall from that cloud. In its default state, this probability could be set to .20 using the value associated with the Cloud.RainProbability property. To run this situation in a rainy environment, the programmer might then wish to create a group of clouds composed of two or more RainCloud objects that have a much higher probability of dropping rain on the earth. Instead of modeling each individual RainCloud as a new object, it would make more sense to have these new objects inherit from the initial Cloud object and extend its functionality by adjusting its default property values and perhaps adding new methods, such as RainCloud. DownPour. If a normal rainy day were required, then the parent's Rain method could also be called by accessing the RainCloud.Rain method inherited from the original Cloud object. Thus, the rain probability for RainCloud objects can be adjusted to .80 so that all new objects created from this class template will have an 80% chance of spawning virtual rain.

This ability to inherit and extend allows customization of generic objects into instance-specific models that inherit base functionality and extend this new object's capabilities in additional directions. Using narrative objects, inheritance can therefore be programmed into a narrative system. First, a collection of base stories are created that contain terminals for the main character in the story, the significant events in the story, and the time and location in which the story took place. A secondary collection of stories would then inherit these base terminals and add additional terminals specifying whether the story took place in a simulated environment or a real world environment. Each inherited narrative frame could then spawn an unlimited number of stories about simulated and real world stories, depending on the type of narrative frame from which they were created.

The similarity of narrative frames to OOP constructs makes them very easy to implement using computational languages since frames translate easily to objects. In this type of model, a frame is represented using a class template, which is a pattern that allows new story objects to be created at will. From a class template, many objects can be created that have the same placeholders (terminals) but with different data stored in these locations. In the next section, we integrate the aforementioned theoretical concepts through the use of Bruner's (1991) essential features of narrative. We do this through a focus on a complex applied training problem in use today: Distributed Simulation-Based Exercises (DSBE). Our goal is to show how these important theoretical developments on story and narrative systems can be realized in a real world training environment, illustrating how a science of learning in distributed environments can be pursued on both epistemological and ecological grounds.

MERGING NARRATIVE SYSTEMS WITH DISTRIBUTED TRAINING ENVIRONMENTS

Distributed simulation-based training is one of the most challenging and resource-intensive training efforts facing the Navy—within services, joint service, and in a coalition with foreign military services. It is extremely personnel and resource intensive, requiring many hours (e.g., role players, trainers, simulation operators, travel funds) to support the implementation of training in high-fidelity simulations. Such a complex training environment is necessary because of the increasing complexity of military operations. Furthermore, there is a recognized need to allow trainees practice in integrating the skills they have acquired with others such that they are able to begin coordinating these skills.

Here we discuss training in the use of DSBEs and illustrate how the narrative form can be seamlessly blended with these complex training environments. In business, for example, narrative has been described as a viable tool for improving organizational communication and facilitating project management across groups (Denning, 2001, 2004; Snowden, 2001). Our specific goal is to highlight the potential value of this construct for the purpose of devising debriefing technologies that are more efficacious for the learner. As the previous review suggests, the narrative concept is applicable to a number of issues cutting across the social and information sciences. Considering the narrative form as just described, along with how the information and computational sciences have been using this construct to design narrative systems, we discuss narrative in the context of the features of narrative as outlined by Bruner (1991). We do this to begin to form the foundation for how it is that narrative systems for DSBEs can be developed. Specifically, within the context of distributed simulations, we suggest that the *story* is what actually happened in a given simulation-based training exercise, but *narrative* can better explain the complexity inherent to this story. At this point, it is important to specify how our interpretation of narrative within the context of training can be distinguished from conceptually similar theorizing, that is, scenario-based training. Scenario-based training has relied on vignettes that are devised to be analogous to actual experiences and environments but that include articulated learning objectives to elicit the use of particular competencies (e.g., Cannon-Bowers et al., 1998; Dwyer, Oser, & Salas, 1998; Dwyer, Oser, Salas, & Fowlkes, 1999; Fowlkes, Lane, Salas, Franz, & Oser, 1994). We do not necessarily see our approach with narrative as being at odds with this. Specifically, the scenarios are themselves constructed around a priori stories created by subject-matter experts and training designers. We suggest that the narrative form be used to convey what actually transpired during simulations, regardless of whether those simulations have been derived from scenario-based training.

In addition to considering the properties of narrative conducive to debriefing applications, we also provide examples of how stories can be used in electronic environments to manipulate simulation and debriefing data using data structures. Following the core capabilities found in many modern programming languages, we chose to consider how narratives can be wrapped around debriefing reports in an object-oriented fashion, thus taking advantage of the four properties of (a) abstraction, (b) encapsulation, (c) polymorphism, and (d) inheritance to store and manipulate debriefing information in narrative form. The function of abstraction is fairly obvious for each feature; the ability to model narratives in any computational form depends on this ability to represent real-world agents and actions in an abstract state. The other three properties, though, can have interesting implications for narrative debriefing. As such, we expand these three additional properties for several of the significant characteristics and features of story.

The features of narrative (from Bruner, 1991) most relevant to our discussion are listed in Table 6.1. Certain components of these features pertain to fiction and the way one uses these features to provide the sense of realism a reader–listener finds so compelling. For example, Bruner wrote

TABLE 6.1
Features of Narrative

Narrative diachronicity	Used to describe how events within a narrative occur over time or the particular patterns of events that unfold over time.
Intentional state entailment	Describes how an actor within a given story has within him or her certain goals or desires that must be attained.
Canonicity and breach	Features within a narrative that make a story interesting enough to tell—that is, a break from a predetermined sequence of events (e.g., a script).
Precipitating event	The factor leading to the breach of the canonical script.
Context sensitivity	Notion of how a reader's background knowledge interacts with the interpretation of the narrative.
Negotiability	The separating out of truth from the story, thus allowing for differing explanations of what occurred based on the idiosyncratic interpretations one may have of what transpired.
Referentiality	Term describing how narrative does not refer to reality; instead, it creates its own reality.

Note. From "The Narrative Construction of Reality," by J. Bruner, 1991, *Critical Inquiry, 18*, pp. 1–21. Copyright 1991 by *Critical Inquiry*. Adapted with permission.

of *referentiality* to describe how narrative does not refer to reality but instead creates its own reality. Although on the surface this may not seem to pertain to DSBE, one could argue that the training community must be ever mindful that it can sometimes create reality rather than represent reality. This is best understood by recognizing that military trainers speak of "ground truth" to describe what actually happened and in recognition that one's interpretation of what happened may deviate from this truth. Within the context of integrating narratology into DSBE debriefing, this is an important issue. Specifically, to effectively diagnose the simulation–story—that is, to correctly interpret what transpired to determine who did what well, and who did what poorly—one must have an accurate understanding of the reality of the situation. This is based on the identification of critical events and their consequences. The resultant story, which is constructed from these critical events and based on the interpretations of the trainers, the diagnoses systems, and techniques they have devised, becomes the reality through which performance is evaluated.

Context Sensitivity and Negotiability

Context sensitivity and *negotiability* are as much philosophical constructs as they are practical necessities. Although context sensitivity, when used in discussions of narrative, easily conveys notions of how the reader's background knowledge interacts with the interpretation of the narrative, Bruner's (1991) notion of negotiability pertains to the separating out of truth from the story. This allows for differing explanations of what occurred based on the idiosyncratic interpretations one may have of what transpired. This does occur at least analogously in what are referred to as *alibis*, which sometimes are offered in unstructured debriefs. In particular, during debriefing team members may generate plausibly sounding yet questionably true excuses for why something went wrong. Referring to our earlier discussion of ground truth, in the absence of an objective evaluation and presentation system, alibis may succeed simply because members of a given team are better able to negotiate their own interpretation of precipitating events and what transpired after these events.

We began with these two features of narrative, that is, referentiality and negotiability, because they strongly illustrate why adding structure to debriefing systems is critical. Along these lines, in the remainder of this section we describe how Bruner's (1991) other features of narrative can be used to create the level of objectivity necessary to efficaciously devise debriefing using narrative. Specifically, we describe the critical features of narrative that can be woven into debriefing, and we describe how computerized narrative systems can help to objectify these data for presentation.

Narrative Diachronicity

The feature of narrative that is perhaps most pertinent to DSBE, and certainly the most foundational feature, has to do with time and the laying out of events in a sequential form, which Bruner (1991) labeled *narrative diachronicity*. Viewing this within the context of DSBE, each simulation unfolds as a particular pattern of events, and we suggest using a story during the debrief to explain this pattern. This story chronology forms the backbone for the narrative system and enables particular elements to be structured for the debrief. We do not mean to suggest that the debrief must follow the story chronology, only that the narrative component of the chronology is implicitly present.

From an object-oriented perspective, narrative diachronicity is a critical feature. To read or listen to a story that is encapsulated within an object, one needs some meaningful way of relating the events that are stored within that object. In other words, if events within a story are returned in a scrambled and nonsequential fashion, the meaning and importance (and perhaps even the logical structure) of the story are lost. Narrative diachronicity must therefore be maintained and uninterrupted when debriefings are converted into an object-oriented electronic format.

Polymorphic characteristics resulting from narrative diachronicity might also be present in story objects. For instance, two stories generated from story frames can each have the same basic transition of events: An unknown situation is encountered, a struggle ensues as the best course of action to address this situation is decided on, and then an outcome is reached based on the final event in the story. If the unknown situation and the final outcome of these stories are the same, but the action taken to reach these similar outcomes is different in each story, then this narrative system can be described as *polymorphic*. Although these stories have the same plot structure, the particular implementation of each action item, although it generates the same end result in its respective story, is different.

In addition to encapsulation and polymorphism, inheritance is a useful feature to enable when considering narrative diachronicity. The ability to inherit a base story's events and add new events may be useful for training purposes. For example, teams of teams interacting within a DSBE have similar and different components of their mission. What makes inheritance a particularly useful notion is that narrative systems can be used to leverage the similarities within a mission but across teams and build the debrief around them. The noninherited components, then, become the idiosyncratic elements of the debrief that pertain to a particular team or team member. Thus, instead of having each team member tell a story that begins and ends in identical fashion, a generic story template or story class can be fashioned that contains similar items (e.g., a central beginning and ending). This custom template thus describes, in common language, the events representing the team's experience during a particular scenario. To operationalize this, each team member could use personalized programs that inherit from these base templates and add functionality that enables the team members to populate the story with relevant data from their own performance within the simulation until the terminal event is reached. In this fashion, object inheritance can be useful for modeling narrative diachronicity within debriefing narratives.

Intentional State Entailment

Intentional state entailment describes the factor whereby an actor within a given story has within him or her certain goals or desires that must be attained. When reading, the reader of a story uses his or her understanding of these intentions to interpret the actions of the actors in a story. Within DSBE the actors, that is, team members, all have intentions within the context of their particular missions. However, these intentions are often thwarted in some way such that mission plans do not always proceed as expected (e.g., through error or the actions of others). As such, this component of narrative helps us to interpret why one behaved as he or she did, that is, why a particular mission parameter that fell within the goals of a team or team member was or was not met.

This feature is also interesting to observe in an electronic environment populated by stories that are represented as objects. Because the encapsulation requirement for object-oriented languages ensures that data and the methods available to manipulate that data remain within the virtual boundaries of each story object, the digitized story can be treated as though it is being observed through a screen with varying levels of transparency. At the minimum level of transparency, the story functions as a black box: The beginning of the story is evident by the characters or agents going into a particular scenario and the end of the story is shown through the existence of some final event and the explanation of a final outcome for the story. The inner workings of the object, though, remain hidden to the listener or the reader. This inner functionality is made up of the various connections between internal plot events within the story. At the maximum level of transparency, the beginning and end of the story are still revealed, along with the inner events that take place in between the introduction and the conclusion of the narrative.

Varying the level of transparent encapsulation as just described can be useful for training pedagogy in that this technique could support attempts to predict which actions generate which types of outcomes for a given simulation exercise. The material for the exercise can be collected from the various narratives written and modeled as objects during the debriefing session. This can be used either as a form for querying predictions of performance or in a more directive lecture fashion. With respect to the former, team members can be queried during debriefs to elicit from them their predictions as to the events driving consequential actions within the scenario. After this, the level of transparency can be increased, thereby revealing whether the user predicted the correct events to generate that particular outcome for a given training scenario. Alternatively, with respect to the latter, the transparency within the scenario can be maximized so these are more readily apparent from the onset; that is, the debriefing leader can choose to more immediately highlight critical events. The decision as to what format to use can be based on practical considerations (e.g., time allotted to debrief) or pedagogically determined (e.g., where in their training the team may be).

Polymorphism can also be a cooperative property for digitized stories used in training situations. Polymorphic features allow for standardized access into key events in a narrative that are relevant to intentional state entailment. Data outlining the mission's objectives will initially be available to provide an outside source for facts that determine what objective should have been met or which action should have been taken for a given team or team member. When one of these objectives is not met, polymorphic searches can be used to determine the particular event or sequence of events in which a team member or an entire team deviated from normal mission goals. Although different story objects may be associated with different debriefing events, polymorphism allows for syntactic regularity when passing messages to any of these individualized data structures. Although the implementation of the search will vary depending on the specific structure of the story being searched, the commands to perform any given search will remain the same, regardless of the story's features or composition.

This polymorphic feature is particularly useful for the analysis of debriefing stories, especially when evaluating the emergent event sequences within these stories. Although each team member may have a different and specific task to perform (representing the causal event sequence, or plot, for that team member's story), polymorphic functionality enables the person analyzing the narrative debriefs to access each possible point of plot departure using common nomenclature. This may also function to divide larger stories into separate units of analysis. For instance, in a single mission each team member might contribute to this larger story with his or her individual experiences made up of a beginning event, a series of intermediate events, and a final event. When any team member is given an individual function within that mission, it can be assigned a label of *Mission* by the script that is used when that team member tells his or her story. When looking for data to indicate why an entire team did not behave as expected, then, an analyst could simply cycle through each story looking for the parts of the narrative that describe these individual missions (again, these substories would be searched in a common fashion because of polymorphic message passing). These missions are in essence treated as mininarratives that begin at the starting event of each Mission event and end at the terminating event during which this personalized objective was completed. Although the details of each particular team member will vary according to that team member's personalized mission roles or goals, polymorphism allows one to access these various series of events, or mininarratives, using a common mode of object dot notation and a standardized naming practice for internal narrative threads. Thus, if the entire team's story were represented in an object named TeamMission, and there were three team members, each with their own embedded stories within that larger narrative, then the mission description for both the group and each team member within the group could be accessed using the same syntax (TeamMission.Mission would return the overall team objective or objectives, whereas TeamMission.Team MemberA.Mission through TeamMission.TeamMemberC.Mission would return individual team member objectives).

Narrative inheritance can similarly be useful to evaluate the level of discrepancy between optimal team projected performance and actual team performance in a simulated environment. A base story can be used as a foundational narrative from which other narratives inherit basic characters and events. The base narrative, in this context, is structured to contain the normal goals or actions performed by actors in a particular story, that is, the teams and team members for a given scenario. If performance diagnosis presented during the debriefing shows that the team's stories do not correlate with the ideal narrative for the scenario, then this ideal from the base narrative is used for comparison. This process involves looking at the differences between the ideal narrative(s) and the actual debriefed narrative(s) to analyze differences in team process and performance. Furthermore, from a training scenario development perspective, when a revised or updated scenario is created, a base story can be inherited and a new ideal narrative formed with the same base expectations for actor performance and outcomes as shown by the foundational story. This facilitates flexibility in the creation of varied scenarios by providing an underlying template for use in performance diagnosis and feedback delivery.

Canonicity and Breach

Canonicity and *breach* are the features within a narrative that make a story interesting enough to tell in the first place. Bruner (1991) used this notion to explain why narrative differs from a predetermined sequence of events (e.g., a script); "for [a story] to be worth telling, a tale must be about how an implicit canonical script has been breached" (p. 11). This breach of the canonical script is referred to as a precipitating event (Bruner, 1991; Herrnstein Smith, 1978). Viewing these constructs within DSBE, the simulation itself is a scripted event that has within it a set of actors who interact with each other and their machines to meet some goal. Viewing this within the lens of narrative, we can use the narrative structure to help interpret why an actor in the story behaved as he or she did. Within the terms of narrative, we can use the notion of breach to help us understand how the script did not go as planned. As with diachronicity, this underlying concept is used to weave together the critical events that are used during a debrief. This then forms the basis for structuring the story used to present the feedback data. Thus, when considering distributed simulation exercises as an unfolding narrative, and the contents of a given simulation as a particular story, the value of our metaphor can be strengthened. In particular, the breach in the canonical script—that is, the precipitating event—becomes the target of feedback.

Because objects require some degree of encapsulation of data by definition, the narrative feature of canonicity and breach therefore requires special consideration in this context. When creating a story frame for modeling a story, and when crafting a story script for soliciting an appropriately formed story, the designer of a narrative software system must take into account that the power of narrative often emerges as the result of a break in the reader's or listener's expectations. As a result, the script used to gather stories should not be so restrictive as to inhibit users from making creative connections between seemingly irrelevant details and the specific milestones related to mission objectives, but the script should not be so permissive as to allow users to overlook important events or to allow them to alter order of occurrences. Debrief stories from a DSBE, then, should be modeled around a core set of events and, subsequently, breaches of events, with a common library of potential characters, but they should also allow for the encoding of special variations in the debriefed narrative. Specifically, given the complexity of distributed simulations, it is not feasible to present the entire mission (i.e., revisit the entire story) during the debrief. As such, the choice needs to be not only objectively determined (i.e., performance data must be gathered to identify the weak areas) but also subjectively determined (i.e., the debriefing leader identifies the element to discuss). This aforementioned liberty would allow a debriefing leader to determine the particular elements of the simulation that are noteworthy, that is, to choose the parts of the story he or she wants to tell or discuss.

The function of inheritance in expressions of canonicity and breach is perhaps more obvious. Because the narrative breach involves a break from a canonical script, the same functionality is mimicked when an inherited narrative breaks from an established base narrative with a normal population of agents, events, time, sequence, and causality. If one of these elements is modified in a compelling enough manner, a breach occurs, and novelty is introduced into the inherited narrative. Here, the foundational narratives are determined by subject-matter expertise and the stated training goals and they are represented as pre-existing narrative objects in an electronic environment.

Narrative objects can also be used to parse precipitating events for several different narratives using polymorphic functionality. For example, in a computerized narrative system one might create a method named *GetResponse* that returns a team member's reaction to an event in the simulation. This reaction would differ depending on this particular team member's prior training and the current mission's objectives. The particular sequence of events during which a team member responds to a situation is different according to each team member's particular training and his or her objective in that mission, but the method for accessing these events would remain the same, that is, from TeamMember[1].GetResponse to TeamMember[n].GetResponse. In this scenario the various team members' stories are represented in a collection of objects from a range of 1, which represents the first team member, to the total number of team members, represented by n. A precipitating event is then discovered when an event or a series of events representing an individual response does not meet normal expectations. In other words, if a given team reacted in Fashion X to a given situation when they should have reacted in Fashion Y, it is possible to quickly scan through several critical parts of the team narrative on an individual level using common method names and dot notation. Any unanticipated individual responses would then represent potential points of departure from the expected team behavior (canonical script) as the actions of one individual might have more global repercussions on their teammates.

In sum, the features of narrative as described by Bruner (1991), and elaborated on here, present an effective means through which we can conceptualize DSBE and how they might be structured for debriefing. Furthermore, through the implementation of OOP we can see how this may be realized in a computational-based narrative system. Our goal was to provide an illustration of how the pedagogically sound concept of narrative can be integrated with the computationally robust technique of OOP to facilitate learning in distributed training environments.

CONCLUSIONS: DEVELOPING THEORY FOR DISTRIBUTED TRAINING

In this chapter, we have sketched a set of concepts and features from narrative theory, a domain that has already influenced a number of areas in the social and computational sciences. Using theoretically derived distinctions, we have parsed components of DSBE to illustrate how teams can be construed of as parts of event layers of a narrative and the team members as the actors and the interaction of these teams as the event structure of a story. When viewing DSBE feedback as a form of narrative system, we suggest that narrative can be the conceptual scaffold that uses stories for transferring critical information. These stories can be construed of as

> the means of packaging and distilling that knowledge into a format suitable for transfer . . . . In other words, a narrative system enables the transfer of knowledge and information using a packaging strategy without ignoring the social factors that help to shape that information. (McDaniel, 2004, pp. 90–91)

In addition to our theoretical consideration of narrative as it applies to a DSBE, we have outlined several characteristics and properties of object-oriented data structures suggesting that these types of programmatic models might be ideal for storing and manipulating narrative information in a computing environment. In connecting the properties of object-oriented languages to several of the important features of narrative, we have shown that narrative objects can exist and coexist in a computational framework without sacrificing the qualities that make the story such a powerful model for storing and classifying world observations and experiences.

As we discussed at the beginning of this chapter, this approach is a continuation of prior work that is building on psychological theory to aid in our understanding of training in distributed environments. The training space conceptualization, developed by Fiore et al. (2003), illustrated how critical learning events should be integrated to enable the linking of training concepts. Through the incorporation of memory theory into techniques to diagnose and debrief performance, Fiore et al. (2004) built on this approach and argued that memory hierarchies enable the development of principled methods for automating performance diagnosis and feedback presentation for distributed mission training. It is important to note that this prior approach for training using memory hierarchies is not at odds with our proposal involving narrative; instead, we view them as completely comple- mentary. In particular, the hierarchical approach can be conceived of as a cross-sectional representation of the narrative, a slice in time across the unfolding story in which the actors are connected in a complex network of nodes. The purpose espoused with the hierarchical approach was to isolate a representation in which particular events can be viewed in parallel. In this chapter, we have built on that work to describe how narrative and story can be used to describe simulation-based exercises not in parallel but in sequence.

The unfolding of events in the distributed simulation and the inter- action of actors within the mission creates the story that needs to be conveyed in a debrief. Narrative readily lends itself as a tool to support not only debriefing but also, more generally, the pre-, in-, and postprocess factors we have described as preparation, execution, and reflection, as one moves through a training space. Narrative can enable this process because it "operates as an instrument of mind in the construction of reality" (Bruner, 1991, p. 6), and in the present case the reality of what occurred in a given distributed simulation-based training exercise. Bruner (1991) ended his influential work on narrative by stating that he has tried to "describe some of the properties of a world of 'reality' constructed according to narrative principles . . . to lay out the ground plan of narrative realities." The daunting task that remains now is to show in detail how, in par- ticular instances, narrative organizes the structure of human experience" (p. 21). Toward this end, we have made one small step by showing how narrative can be used to construct and convey the complex reality that unfolds during training so as to support a science of learning in distributed environments.

REFERENCES

Abbott, H. P. (2003). Unnarratable knowledge. In D. Herman (Ed.), *Narrative theory and the cognitive sciences* (pp. 143–162). Stanford, CA: Center for the Study of Language and Information.

Abrahamson, C. (1998). Storytelling as a pedagogical tool in higher education. *Education, 118,* 440–451.

Anderson, J. R., & Schunn, C. D. (2000). Implications of the ACT-R learning theory: No magic bullets. In R. Glaser (Ed.), *Advances in instructional psychology: Educational design and cognitive science, Vol. 5.* (pp. 1–33). Mahwah, NJ: Lawrence Erlbaum Associates.

Bal, M. (1997). *Narratology: Introduction to the theory of narrative.* Toronto, Ontario, Canada: University of Toronto Press.

Bartlett, F. C. (1932). *Remembering: An experimental and social study.* Cambridge, England: Cambridge University Press.

Berg, G. (2000). Cognitive development through narrative: Computer interface design for educational purposes. *Journal of Educational Multimedia and Hypermedia, 9,* 3–17.

Body, R., & Perkins, M. R. (1998). Ecological validity in assessment of discourse in traumatic brain injury: Ratings by clinicians and non-clinicians. *Brain Injury, 12,* 963–976.

Bond-Chapman, S., Levin, H. S., Matejka, J., Harward, H., & Kufera, J. A. (1995). Discourse ability in children with brain injury: Correlations with psychosocial, linguistic and cognitive factors. *Journal of Head Trauma Rehabilitation, 10,* 36–54.

Bousfield, W. A. (1953). The occurrence of clustering in the recall of randomly arranged associates. *Journal of General Psychology, 49,* 229–240.

Bower, G. H., Clark, M. C., Lesgold, A. M., & Winzenz, D. (1969). Hierarchical retrieval schemes in recall of categorical word lists. *Journal of Verbal Learning and Verbal Behavior, 8,* 323–343.

Bower, G. H., & Morrow, D. G. (1990, January 5). Mental models in narrative comprehension. *Science, 247,* 44–48.

Bransford, J. D., & Franks, J. J. (1971). The abstraction of linguistic ideas. *Cognitive Psychology, 2,* 331–350.

Brookshear, J. G. (2000). *Computer science: An overview.* Reading, MA: Addison-Wesley.

Bruner, J. (1991). The narrative construction of reality. *Critical Inquiry, 18,* 1–21.

Cannon-Bowers, J. A., Rhodenizer, L., Salas, E., & Bowers, C. A. (1998). A framework for understanding pre-practice conditions and their impact on learning. *Personnel Psychology, 51,* 291–320.

Chapman, S. B., Culhane, K. A., Levin, H. S., Harward, H., Mendelsohn, D., Ewing-Cobbs, L., et al. (1992). Narrative discourse after closed head injury in children and adolescents. *Brain and Language, 43,* 42–65.

Chi, M. T. H. (2000). Self-explaining: The dual processes of generating inference and repairing mental models. In R. Glaser (Ed.), *Advances in instructional psychology: Educational design and cognitive science* (Vol. 5, pp. 161–238). Mahwah, NJ: Lawrence Erlbaum Associates.

Chi, M. T. H., Bassok, M., Lewis, M. W., Reimann, P., & Glaser, R. (1989). Self-explanations: How students study and learn examples in learning to solve problems. *Cognitive Science, 13,* 145–182.

Chi, M. T. H., de Leeuw, N., Chiu, M. H., & LaVancher, C. (1994). Eliciting self-explanations improves understanding. *Cognitive Science, 18,* 439–477.

Coelho, C. A., Liles, B. Z., & Duffy, R. J. (1995). Impairments of discourse abilities and executive functions in traumatically brain-injured adults. *Brain Injury, 9,* 471–477.

Denning, S. (2001). *The springboard: How storytelling ignites action in knowledge-era organizations.* Boston: Butterworth Heinemann.

Denning, S. (2004). *Squirrel Inc: A fable of leadership through storytelling.* San Francisco: Wiley.

Don, A. (1990). Narrative and the interface. In B. Laurel (Ed.), *The art of human–computer interface design* (pp. 383–391). Reading, MA: Addison-Wesley.

Dwyer, D. J., Oser, R. L., Salas, E., & Fowlkes, J. E. (1999). Performance measurement in distributed environments: Initial results and implications for training. *Military Psychology, 11,* 189–215.

Fiore, S. M., Jentsch, F., Becerra-Fernandez, I., Salas, E., & Finkelstein, N. (2005). Integrating field data with laboratory training research to improve the understanding of expert human-agent teamwork. *IEEE Proceedings of the 38th Hawaii International Conference on System Sciences* [CD-ROM]. Los Alamitos, CA: IEEE Computer Society Press.

Fiore, S. M., Johnston, J., & McDaniel, R. (2005). Applying the narrative form and Xml metadata to debriefing distributed simulation-based exercises. In *Proceedings of the Human Factors and Ergonomics Society 49th Annual Meeting* (pp. 2135–2139). Santa Monica, CA: Human Factors and Ergonomics Society.

Fiore, S. M., Johnston, J., & Van Duyne, L. (2004). Conceptualizing the *Training Space*: Constructing Hierarchies to Integrate Time and Space for Debriefing Distributed Simulation-Based Exercises. In *Proceedings of the 48th Annual Meeting of the Human Factors and Ergonomics Society* (pp. 2562–2566). Santa Monica, CA: Human Factors and Ergonomics Society.

Fiore, S. M., & McDaniel, R. (2006). Building bridges: Connecting virtual teams using narrative and technology. *THEN: Journal of Technology, Humanities, Education and Narrative, 3*(1). Retrieved January 02, 2006, from http://thenjournal.org/commentary/95/

Fiore, S. M., Metcalf, D. S., & McDaniel, R. (2007). Simulating narrative: On the application of narrative theory for experiential learning. In M. Silberman (Ed.), *The handbook of experiential learning* (pp. 33–58). San Francisco, CA: Pfeiffer.

Fiore, S. M., Salas, E., & Cannon-Bowers, J. A. (2001). Group dynamics and shared mental model development. In M. London (Ed.), *How people evaluate others in organizations: Person perception and interpersonal judgment in industrial/ organizational psychology* (pp. 309–336). Mahwah, NJ: Erlbaum.

Fiore, S. M., Salas, E., Cuevas, H. M., & Bowers, C. A. (2003). Distributed coordination space: Toward a theory of distributed team process and performance. *Theoretical Issues in Ergonomic Science, 4*, 340–363.

Fowlkes, J., Dwyer, D. L., Oser, R. L., & Salas, E. (1998). Event-based approach to training (EBAT). *International Journal of Aviation Psychology, 8*, 209–221.

Fowlkes, J. E., Lane, N. E., Salas, E., Franz, T., & Oser, R. (1994). Improving the measurement of team performance: The TARGETs methodology. *Military Psychology, 6*, 47–61.

Gagne, R., & Glaser, R. (1987). Foundations in learning research. In R. Gagne (Ed.), *Instructional technology: Foundations* (pp. 49–83). Hillsdale, NJ: Erlbaum.

Gerrig, R. J., & Egidi, G. (2003). Cognitive psychological foundations of narrative experiences. In D. Herman (Ed.), *Narrative theory and the cognitive sciences* (pp. 33–55). Stanford, CA: Center for the Study of Language and Information.

Gershon, N., & Page, W. (2001). What storytelling can do for information visualization. *Communications of the ACM, 44*(8), 31–37.

Hartley, L. L., & Jensen, P. J. (1991). Narrative and procedural discourse after closed head injury. *Brain Injury, 5*, 267–285.

Hemphill, L., Feldman, H. M., Camp, L., Griffin, T. M., Miranda, A. B., & Wolf, D. P. (1994). Developmental changes in narrative and non-narrative discourse in children with and without brain injury. *Journal of Communicative Disorders, 27*, 107–133.

Herman, D. (2003). Stories as a tool for thinking. In D. Herman (Ed.), *Narrative theory and the cognitive sciences* (pp. 163–192). Stanford, CA: Center for the Study of Language and Information.

Herrnstein Smith, B. (1978). *On the margins of discourse: The relation of literature to language.* Chicago: University of Chicago Press.

Hirumi, A., Knowland, K., & Pounds, K. (2004, October). *The professional development of online distance educators: A study of K12, university and corporate collaboration.* Paper presented at the Association for Educational Communications and Technology Conference, Chicago.

Hughes, C. E., Konttinen, J., & Pattanaik, S. N. (2004). *The future of mixed reality: Issues in illumination and shadows.* Proceedings of the 2004 Interservice/Industry Training, Simulation, and Education Conference [CD-ROM]. Orlando, FL: National Training Systems.

King, A. (1992). Facilitating elaborative learning through guided student-generated questioning. *Educational Psychologist, 27*, 111–126.

Knerr, B., Lampton, D., Martin, G., Washburn, D., & Cope, D. (2002). Dismounted Infantry Virtual After Action Review System. *Proceedings of Interservice/Industry Training, Simulation and Education Conference* [CD-ROM]. Orlando, FL: National Training Systems.

Mandler, G. (1967). Organization and memory. In K. W. Spence & J. T. Spence (Eds.), *The psychology of learning and motivation* (Vol 1, pp. 327–372). New York: Academic Press.

Mandler, J. M. (1984). *Stories, scripts, and scenes: Aspects of schema theory.* Hillsdale, NJ: Erlbaum.

Mateas, M., & Sengers, P. (1999). Narrative intelligence: An introduction to the NI Symposium. In M. Mateas & P. Sengers (Eds.), *Working notes of the Narrative Intelligence Symposium, AAAI Fall Symposium Series.* Menlo Park, CA: American Association for Artificial Intelligence Press.

Mathison, C., & Gallego, M. (2002). School stories: The power of narrative in teacher education. *Reading Online, 5*(8), 1–10.

McDaniel, R. (2004). *A software-based knowledge management system using narrative texts.* Unpublished doctoral dissertation, University of Central Florida, Orlando.

Mckenna, C., Pounds, K., & Hirumi, A. (2004, October). *Storytelling: A strategy for promoting online learner engagement.* Paper presented at the Association for Educational Communications and Technology Conference, Chicago.

Metcalf, D. S. (2006). *mLearning: Mobile learning and performance in the palm of your hand.* Amherst, MA: HRD Press.

Minsky, M. (1985). *The society of mind.* New York: Simon & Schuster.

Norman, D. (1993). *Things that make us smart.* Reading, MA: Perseus Books.

Rosenshine, B., Meister, C., & Chapman, S. (1996). Teaching students to generate questions: A review of the intervention studies. *Review of Educational Research, 66,* 181–221.

Rumelhart, D. E. (1980). Schemata: The building blocks of cognition. In R. J. Spiro, B. Bruce, & W. F. Brewer (Eds.), *Theoretical issues in reading and comprehension* (pp. 38–58). Hillsdale, NJ: Erlbaum.

Ryokai, K., Vaucelle, C., & Cassell, J. (2003). Virtual peers as partners in storytelling and literacy learning. *Journal of Computer Assisted Learning, 19,* 195–208.

Schank, R. C. (1998). *Tell me a story: Narrative and intelligence.* Evanston, IL: Northwestern University Press.

Schank, R. C., & Abelson, R. P. (1977). *Scripts, plans, goals, and understanding: An inquiry into human knowledge structures.* Hillsdale, NJ: Erlbaum.

Smith-Jentsch, K. A., Zeisig, R. L., Acton, B., & McPherson, J. A. (1998). Team dimensional training. In J. A. Cannon-Bowers & E. Salas (Eds.), *Making decisions under stress: Implications for individual and team training* (pp. 271–297). Washington, DC: American Psychological Association.

Snowden, D. (2001). Narrative patterns: The perils and possibilities of using story in organisations. *Knowledge Management Ark*. Retrieved January 15, 2006, from http://www.kwork.org/Stars/narrative_snowden.html.

Stapleton, C. B., & Hughes, C. E. (2003). Interactive imagination: Tapping the emotions through interactive story for compelling simulations. *IEEE Computer Graphics and Applications, 24*, 11–15.

Stapleton, C. B., Hughes, C. E., Moshell, J. M., Micikevicius, P., & Altman, M. (2002). Applying mixed reality to entertainment. *IEEE Computer, 35*, 122–124.

Sturm, B. W. (1999). The enchanted imagination: Storytelling's power to entrance listeners. *American Library Association School Library Media Annual, 2*.

Togher, L., & Handoe, L. (1999). The macrostructure of the interview: Are traumatic brain injury interactions structured differently to control interactions? *Aphasiology, 13*, 709–723.

Trabasso, T., & Sperry, L. L. (1985). Causal relatedness and importance of story events. *Journal of Memory and Language, 24*, 595–611.

Turner, M. (2003). Double-scope stories. In D. Herman (Ed.), *Narrative theory and the cognitive sciences* (pp. 117–142). Stanford, CA: Center for the Study of Language and Information.

Wittenbaum, G. M., Vaughan, S. I., & Stasser, G. (1998). Coordination in task-performing groups. In R. S. Tindale & L. Heath (Eds.), *Theory and research on small groups: Social psychological applications to social issues* (Vol. 4, pp. 177–204). New York: Plenum Press.

7

DISTRIBUTED MISSION ENVIRONMENTS: EFFECTS OF GEOGRAPHIC DISTRIBUTION ON TEAM COGNITION, PROCESS, AND PERFORMANCE

NANCY J. COOKE, JAMIE C. GORMAN, HARRY PEDERSEN, AND BRIAN BELL

In this chapter, we empirically examine the effects of geographic distribution on team performance, process, and cognition in a command-and-control setting. The particular command-and-control setting in which our investigation takes place is that of unmanned aerial vehicle (UAV) ground control. Teams in this setting are heterogeneous with respect to their knowledge, skills, and abilities; the task is highly complex and dynamic; and interactions are synchronous. These factors make this setting different from many of the scenarios typically tested by social and organizational psychologists who use homogeneous groups and relatively simple tasks (e.g., Hinsz,

This work was supported by AFOSR Grants F49620-01-1-0261 and F49620-03-1-0024 awarded to the first author at New Mexico State University and Arizona State University, respectively.

1999) and lend ecological validity in terms of the characteristics of distributed team task performance.

Highly complex tasks often involve a unique division of labor, often covering a global terrain of operations coordinated by specialized team members distributed across the landscape. Distributed teams pervade the military. Although individuals may be distributed in space, distributed teams can make decisions, communicate, and share information over an interconnected network. Warfare in this environment has been termed *network centric*, such that the battlefield is not only geographically dispersed over terrain but also dispersed over the Internet, or some other communication network, as well as individual team member competencies (cf. *heterogeneous* teams). Thus, in the military, team tasks are performed by individuals who may have never met; who are not sitting in the same room; who may share information only by computer or other media, such as radios or telephones; and who may come from rather distinct backgrounds in terms of training or knowledge. In addition, these arrangements apply not only to teams of individuals but also to teams of teams (i.e., hierarchical layers of teams) in which the task is shared by an intricate distributed network of collaborating individuals who are required to coordinate voluminous amounts of information.

However, heterogeneous groups interacting in a distributed manner to perform complex tasks are not unique to the military. This type of team task is increasingly common in venues ranging from business meetings and emergency operations to remote telemedicine and collaborations in distance education. The degree to which geographically distributed as opposed to colocated work environments affect team performance and cognition in these settings has critical implications for training and design in support of distributed work. Another characteristic these complex distributed tasks have in common is that most, if not all, of the work entails cognitive, rather than physical, activity. The performance of cognitive activities at the team or group level gives rise to the concept of team cognition (Cooke, Salas, Cannon-Bowers, & Stout, 2000; Salas & Fiore, 2004).

WHAT IS TEAM COGNITION?

Teams think, make decisions, assess situations, remember, plan, and solve problems as an integrated unit. These cognitive activities are increasingly prevalent in team tasks in general and dominate activities in distributed mission environments. We assume that team cognition provides the psychological basis for team performance and therefore is a prime target for training or design interventions to improve team performance. Similarly, we assume

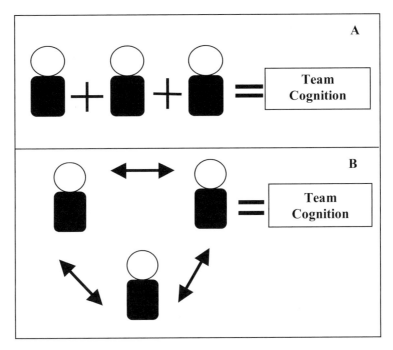

Figure 7.1. Panel A represents traditional collective views of team cognition. Panel B represents a more process-oriented holistic view of team cognition.

that factors such as geographic distribution can have profound effects on team cognition.

Traditional views of team cognition are collective in that they assume that team cognition is a linear, or additive, by-product of the knowledge residing in each team member's head (cf. Steiner, 1972). In some sense, the collective model predicts that team member cognition is less than or equal to the sum of its parts, in this case, individual team member knowledge. This view is represented in Panel A of Figure 7.1. Measures of team cognition (e.g., shared mental models) based on aggregating individual cognitive measures across team members reflect the collective view (e.g., Langan-Fox, Code, & Langfield-Smith, 2000).

There are two main limitations to the collective view and measures derived from it. First, aggregation and its associated constructs and metrics (e.g., shared mental models) assume homogeneous cognition (i.e., identical or at least similar parts), a view that does not strictly apply to heterogeneous teams (Cooke & Gorman, 2006). For example, the assumption that one can compare the (task) effective knowledge of a surgeon with the knowledge of an anesthesiologist, or somehow sum the two to estimate the knowledge of the two in coordination, is a collective assumption. Second, collective views and metrics omit, or at least oversimplify, the processing component of team cognition and therefore do not accurately reflect team cognition (Cooke et al., 2000). Thus a linear, or additive-factors approach to understanding team cognition belies the intrinsic importance of team member interactions to team cognition such that the team's parts as well as the team members' interactions are important in generating an emergent whole (see Figure 7.1A). The shared mental models view of team cognition has traditionally been a collective view that may be limited, especially for heterogeneous teams.

In general, we define *team cognition* as the emergent product of the interplay between the local cognition of each team member and team process behaviors (Cooke et al., 2000; Cooke, Salas, Kiekel, & Bell, 2004). That is, team members each have a unique responsibility for their own particular labor division: a local environment, which they perceive and maintain and on which they act. Through interaction, team members can share changes in their own local environments with other team members, potentially making significant contributions to the information available in the environments of other, reciprocating team members. In this case, the emphasis is on the act of sharing knowledge as opposed to the collective knowledge product often referred to as a *shared mental model*. Team members interact with respect to time through communication, coordination, and other process behaviors, thereby building actionable team knowledge. Thus, no team member is responsible for the global patterns underlying team cognition; instead, team cognition emerges from the interplay of the parts, each member responsible for his or her own local environment (see Panel B of Figure 7.1). In terms of understanding complexity, this viewpoint is called *self-organization*, but here we use Cooke et al.'s (2000) terminology, referring to it instead as a *holistic* perspective.

Metrics of team cognition applicable at the group or team level should also be relevant in terms of a holistic view of team cognition. For example, team members in a military aviation setting may individually have information about an impending threat, but without adequate communication that helps to produce the integration or fusion of the pieces of information at a very global level, the team's knowledge would be lacking and the team would fail to act on the impending threat. In this case, collective knowledge metrics would inaccurately represent the team as having knowledge about the impending threat, whereas holistic metrics would better reflect the team's actual knowledge.

One of our approaches to measuring team cognition has focused on obtaining and comparing collective and holistic measures of team cognition. Collective measurements can be obtained using a number of aggregation procedures, such as averaging individual responses. Holistic measurement requires that one assesses team knowledge at the team level. We have explored the use of communication data as a holistic approach to measuring team cognition (Kiekel, Cooke, Foltz, Gorman, & Martin, 2002). Communication can actually be viewed as cognitive processing at the team level but has the benefit of being a natural by-product of most team interactions. Another approach to assessing team knowledge at the holistic level is to present the same measurement tasks used at the individual level to the group as a whole (Cooke et al., 2004). For instance, we have asked team members to discuss material over headsets and come to a consensus on the team's responses to questions about taskwork. We assume that the team interaction that is required to come to a consensus involves some of the same team process behaviors that the team exercises in the operational environment and that the output of this measure is postprocessed knowledge.

In much of the remainder of this chapter, we empirically examine the effects of geographic distribution on team process behaviors, team cognition (both collective and holistic views), and team performance in a command-and-control UAV setting.

PREDICTED INFLUENCES OF GEOGRAPHIC DISTRIBUTION

Very little research has examined the effects of distributed mission environments on team performance, process behaviors, or cognition. Although Kleinman and Serfaty (1989) studied a military-based synthetic task environment that represented a geographically distributed Airborne Warning and Control Systems environment, there were no direct comparisons of team behavior, performance, and cognition between this setting and a colocated environment.

Whereas there has been little or no research on the impact of geographic distribution on team performance or cognition in military settings, research in the human–computer interaction community has addressed mode of communication, a topic relevant to distributed work. This research has compared face-to-face or audio communication with computer-mediated communication, such as e-mail, Group Decision Support Systems, or other tools. Several of these studies have found problems with computer-mediated communication. For example, Mantovani (1996) found that computer-mediated communication can hinder the creation of meaning, although Hedlund, Ilgen, and Hollenbeck (1998) found that computer-mediated communication can lead to lengthy decision making compared with face-to-face communication. Unfortunately, these studies did not measure the performance of heterogeneous teams working on complex tasks for an extended period of time during which team member familiarity may confer an advantage. Some researchers have found that specific group norms are critical when higher team member familiarity among colocated teams produces better performance compared with distributed teams (Contractor, Seibold, & Heller, 1996; Postmes & Spears, 1998; Postmes, Spears, & Lea, 1998).

Team members in distributed environments are less likely to be familiar with each other, because they must often communicate in ways that are less direct (i.e., never face to face), and they may not be able to share displays or convey information visually through gestures or facial expressions. This opacity is likely to affect team process behaviors (e.g., communication, coordination, and planning) that in turn affect team performance during initial team missions and when workload is high (Fiore, Salas, Cuevas, & Bowers, 2003; Levine & Choi, 2004; Robertson & Endsley, 1997). These factors may also affect the acquisition of a team member's knowledge about the task or team, with colocated team members better able to acquire interpositional knowledge than distributed team members (Fiore et al., 2003). For instance, team members in distributed environments may have less of an understanding of the tasks of other team members simply because they cannot view the work environment of their teammates. In addition, communication limitations can affect the ability of team members to develop a shared understanding of the task or of the immediate situation. This knowledge difference at the individual level can ultimately affect knowledge at the team level.

We hypothesize that process limitations of a distributed learning and work environment will lead to deficits in the development of team cognition and, ultimately, team performance.

EXAMINING THE IMPACT OF GEOGRAPHIC DISTRIBUTION

To investigate the effect of geographic distribution on team performance, process, and cognition, we conducted a study on the context of the Cognitive Engineering Research on Team Tasks Laboratory Unmanned Aerial Vehicle Synthetic Task Environment (UAV-STE; Cooke & Shope, 2004). The Cognitive Engineering Research on Team Tasks Laboratory UAV-STE task is an abstraction of the Air Force's Predator UAV ground operations task (Cooke, Rivera, Shope, & Caukwell, 1999). The team's goal is to fly the UAV to designated target areas to take acceptable photos of the areas.

This comprises a heterogeneous task environment in which there are three distinct roles: (a) air vehicle operator (AVO; pilot); (b) payload operator (PLO; photographer); and (c) data exploitation, mission planning and communication operator (DEMPC; navigator). Thus, the UAV-STE is a good example of a heterogeneous task because each team member performs different although interdependent functions: The AVO controls airspeed, heading, and altitude and monitors UAV systems. The PLO adjusts camera settings (in accord with airspeed and altitude), takes photographs, and monitors the camera equipment. The DEMPC oversees the mission and determines the flight paths under various constraints. Thus, each team member has unique yet interdependent roles and is provided with distinct, although slightly overlapping training and information during the mission. To complete the mission, the team members need to coordinate information with one another in a timely and adaptive fashion. Most communication is done with microphones and headsets, although some involve computer messaging.

In the experiment discussed in this chapter, 20 teams engaged in seven 40-minute missions in either a colocated or a geographically distributed team environment. On the one hand, colocated team members worked at individual consoles in the same room, and although they could see each other, during missions they communicated over headsets. Distributed team members, on the other hand, could not see each other because they were separated for the entire experiment by partition walls or, in the case of the DEMPC, by separate rooms. (Note that this manipulation is subtle in that communication mode [i.e., over headsets and microphones] remains constant.) The first four missions were low workload in that there were nine targets to photograph. Missions 5 through 7 were high-workload missions with 20 targets each and additional scenario constraints.

On the basis of the extant literature (e.g., Hedlund et al., 1998; Mantovani, 1996), we hypothesized that distributed teams would exhibit impaired process behaviors compared with colocated teams and that this in turn would negatively affect team cognition and performance for distributed teams compared with colocated teams. We also hypothesized that the impact of distribution would be greater under conditions of high workload than low workload.

Measures

The study presented here is part of a larger project that investigated not only the effects of distributed versus colocated mission environments on team performance and cognition but also various techniques for measuring aspects of team cognition and performance. Thus, a variety of measures were taken, including Situational Awareness Rating Technique (subjective situation awareness), Situation Present Assessment Method (situation awareness; Durso et al., 1998), National Aeronautics and Space Administration Task Load Index (subjective workload), social desirability, teamwork knowledge measures, experimenter ratings of team process behavior, and working memory measures. The analyses presented in this chapter focus on the measures most central to our hypotheses (i.e., team performance, team knowledge, and team process behavior). Measures of team performance and process were taken unobtrusively during each mission. The taskwork knowledge measure was taken apart from the mission in two sessions: one immediately following training and another after the last mission (i.e., Mission 7).

Team performance was measured using a composite score based on several mission outcome variables most relevant to the team objective, including time each individual spent in an alarm state (e.g., airspeed beyond an acceptable range—pilot), time each individual spent in a warning state (e.g., camera battery low—photographer), rate at which critical waypoints were visited, and the rate at which targets were successfully photographed. Penalty points for these components were weighted a priori in accord with importance to the task and subtracted from a maximum score of 1,000. Team performance data were collected for each of the seven missions.

Team process behavior was scored independently by each of two experimenters who attended to specific process behaviors at critical events and thus is referred to as *critical incident process* (CIP). For each mission, the experimenters observed team behavior and responded to a series of six questions. Three of these items concerned team behaviors that did or did not occur at designated event triggers in each mission (e.g., within 5 minutes after the end of the mission, the team members discuss and assess their performance). These items were scored as either present or not present. The other three items also assessed team behaviors that did or did not occur at designated event triggers in each mission, but these items were scored on a scale that ranged from *very poor/none* (0) to *good* (2) (or, in the case of one item, to *very good* [3]). The sum of scores on these six items was expressed as a ratio of total possible points out of 10 for a given mission. This ratio formed the CIP score for each mission.

A taskwork knowledge measure was administered by presenting 55 concept pairs, 1 pair at a time, to participants. Items for each pair were drawn from 11 task-related terms, such as *altitude* and *airspeed*. Team members made relatedness ratings of the 55 concept pairs on a 6-point scale that ranged from *unrelated* to *highly related*. On the basis of these ratings, the Pathfinder network scaling procedure (Schvaneveldt, 1990) was used to develop an individual knowledge network for each of the team members on a team. Network similarities were computed that ranged from 0 to 1 and represented the proportion of shared links between two networks.

Intrateam similarity was based on the mean of network similarity values for all pairs of team member networks. An overall accuracy value was computed for each team member by computing the similarity between the individual network and an overall knowledge referent (derived from task expert ratings). These similarities were averaged across the three team members for a collective measure of taskwork accuracy. Individual taskwork knowledge was also scored against referents specific to each role (Cooke et al., 2004). Thus, each individual obtained a score reflecting accuracy relative to the AVO, PLO, and DEMPC positions. From these scores, estimates of positional and interpositional knowledge accuracy could be determined (e.g., each DEMPC was scored against a DEMPC key for positional accuracy, and interpositional accuracy was estimated as the average when scored against the PLO and AVO keys).

A holistic measure of taskwork accuracy involved having teams reach a consensus on the items that were presented to individual team members. For each pair, the rating entered in the prior session by each team member was displayed on the computer screen of each team member. The three team members discussed each pair over their headsets until a consensus was reached. As a team, the individuals had to agree on relatedness ratings for the concepts. The team was scored for holistic accuracy on the same scale used for overall individual accuracy, by comparison of the team's network to a referent.

Participants

Twenty 3-person teams of New Mexico State University students voluntarily participated in two 5-hour sessions separated by 48 hours. Forty of the participants were male. Individuals were compensated for their participation by payment of $6 per person-hour to their organization. In addition, the 3 members on the team with the highest team performance score were each awarded a $50 bonus. At the beginning of each experiment, the participants were randomly assigned (with constraints of 3 persons per team) to teams and to roles (with the constraint of 1 AVO, PLO, or DEMPC per team), with the teams randomly assigned (but maintaining equivalent number of teams per condition) to either the colocated or the distributed mission environment.

Procedure

Each experimental session was overseen by two experimenters. Communication occurred mostly over headsets, with some minimal computer messaging (e.g., the DEMPC could send the AVO a current route plan). Participants were first given a brief overview of the task and then started training. During training, all of the participants were separated by partitions regardless of the condition to which they were assigned. Team members studied three PowerPoint training modules at their own pace and were tested with a set of multiple-choice questions at the end of each module. Once all team members had completed the tutorial and correctly answered the test questions, skills were tested. Experimenters had participants practice aspects of the individual tasks, checking off skills that were mastered (e.g., the AVO needed to change altitude and airspeed, the PLO needed to take a good photograph of a target) and assisting in cases of difficulty. This continued until all skills were mastered. Training took a total of 1.5 hours.

After a short break, the taskwork measure was administered, after which the partitions were removed for colocated teams, and the first 40-minute mission was begun. The first experimental session contained three low-workload missions. The second session (48 hours later) contained one low-workload mission and three high-workload missions. Team performance and process measures were administered during each mission. The taskwork knowledge measure was again administered at the end of the second session (after Mission 7).

Each mission was completed at the end of a 40-minute interval or when team members believed that their mission goals had been completed. Immediately after each mission, participants were shown their individual and team performance scores and were able to compare these scores to the means of previous teams in the same experiment.

RESULTS

Our results can be broken down into three distinct areas: (a) team process, (b) team performance, and (c) taskwork knowledge.

Team Process

We hypothesized that distributed teams should have more trouble with communication, coordination, and planning compared with colocated teams because of the inability to see each other and view team members' computer screens. As discussed in the Measures section, the sum of scores on the six CIP items was expressed as a ratio of points out of 10. When the team did not reach a designated event trigger, and therefore had missing data for that item, the ratio was calculated without that item. In this way, the team's process score was not affected by an event that is better captured by the team's performance score. Thus, the CIP ratios range from 0 to 1.

A 7 (mission) × 2 (distribution condition) analysis of variance (ANOVA) was conducted, with mission manipulated within teams and distribution manipulated between teams. The main effect of mission was significant, $F(6, 108) = 4.77$, $p < .01$, implying that CIP scores were statistically different across the seven missions. The main effect of condition was also significant, $F(1, 18) = 18.41$, $p < .01$. Figure 7.2 illustrates that colocated teams had significantly higher CIP over missions. Figure 7.2 supports the statistical finding that distribution effect was largely independent of mission, $F(6, 108) < 1$.

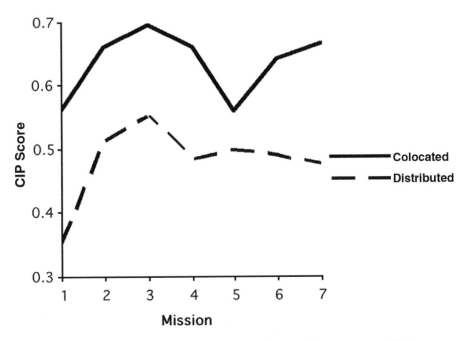

Figure 7.2. Mean colocated and distributed critical incident process (CIP) scores over missions.

A planned comparison between Missions 4 and 5 was conducted to examine the impact of the increase in workload from Mission 4 to 5. As expected, the results indicate a significant main effect of condition, $F(1, 18) = 5.53$, $p < .05$, between these missions, with the colocated teams continuing to earn higher CIP scores. The main effect of mission, however, was not significant, $F(1, 18) = 1.86$. An inspection of Figure 7.2 suggests that the reason this main effect was not significant is likely because the process of distributed teams was not impaired by the higher workload. A post hoc simple comparison revealed that colocated teams did show significant decrease on CIP between Missions 4 and 5, $F(1, 9) = 4.37$, $p = .07$. (Note that in this study we consider alpha levels of $\leq .10$ statistically significant, opting to err in the direction of increased Type I errors to identify any potentially interesting measures or effects.) It is not surprising, then, that the planned interaction contrast using Missions 4 and 5 was also significant, $F(1, 18) = 3.01$, $p = .10$. Apparently, colocated and distributed teams' CIP scores were differentially affected by the transition from low to high workload between Missions 4 and 5. In Figure 7.2, this difference is illustrated by the sharp drop in colocated CIP at Mission 5 relative to the steady, albeit low, level of CIP at Missions 4 and 5 for distributed teams.

TABLE 7.1
Results of Discriminant Analysis

Process Item	Wilks's lambda	F	dfnum	dfden	p	Standardized weights
1	.90	13.31	1	124	.00	.16
2	1.00	.00	1	124	.99	-.11
3	.94	7.38	1	124	.01	.28
4	1.00	0.50	1	124	.48	-.06
5	1.00	.01	1	124	.92	-.11
6	.34	244.84	1	124	.00	.98

Note: *df*num = numerator degrees of freedom; *df*den = denominator degrees of freedom.

To more deeply explore the source of the process differences between colocated and distributed teams, we conducted a discriminant analysis model using the critical incident items as predictors and colocated (0) or distributed (1) as the dependent grouping variable. Wilks's lambda and the F analogue of the weights assigned to each item in the discriminant function are presented in Table 7.1.

CIP Item 6 clearly is the largest discriminator, followed by Items 1 and 3, in that order. It is interesting to note that these items involve communications that are not explicitly necessary to accomplish their task. For example, Items 6 and 1 involved teams discussing their performance after and at the beginning of, respectively, their missions. Item 3 concerned whether teams explicitly noted called-in (i.e., ad hoc) targets before getting to a called-in Restricted Operating Zone area. Items 2, 4, and 5 involve communications that are explicitly necessary during the course of a mission (e.g., AVO and PLO coordinating on a specific target). We thus theorize that the significantly better process behaviors exhibited by colocated teams were due to teams' differences in assessing performance before and after each mission (Items 1 and 6) and, to some extent, explicitly noting mission parameters that emerge during the course of a mission (Item 3).

To summarize, the results suggest that teams in the colocated condition exhibit better team process behaviors at our predefined trigger points and thus support our hypothesis. Given that our participants in the colocated condition are geographically proximal, the simple explanation is that something about being located in the same room facilitates certain types of process behaviors. The specific process behaviors exhibited by colocated teams but not by distributed teams included pre- and postmission process planning and adaptive process behaviors. In terms of CIP, although colocated teams exhibited a more drastic decrease at the onset of high workload, they still displayed higher CIP scores than distributed teams under the same conditions.

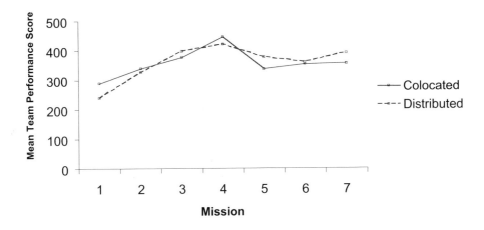

Figure 7.3. Mean colocated and distributed team performance across missions.

Team Performance

Team performance scores across the seven missions are displayed in Figure 7.3. Teams steadily improved during the initial four missions and then performed more poorly at the point at which the high-workload manipulation was introduced. A two-factor ANOVA with mission as the repeated measure and distribution as the between-teams variable revealed a detectable effect of mission, $F(6, 108) = 19.10$, $p < .01$, but no effect of distribution (i.e., colocated or distributed), $F(1, 18) < 1$. There was also an interaction between mission and distribution, $F(6, 108) = 1.94$, $p = .08$.

Further exploration of the Mission × Distribution interaction for the transition from low to high workload (Missions 4 to 5) indicated that increased workload produced a decline in performance between the last low-workload mission (Mission 4) and the first high-workload mission (Mission 5), $F(1, 18) = 31.47$, $p < .01$, with a detectable interaction between distribution and mission, $F(1, 18) = 6.05$, $p = .02$, suggesting that the decline in performance was affected by distribution. Means in this single-degree-of-freedom interaction revealed that the direction of the distribution effect changed from Mission 4 to Mission 5, with distributed teams performing better than colocated teams in Mission 5 and with colocated teams suffering the most from increased workload.

We also compared colocated teams to distributed teams on Mission 4, the last low-workload mission, and on Mission 7, the last high-workload mission, to see whether teams had recovered from the workload manipulation by the end of the experiment. There was a main effect of mission, $F(1, 18) = 13.74$, $p < .01$, with teams performing worse on Mission 7 than on Mission 4. Also, there was an interaction between distribution and

TABLE 7.2
Descriptive Statistics on Taskwork Knowledge Metrics in Colocated and
Distributed Conditions for Knowledge Session 1 and Knowledge Session 2

Metric and knowledge session	M		SD		Minimum		Maximum	
	Col.	Dist.	Col.	Dist.	Col.	Dist.	Col.	Dist.
Overall accuracy								
1	.44	.48	.06	.04	.37	.41	.56	.53
2	.50	.47	.05	.04	.39	.40	.59	.54
Positional accuracy								
1	−.19	−.07	.55	.60	−.96	−.96	.52	.57
2	.15	.13	.56	.65	−.51	−.94	1.18	1.15
Interpositional accuracy								
1	−.20	−.08	.55	.40	−.70	−.84	1.24	.62
2	.32	.00	.46	.43	−.62	−.90	.68	.49
Intrateam similarity								
1	.36	.38	.06	.06	.30	.28	.49	.47
2	.43	.41	.07	.07	.34	.27	.56	.53
Holistic accuracy								
1	.53	.59	.07	.05	.39	.50	.63	.69
2	.62	.56	.06	.08	.52	.44	.71	.71

Note. Col. = colocated; Dist. = distributed.

mission, $F(1, 18) = 3.65$, $p = .07$, indicating a change in valence for the distribution effect between Mission 4 and Mission 7, with distributed teams outperforming colocated teams in Mission 7 but not in Mission 4.

In sum, our hypotheses regarding performance deficits of distributed teams were not supported by our findings. Colocated and distributed teams performed nearly equivalently, and colocated teams, but not distributed teams, were negatively affected by the workload change. In fact, the minimal differences between high-workload Missions 5 and 7 attribute workload deficits more so to the colocated teams.

Taskwork Knowledge

The means and standard deviations, as well as the minimum and maximum scores for the various taskwork knowledge metrics, can be seen in Table 7.2. Taskwork data collected during Knowledge Session 2 was missing for one team (Team 7). With regard to overall taskwork accuracy, a two-factor ANOVA revealed a significant interaction between distribution condition (between subjects) and knowledge session (within subject), $F(1, 17) = 5.17$, $p = .04$. A main effect of knowledge session was also found, $F(1, 17) = 4.05$, $p = .06$, where overall accuracy was higher in Knowledge

Session 2. There was no main effect of distribution, $F(1, 17) < 1$. As post hoc tests reveal, colocated teams improved in overall accuracy from Knowledge Session 1 to Knowledge Session 2, $F(1, 8) = 6.62, p = .03$, but distributed teams' overall accuracy scores did not change, $F(1, 9) < 1$.

Table 7.2 also displays the descriptive statistics for taskwork positional knowledge. A two-factor ANOVA revealed no significant interaction between distribution and knowledge session, $F(1, 17) < 1$, or a significant effect of distribution, $F(1, 17) < 1$. There was no significant difference across knowledge sessions in terms of positional knowledge, $F(1, 17) = 1.97$.

Taskwork interpositional knowledge was also analyzed for both sessions as a function of the colocated/distributed manipulation (see Table 7.2). As with overall accuracy, there was a significant interaction between knowledge session and distribution, $F(1, 17) = 3.29, p = .09$, as well as a significant main effect of knowledge session, $F(1, 17) = 6.09, p = .03$. No main effect of distribution was found, $F(1, 17) < 1$. Again, post hoc tests confirmed that colocated teams improved in interpositional knowledge across knowledge sessions, $F(1, 8) = 8.86, p = .02$, whereas distributed teams' interpositional knowledge did not significantly improve from Knowledge Session 1 to Knowledge Session 2, $F(1, 9) < 1$.

We also examined taskwork intrateam similarity (the descriptive data are displayed in Table 7.2). There was no significant interaction between distribution and knowledge session, $F(1, 17) = 2.67$, but a significant effect of session was found, $F(1, 17) = 14.39, p < .01$, with both colocated and distributed teams becoming more similar over time. The distribution main effect was not significant, $F(1, 17) < 1$.

The final taskwork variable we examined was holistic taskwork accuracy. Descriptive data are displayed in Table 7.2. For this variable, there was a significant interaction between distribution and session, $F(1, 16) = 12.27, p < .01$. A significant main effect of session was detected, $F(1, 16) = 3.07, p = .10$, indicating that across teams, holistic accuracy was higher at Knowledge Session 2. There was no significant main effect of distribution, $F(1, 16) < 1$. Post hoc tests indicated that colocated teams became more accurate from Knowledge Session 1 to Knowledge Session 2 on the holistic measure, $F(1, 8) = -17.99, p < .01$, whereas distributed teams' holistic accuracy did not significantly change across sessions, $F(1, 8) = 1.24$.

In summary, with the exception of positional knowledge, there was general improvement in taskwork knowledge scores from Session 1 to 2. This improvement is mostly attributable to colocated teams (however, both colocated and distributed teams became more similar over sessions). The pattern of results suggests that colocated teams acquired interpositional knowledge (i.e., knowledge about the tasks of their fellow team members), which also influences overall accuracy and holistic accuracy scores.

TABLE 7.3
Statistics for the Comparison of the Number of Utterances Between Colocated and Distributed Conditions

Role	M_{col}	M_{dist}	F	df_{num}	df_{den}	p	η^2
AVO	99.11	68.31	11.349	1	16.12	.004	.412
PLO	81.61	55.65	5.459	1	16.13	.033	.253
DEMPC	93.74	71.13	5.000	1	16.18	.040	.236

Note. M_{col} = mean colocated; M_{dist} = mean distributed; df_{num} = numerator degrees of freedom; df_{den} = denominator degrees of freedom; AVO = Air Vehicle Operator; PLO = Payload Operator; DEMPC = Data Exploitation, Mission Planning and Communication Operator.

DISCUSSION OF THE GEOGRAPHIC DISTRIBUTION STUDY

As predicted, geographic distribution of team members affected team process and team cognition. Specifically, teams that were colocated as opposed to distributed engaged in more pre- and postmission process communication behaviors. These behaviors involved adaptation and planning. Indeed, some preliminary analyses of communication data collected in the same study indicate that colocated teams spend more time, in general, communicating compared with distributed teams. In particular, team members in every role made more utterances in the colocated condition than in the distributed condition (see Table 7.3).

Some researchers have tied these kinds of pre- and postmission process behaviors theoretically to the building of shared knowledge (Fiore et al., 2003; Levine & Choi, 2004). There is support for the connection between process and knowledge in that the colocated teams more readily acquired knowledge about the task from the perspective of other team members than distributed teams. This pattern suggests that the process behaviors favored by colocated teams may have facilitated a common understanding (i.e., shared mental model) of the task.

However, we found no evidence to support the notion that geographic distribution affected performance on the UAV team task. So, although distributed teams appear to be scoring lower on team process than colocated teams and failing to acquire knowledge of the others' tasks, they maintain performance equivalent to, and in some cases better than, colocated teams (e.g., during the switch to high workload). How do we explain such process and knowledge differences with no concomitant performance effects? What about the finding that common knowledge mitigates the detrimental effects of high workload (e.g., Stout, Cannon-Bowers, Salas, & Milanovich, 1999)? This is puzzling unless we take the view that teams in these two conditions can adapt differently given the constraints of their special environments and that differences in team behavior and team cognitions that result are appropriate for their unique setting, that there exists a principle of equifinality, with different teams taking different routes to what comprises qualitatively the same outcome.

A colocated environment allows team members to interact more directly and share computer displays, which means that colocated teams can develop interpositional taskwork knowledge. In turn, this kind of broadly overlapping understanding of the task environment allows team members to anticipate what other team members need or will do (Entin & Serfaty, 1999; Stout et al., 1999), enabling them to coordinate their activities appropriately, further enhancing team process.

However, in this study distributed teams successfully adapted to an environment that more readily constrained team member interactions (e.g., there were no opportunities for face-to-face interactions). Unlike colocated teams, the members of which interact more freely outside of what their task dictates and who thereby acquire interpositional knowledge, distributed teams interact only as the task necessitates (or perhaps exhibited different process behaviors that were not anticipated and thus not captured by our CIP measure). Along with this highly constrained medium of interaction, distributed team members became more similar over time in their understanding of the task; however, this did not necessarily entail a better understanding of the nuances of other task roles (interpositional knowledge). We might think of this form of adaptation as developing a much more rigid but efficient team cognition, whereas colocated teams have more "play" in the system, from which they can develop expectancies about what it means to play a different role on the team. However, this was clearly not always adaptive, given the findings of performance decrement under high workload. Indeed, the distributed modes of interaction seemed to be most impervious to the demands of high workload compared with the more easygoing interaction of colocated teams.

Other results from our laboratory similarly support the adaptation explanation. On the one hand, in a previous study that manipulated the ability to share knowledge in the same UAV task environment, Cooke, Shope, and Kiekel (2001) found that teams with different knowledge structures did not differ in terms of team performance. On the other hand, team members who were allowed to freely share knowledge had more accurate taskwork knowledge scores than those who were restricted from information sharing.

Overall, these results suggest that there is not a single form of team cognition to which teams should aspire. Instead, team cognition, like individual cognition, is more parsimoniously considered an adaptation to the environment.

One other possibility is that there may be a cost associated with the colocated condition that overrides any potential benefits of pre- and postprocessing. According to Penner and Craiger (1992), the presence of others can produce higher levels of arousal, which in turn may produce poorer performance on a complex task. Although colocated team members may have a richer understanding of the task, the presence of others may also increase evaluative pressures or produce a distraction that prevents individuals from fully attending to the task. It is interesting to note that we have some evidence in our secondary measures to support this cost of colocation in our task. Specifically, on the basis of the NASA TLX results, DEMPCs experienced greater workload demands than distributed DEMPCs during Mission 4, $F(1, 19) = 8.62$, $p < .01$, and Mission 5, $F(1, 19) = 6.82$, $p < .05$.

IMPLICATIONS FOR DISTRIBUTED LEARNING

Distributed team environments have many advantages, from dispersing assets on the battlefield and minimizing the risks of concentrating resources in a single location that may be attacked to reducing the logistical problems of bringing team members to a single location for a business meeting. However, what are the costs? The results from our experiment in a UAV command-and-control environment suggest that teams are able to adapt their interactions to these environments to achieve successful performance. Our research suggests that team performance will not necessarily suffer when team members are geographically dispersed; in fact, they may demonstrate superior performance compared with colocated teams through differential mechanisms of learning and team member interaction.

Our research suggests that distributed teams are different from colocated teams in terms of their process behavior and taskwork-relevant knowledge. Although these differences seem adaptive for the situations tested in our experiment, it may be the case that they would not be for other novel situations. In fact, the colocated teams who displayed more pre- and postmission process behaviors and more interpositional knowledge were less able to adapt to a more intense high-workload task. In other cases, for example, when team members must be completely interchangeable, the distributed mode of interaction may be more difficult to adapt. Future work should be directed at identifying factors that facilitate or inhibit the adaptiveness of certain team process behaviors as well as team member knowledge. Accordingly, research should also address the relative importance of team process and team knowledge in this adaptation.

It is also possible that knowledge differences were simply a by-product of different process behaviors, but not critically tied to team performance. For instance, the development of interpositional knowledge by colocated teams may not produce significant benefits in performance compared with distributed teams when all team members in both settings are allowed to freely communicate, thereby sharing knowledge in real time (Stout, Cannon-Bowers, and Salas, 1996). Put differently, interpositional knowledge may not always be critical, given, for example, a highly specialized division of labor, as found in an operating room context. Given the other extreme, however, in which team members are highly interchangeable, communication restrictions such as requiring team members to communicate by computer messaging or restricting the amount of communication allowed may produce a greater decline in performance for distributed teams compared with colocated teams, who presumably can develop expectancies about the needs of other team members.

These results also suggest that distributed teams may derive benefits from interventions targeting pre- and postmission process coordination behaviors. If interpositional knowledge is necessary for adapting to some settings, then this type of intervention might foster the types of process behaviors that facilitate the development of this sort of knowledge in distributed teams, for example, through instituting pre- and postmission planning sessions.

From a more global perspective, our conclusions pertain to the kind of distributed scenario characterized by our UAV-STE. Communication took place primarily over headsets, even in the colocated condition; the task was a highly structured command-and-control task; and there was significant interdependence among team members. Therefore, differences in process and cognition should not be attributed to mode of communication but, rather, to the subtle differences associated with copresence.

Although various methodological concerns may prevent us from generalizing broadly to other task environments, we can conclude that geographic distribution changes team cognition and team process but apparently has little effect on team performance. Whereas in this task the benefits of using distributed teams appear to outweigh any minor costs of geographic distribution, in another task in which communication is hampered or interpositional knowledge is critical the costs may be significant. We hope that in this chapter we have at least provided researchers in applied domains such as command and control and particularly network-centric warfare with some theoretical footing in terms of the issues, factors, and considerations in assessing the effects of distributed mission environments on team cognition, process, and performance.

REFERENCES

Contractor, N. S., Seibold, D. R., & Heller, M. A. (1996). Interactional influence in the structuring of media use in groups: Influence in members' perceptions of group decision support system use. *Human Communication Research, 22,* 451–481.

Cooke, N. J., & Gorman, J. C. (2006). Assessment of team cognition. In P. Karwowski (Ed.), *International encyclopedia of ergonomics and human factors* (2nd ed.), pp. 270–275. Oxford, England: Taylor & Francis.

Cooke, N. J., Rivera, K., Shope, S. M., & Caukwell, S. (1999). A synthetic task environment for team cognition research. *Proceedings of the Human Factors and Ergonomics Society 43rd Annual Meeting* (pp. 303–307). Santa Monica, CA: Human Factors and Ergonomics Society.

Cooke, N. J., Salas, E., Cannon-Bowers, J. A., & Stout, R. (2000). Measuring team knowledge. *Human Factors, 42*, 151–173.

Cooke, N. J., Salas, E., Kiekel, P. A., & Bell, B. (2004). Advances in measuring team cognition. In E. Salas & S. M. Fiore (Eds.), *Team cognition: Understanding the factors that drive process and performance* (pp. 83–106). Washington, DC: American Psychological Association.

Cooke, N. J., & Shope, S. M. (2004). Designing a synthetic task environment. In S. G. Schiflett, L. R. Elliott, E. Salas, & M. D. Coovert (Eds.), *Scaled worlds: Development, validation, and application* (pp. 263–278). Surrey, England: Ashgate.

Cooke, N. J., Shope, S. M., & Kiekel, P. A. (2001). *Shared-knowledge and team performance: A cognitive engineering approach to measurement.* Technical Report for Air Force Office of Scientific Research Grant F49620-98-1-0287.

Durso, F. T., Hackworth, C. A., Truitt, T. R., Crutchfield, J., Nikolic, D., & Manning, C. A. (1998). Situation awareness as a predictor of performance in en route air traffic controllers. *Air Traffic Control Quarterly, 5*, 1–20.

Entin, E. E., & Serfaty, D. (1999). Adaptive team coordination. *Human Factors, 41*, 312–325.

Fiore, S. M., Salas, E., Cuevas, H. M., & Bowers, C. A. (2003). Distributed coordination space: Toward a theory of distributed team process and performance. *Theoretical Issues in Ergonomic Science, 4*, 340–364.

Hedlund, J., Ilgen, D. R., & Hollenbeck, J. R. (1998). Decision accuracy in computer-mediated versus face-to-face decision making. *Organizational Behavior and Human Decision Processes, 76*, 30–47.

Hinsz, V. B. (1999). Group decision making with responses of a quantitative nature: The theory of social decision schemes for quantities. *Organizational Behavior and Human Decision Processes, 80*, 28–49.

Kiekel, P. A., Cooke, N. J., Foltz, P. W., Gorman, J. C., & Martin, M. J. (2002). Some promising results of communication-based automatic measures of team cognition. In *Proceedings of the Human Factors and Ergonomics Society 46th Annual Meeting* (pp. 298–302). Santa Monica, CA: Human Factors and Ergonomics Society.

Kleinman, D. L., & Serfaty, D. (1989). Team performance assessment in distributed decision making. In R. Gibson, J. P. Kincaid, & B. Godiez (Eds.), *Proceedings: Interactive Networked Simulation for Training Conference* (pp. 22–27). Orlando, FL: Institute for Simulation and Training.

Langan-Fox, J., Code, S., & Langfield-Smith, K. (2000). Team mental models: Techniques, methods, and analytic approaches. *Human Factors, 42*, 242–271.

Levine, J. M., & Choi, H. (2004). Impact of personnel turnover on team performance and cognition. In E. Salas & S. M. Fiore (Eds.), *Team cognition: Understanding the factors that drive process and performance* (pp. 83–106). Washington, DC: American Psychological Association.

Mantovani, G. (1996). *New communication environments from everyday to virtual.* Bristol, PA: Taylor & Francis.

Penner, L. A., & Craiger, J. P. (1992). The weakest link: The performance of individual team members. In R. W. Swezey & E. Salas (Eds.), *Teams: Their training and performance* (pp. 57–73). Norwood, NJ: Ablex.

Postmes, T., & Spears, R. (1998). Deindividuation and antinormative behavior: A meta-analysis. *Psychological Bulletin, 123*, 238–259.

Postmes, T., Spears, R., & Lea, M. (1998). Breaching or building social boundaries? SIDE-effects of computer-mediated communication. *Communication Research, 25*, 689–715.

Robertson, M. M., & Endsley, M. R. (1997). Development of a situation awareness training program for aviation maintenance. In *Proceedings of the Human Factors and Ergonomics Society 41st Annual Meeting* (pp. 1163–1167). Santa Monica, CA: Human Factors and Ergonomics Society.

Salas, E., & Fiore, S. M. (Eds.). (2004). *Team cognition: Understanding the factors that drive process and performance.* Washington, DC: American Psychological Association.

Schvaneveldt, R. W. (1990). *Pathfinder associative networks: Studies in knowledge organization.* Norwood, NJ: Ablex.

Steiner, I. D. (1972). *Group processes and productivity.* New York: Academic Press.

Stout, R., Cannon-Bowers, J. A., & Salas, E. (1996). The role of shared mental models in developing team situation awareness: Implications for training. *Training Research Journal, 2*, 85–116.

Stout, R. J., Cannon-Bowers, J. A., Salas, E., & Milanovich, D. M. (1999). Planning, shared mental models, and coordinated performance: An empirical link is established. *Human Factors, 41*, 61–71.

III

COGNITIVE PROCESSES AND PRODUCTS IN DISTRIBUTED LEARNING ENVIRONMENTS

8

FIVE FEATURES OF EFFECTIVE MULTIMEDIA MESSAGES: AN EVIDENCE-BASED APPROACH

RICHARD E. MAYER

Online courses, like traditional courses, often present to-be-learned material in verbal form (e.g., on-screen text). For example, Exhibit 8.1 presents a brief explanation of how a car's braking system works (Mayer, Mathias, & Wetzell, 2002, p. 150). Research shows that most inexperienced learners do not learn much from this kind of presentation, whether it is presented as printed text on paper or as on-screen text on a computer screen (Mayer, 2001a, 2001b). Given the potential of computer graphics and the limitations of text as an instructional medium, it is tempting to consider adding graphics to text-based lessons. For example, Figure 8.1 shows some frames from an animation depicting how a car's braking system works. The goal of this chapter is to examine the conditions under which graphics (such as in Figure 8.1) can be used to help people understand verbal explanations (such as in Exhibit 8.1). Building effective multimedia instruction is a basic challenge for instructional design in distributed environments.

Preparation of this chapter was supported by Office of Naval Research Grant N00014-01-1-1039 and National Science Foundation Grant 99-0705-01.

How a Car's Braking System Works

When the driver steps on the car's brake pedal, a piston moves forward in the master cylinder. The piston forces brake fluid out of the master cylinder and through the tubes to the wheel cylinders. In the wheel cylinders, the increase in fluid pressure makes a smaller set of pistons move. These smaller pistons activate the brake shoes. When the brake shoes press against the drum, both the drum and the wheel stop or slow down.

After a brief introduction, I examine five features of effective computer-based explanative multimedia messages: (a) systematicity, (b) referencing, (c) conciseness, (d) sociability, and (e) conserving. *Systematicity* means that the graphic shows the location and names of the key components of the

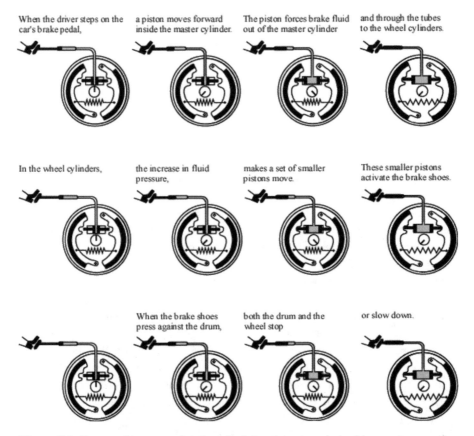

Figure 8.1. Frames from an animation depicting how a car's braking system works. From "The Instructive Animation: Helping Students Build Connections Between Words and Pictures in Multimedia Learning," by R. E. Mayer and R. B. Anderson, 1992, *Journal of Educational Psychology, 84,* p. 446. Copyright 1992 by the American Psychological Association.

EXHIBIT 8.2
Characteristics of Multimedia Messages That Promote Deep Learning

Systematicity: Help the learner build a mental model. Create a graphic that shows each component in the system, indicates the potential action (state changes) of each component, and expresses the causal relations among the actions.

Referencing: Help the learner build referential connections between words and pictures. Place printed words near corresponding portions of graphics or present spoken words at same time as presenting corresponding segments of graphics.

Conciseness: Help the learner stay focused. Avoid irrelevant material and provide cues that guide the learner's attention.

Sociability: Activate a sense of social presence. Use a friendly, human voice that speaks in a conversational style.

Conserving: Help the learner to avoid overloading his or her visual channel. Present words as spoken text so they do not compete with graphic for the learner's visual attention.

---

system (e.g., pedal, piston, brake fluid), the potential behavior of the components (e.g., the pedal can be up or down, the piston can be forward or back), and the causal relations among the behaviors of the components (e.g., when the pedal goes down, the piston moves forward). This helps the learner in his or her attempt to build a mental model of the system. *Referencing* means that elements of the graphic are connected to corresponding words (e.g., placing on-screen text next to corresponding parts of a graphic or presenting voice-over narration concurrently with relevant graphics). This helps the learner in his or her attempt to build connections between corresponding verbal and pictorial representations. *Conciseness* means that the graphic does not contain irrelevant details (e.g., using simple line drawings) or contains words that direct the learner's attention. This helps the learner focus on the important material in the multimedia message. *Sociability* means that the words are spoken in a friendly human voice that uses an informal, conversational style. This encourages the learner to accept the computer as a social partner and thus to try hard to understand the computer's communication. *Conserving* means that the words and pictures do not compete for attention in the visual channel. This helps the learner in his or her efforts to keep the visual and verbal channels free from overload. These five features are summarized in Exhibit 8.2.

INTRODUCTION

Multimedia messages are presentations containing words and pictures. The words can be printed (as on-screen text) or spoken (as narration). The pictures can be static graphics (including illustrations and photos) or dynamic graphics (including animation and video). For example, a lesson on earth science may contain a 2-minute narrated animation explaining the process of lightning formation, or an educational game on environmental science may contain a 45-second narrated animation explaining how photosynthesis works.

In this chapter, I focus on multimedia messages that consist of explanative words and pictures, such as in Exhibit 8.1 and Figure 8.1, respectively. Explanative words and pictures explain how some system or process works by describing or depicting a series of principle-based causal relations in which a state change in one part is causally related to a state change in another part and so on (Mayer, 1993). The causal links depicted in a multimedia explanation form a causal chain of the form "If A, then B; if B, then C; if C, then D . . . ," in which the letters refer to state changes. For example, some of the links in the causal chain for the braking system are presented in Exhibit 8.1 and Figure 8.1:

> If the brake pedal moves from up to down, then a piston moves from back to forward in the master cylinder; if the piston moves from back to forward in the master cylinder, then the brake fluid changes from uncompressed to compressed; if the brake fluid changes from uncompressed to compressed, then smaller pistons move from back to forward in the wheel cylinder; if smaller pistons move from back to forward in the wheel cylinder, then the brake shoe moves from inward to outward; when the brake shoe moves from inward to outward, then the brake drum changes from not being pressed against to being pressed against; when the brake drum changes from not being pressed against to being pressed against, then the brake drum changes from faster moving to slower moving.

This can be called a *causal model* because it consists of a chain of cause-and-effect events.

Explanative multimedia messages are intended to help learners form mental models—that is, knowledge of how a causal system works.[1] Helping learners understand how things work is a core goal in many lessons in science and mathematics as well as other domains. In addition, explanative multimedia messages may be a particularly fertile area for research on the role of graphics as aids to human understanding. Thus, my goal in this chapter is to explore how to design explanative multimedia messages that promote understanding in learners.

---

[1]Forming a mental model (or developing a causal model) is an example of understanding (or deep learning). A mental model is a type of conceptual knowledge. The goal of this chapter is to examine instructional design techniques that promote understanding (or deep learning) by helping students form a mental model (which is a type of conceptual knowledge). In the interests of staying focused, I use these terms interchangeably.

The overarching principle guiding this work is that multimedia messages should be designed as an aid to how people learn. Thus, the starting point is to consider the learner's cognitive processing, and the goal is to determine how multimedia messages can be designed to facilitate the learner's cognitive processing. In the remainder of this chapter, I explore five aspects of cognitive processing and how they can be supported through proper design of multimedia instruction.

SYSTEMATICITY: HELP THE LEARNER BUILD A MENTAL MODEL

In our research, my colleagues and I have focused on helping learners build one kind of learning outcome: a mental model of how some system works. Thus, we begin with the idea that the learner is struggling to build a mental model of how something works, so the job of an instructional designer is to facilitate this process. A *mental model* is the learner's representation of how a cause-and-effect system works, that is, a set of components that interact with one another in systematic ways. Examples include how a bicycle tire pump works, how a car's braking system works, how lightning storms develop, how the human respiratory system works, how plants grow, how airplanes achieve lift, and how ocean waves form (Mayer, 2001a, 2001b). In short, we focus on scientific explanations of how things work that are intended to help learners build conceptual knowledge (Anderson et al., 2001).

Consider how a car's braking system works, as described in Exhibit 8.1. The components in the braking system include a brake pedal that can be up or down, a piston in the master cylinder that can be forward or back, fluid in the brake tubes that can be compressed or not compressed, smaller pistons in the wheel cylinders that can be forward or back, brake shoes that can be pressed or not pressed against the drum, and the drum, which can be rotating or not rotating.

According to the *two-stage theory of mental model construction* (Mayer et al., 2002), building a mental model requires building a component model for each major part and building a causal model of the entire system. A *component model* includes viewing the component as a unit that has a name, knowing the location of the component within the system, and knowing the possible states of the component. The *causal model* is a causal chain in which a change in the state of one part causes a principle-based change in the state of another part, and so on.

Our research, which has been conducted mainly with college students as participants, has shown that the process of mental model construction is often difficult for novices when explanations are presented solely in words but is greatly improved when corresponding pictures are added (Mayer, 2001a, 2001b). For example, in a series of three studies involving pumps and brakes, students learned more deeply from an animation and narration than from narration alone (Mayer & Anderson, 1992); in a series of two studies involving brakes, students learned more deeply from printed words and frame-by-frame illustrations than from printed words alone (Mayer, 1989); and in a series of three studies involving brakes, pumps, and generators, students learned more deeply from printed text and frame-by-frame illustrations than from printed text alone (Mayer & Gallini, 1990). In all our studies, deep learning is measured by asking students to solve transfer problems, and tallying the number of acceptable answers they produce. *Transfer* refers to the ability to apply what was learned to new situations. For example, a transfer problem for the brakes lesson is to ask the learner to troubleshoot the system (e.g., "Suppose a driver steps on a car's brake pedal, but the car does not stop. What could have gone wrong?") or to redesign the system (e.g., "How could you make car brakes more reliable, that is, make sure they would not fail?"). Our studies show that graphics—such as animation or frame-by-frame illustrations—can help learners build component models by showing the location and possible states of each component. Having component models makes it easier for learners to understand the verbal description of the causal model.

A more direct way to promote the process of mental model construction is to provide pretraining in the components of the model. For example, in a series of two studies on brakes, students viewed a narrated animation explaining how a car's braking system works (Mayer et al., 2002). Some students received pretraining in which they saw a graphic with each part labeled or a short computer-based animation of the behavior of each part. The pretraining was intended to help students build component models for each part of the braking system—such as understanding the location of the piston in the master cylinder and what it means for it to be forward or back. In two studies, students who had pretraining before receiving the narrated animation about brakes learned more deeply—as measured by transfer tests—than students who received only the narrated animation (Mayer et al., 2002). In a follow-up study, students who received pretraining in operating a real bicycle tire pump learned more deeply from a narrated animation explaining how a bicycle tire pump works than did students who had not received pretraining (Mayer et al., 2002). In a related study, as pretraining we allowed some students to view each segment of a multimedia explanation of lightning formation, and then click a button to continue, so they could build component models. Other students saw the entire multimedia lesson as a continuous presentation. Then, all students saw the entire presentation as a continuous presentation. Students who received the part-by-part pretraining learned more deeply than students who received the whole pretraining (Mayer & Chandler, 2001).

Overall, my colleagues and I have identified two useful techniques for promoting mental model construction: (a) using graphics that show the location and possible states of each component in the system and (b) providing pretraining in which graphics or real objects show the location and possible states of each component in the system. Thus, instructional designers in distributed environments should see their job as facilitating the learner in his or her attempt to construct a mental model of the to-be-learned system. Instructional designers can do this by using appropriate graphics—that is, graphics providing information on the potential states of a system are used. Similarly, pretraining can be used to provide the development of a rudimentary framework on which this type of information is built.

REFERENCING: HELP THE LEARNER BUILD CONNECTIONS BETWEEN WORDS AND PICTURES

The learner needs help in building mental connections between words and pictures, something Paivio (1986) termed *building referential connections*. For example, when viewing a narrated animation on lightning formation, the learner may hear the phrase "negatively charged particles fall to the bottom of the cloud," and may see a narration segment in which small circles containing minus signs move from the top to the bottom of a cloud. According to the cognitive theory of multimedia learning (Mayer, 2001a, 2001b), deep understanding occurs when the learner makes connections between corresponding verbal and visual representations—such as spoken text describing negative particles moving to the bottom of the cloud and an animation segment showing negative particles moving to the bottom of the cloud.

In our research, my colleagues and I have investigated two ways of aiding the learner's process of building referential connections: (a) placing the corresponding printed words and illustrations near each other on the page or screen (which we call *spatial contiguity*) or (b) presenting corresponding narration and animation at the same time (which we call *temporal contiguity*). First, consider the benefits of spatial contiguity. In a set of five studies involving lightning and brakes, students learned more deeply when printed words were placed within the illustrations that they described than when the printed words and illustrations were presented far apart on the page or screen (Mayer, 1989; Mayer, Steinhoff, Bower, & Mars, 1995; Moreno & Mayer, 1999).

Second, consider temporal contiguity. In a set of eight studies concerning lightning, brakes, pumps, or lungs, students understood a narrated animation more deeply when they received concurrent narration and animation than when they received the same animation and narration successively (Mayer & Anderson, 1991, 1992; Mayer, Moreno, Boire, & Vegge, 1999; Mayer & Sims, 1994).

Overall, our research—conducted with adults, most of whom were college students—is consistent with the idea that learners may need help in making referential connections between corresponding words and pictures. Instructional design in distributed environments requires the creation of environments that assist learners in their efforts to build referential connections between corresponding words and pictures. This goal can be accomplished by presenting the words and pictures near each other on the screen (spatial contiguity) or near each other in time (temporal contiguity).

CONCISENESS: HELP THE LEARNER STAY FOCUSED

A learner easily can be distracted, so an additional goal for instructional design in distributed environments should be to guide the learner's cognitive processing while minimizing what may be distracting. For example, it may be tempting to add "bells and whistles" to a multimedia presentation in an attempt to make the material more interesting; however, our research has shown that adding interesting but irrelevant words and pictures to a multimedia presentation—which can be called "seductive details" (Garner, Gillingham, & White, 1989)—can distract the learner and lead to poorer learning (Mayer, 2001a, 2001b).

Let's consider one way to help learners stay focused on making sense of the essential material—minimizing extraneous material. First, what happens when we add interesting facts and interesting illustrations to a narrated animation or annotated illustrations explaining the formation of lightning? In six studies, students learned more deeply when the interesting facts and illustrations were excluded rather than included (Harp & Mayer, 1997, 1998; Mayer, Heiser, & Lonn, 2000). Second, what happens when we add interesting sounds and background music to a narrated animation about lightning formation or brakes? In two studies, students learned more deeply when interesting sounds and music were excluded rather than included (Moreno & Mayer, 2000a). Third, what happens when we revise a lesson consisting of annotated illustrations so that the words present a summary of how lightning forms? In three studies, the summarized version resulted in deeper learning than the full version (Mayer, Bove, Bryman, Mars, &

Tapangco, 1996). These studies lead us to conclude that in some cases, less is more—that is, students are better able to focus on the essential material when extraneous material is eliminated from a multimedia presentation.

Another approach to helping students focus on essential material is to provide signals that cue the reader's attention. For example, the speaker in a narrated animation explaining how airplanes achieve lift highlighted the important information by speaking in a deeper voice; by inserting pointer words, such as *first*, *second*, *third*, and so on; by inserting an outline listing the main sections; and by inserting headings for each section summarizing the main point. Students who received this signaled version of the multimedia presentation performed better on transfer tests than did students who received a nonsignaled version containing the same factual information (Mautone & Mayer, 2000). The signals helped the learners pay attention to main steps in the process of lift, rather than some of the less important details in the lesson.

Overall, learners seem to need some guidance in how to process the presented material. In distributed learning environments, part of the instructional designer's job is to provide the needed guidance by minimizing extraneous material and signaling the important material.

SOCIABILITY: ACTIVATE A SENSE OF SOCIAL CONVERSATION

A further goal of our research program has been to investigate how encouraging the learner to view the computer as a social partner can facilitate learning. This may seem like a strange goal in light of the fact that learners know that the computer is not really a person. However, there is a growing body of research showing that people are easily convinced to treat computers as social beings (Reeves & Naas, 1996). People are used to the idea that communication is a social activity subject to basic rules of conversation. These rules include what Grice (1975) called the *cooperation principle* and its four conversational maxims, that is, listeners expect the speaker to be (a) informative, (b) accurate, (c) relevant, and (d) concise.

According to social agency theory, "social cues in multimedia messages can prime the social conversation schema in learners" (Mayer, Sobko, & Mautone, 2003, p. 419). Once the social conversation is primed in a multimedia learning environment, the learner uses the social rules of human-to-human conversation. Thus, if the learner interprets the multimedia learning situation as a case of social conversation, then he or she will work harder to make sense of what the computer is saying. In contrast, if the learner interprets the multimedia learning situation as a case of information delivery, then he or she will not work as hard to make sense of what the computer is saying.

I offer two examples of how to create a sense of social conversation in multimedia messages. First, consider the quality of the speaker's voice. In one set of studies, my colleagues and I presented a short multimedia explanation of how lightning storms develop and then asked students to take a transfer test. Students learned more deeply—and rated the speaker more positively—when the computer spoke to them in a human voice rather than in a machine-synthesized voice (Mayer et al., 2003). Even when the computer spoke in a human voice, students learned more deeply—and rated the speaker more positively—when the voice had a standard accent rather than a foreign accent (Mayer et al., 2003).

Second, consider the conversational style of the speaker. In a set of three studies, students played an educational game in which an on-screen character named Herman-the-Bug explained environmental science principles. They were later tested on their ability to use what they had learned to solve new problems. When Herman spoke in an informal conversational style, using the first- and second-person point of view (e.g., *I* and *you*), students learned more deeply—and rated the program more positively—than when Herman-the-Bug spoke in a formal style, using the third-person point of view only (Moreno & Mayer, 2000b). In another set of two studies, students received an instructional message explaining the formation of lightning and then took a transfer test. Students learned more deeply when the voice in the multimedia message spoke in an informal style, using the first- and second-person point of view than when the voice spoke in a formal style, using only the third-person point of view (Moreno & Mayer, 2000b). In two additional studies, having Herman-the-Bug speak in an informal style resulted in deeper learning than having him speak in a formal style, even though identical information was presented (Moreno, Mayer, Spires, & Lester, 2001).

Overall, our research has shown that voice carries a lot of weight in encouraging the learner to form a sense of social partnership with the computer. In fact, our research has shown that it is not even necessary for an image of the speaker to be on the screen (Moreno et al., 2001). In a series of two studies, presenting (or not presenting) the image of Herman-the-Bug as a cartoon character or as a human did not affect student learning in an educational game—but the voice of the speaker did (Moreno et al., 2001). Research on how to promote social partnership is in its infancy, but preliminary research shows that much can be gained by having the computer speak in a standard human voice using an informal conversational style. From a theoretical standpoint, attempts to build social agency are based on an integration of cognitive and social psychology within the learning sciences.

CONSERVING: HELP THE LEARNER TO AVOID OVERLOADING HIS OR HER VISUAL CHANNEL

According to the cognitive theory of multimedia learning, learners process information in two somewhat separate channels: (a) a visual–pictorial channel, which takes pictures and printed words as input, (b) and an auditory–verbal channel, which takes spoken words as input (Mayer, 2001a, 2001b). Each channel is limited in the amount of material that the learner can process at any one time. In multimedia presentations, the learner's visual channel can easily become overloaded, so vital material can be lost. Sweller and colleagues (Paas, Renkl, & Sweller, 2003; Sweller, 1999) have come to the same conclusions in applying cognitive load theory to instructional design.

For example, consider what happens when a learner receives a multimedia presentation consisting of an animation depicting the steps of lightning formation along with concurrent on-screen text at the bottom of the screen describing the steps in lightning formation. This situation creates what Sweller (1999) called a *split attention effect*, in which the learner's visual attention is split between watching the animation and reading the printed words. What can be done to overcome this problem? One answer is to offload the words from the visual channel to the verbal channel by presenting them as narration (Mayer & Moreno, 2003).

Does offloading work? In a set of eight studies involving lightning, brakes, and an educational game on plant growth, my colleagues and I found consistent evidence that students learned more deeply from animation and narration than from animation and text (Mayer & Moreno, 1998; Moreno & Mayer, 1999, 2002a; Moreno et al., 2001). Mousavi, Low, and Sweller (1995) reported similar results.

In spite of these overwhelming results, one might be tempted to think that the best situation would involve animation, narration, and on-screen text. However, our research shows that redundant printed and spoken text can create overload because learners waste cognitive effort in trying to reconcile the spoken and printed text while ignoring portions of the animation. In three studies involving multimedia presentations on lightning, students learned better from animation and narration than from animation, narration, and on-screen text (Mayer et al., 2000; Moreno & Mayer, 2002b).

CONCLUSION

Suppose you wanted to create multimedia instruction to help learners understand scientific explanations. If you take a learner-centered approach to this problem, then the task of instructional design is not solely to present relevant information; in addition, an important goal is to help the learner process the information productively, that is, to assist the learner in his or her cognitive processing of the presented material. I have presented five general kinds of cognitive processing that can be influenced by the design of multimedia messages: (a) helping the learner build a mental model, (b) helping the learner see connections between words and pictures, (c) helping the learner stay focused, (d) activating a sense of social conversation, and (e) helping learners avoid overloading their visual channel.

As you can see, I start with a conception of the learner who is actively struggling to engage in cognitive processes, such as building a mental model (i.e., asking "How does this work?"), building referential connections between words and pictures (i.e., asking "How does that graphic relate to those words?"), trying to pay attention to what is most important (i.e., asking "What should I pay attention to?"), willing to see the computer as a social partner (i.e., asking "Do I like communicating with this computer?"), and trying to avoid overloading his or her visual and verbal channels (i.e., asking "Am I having difficulty keeping up with the message?"). My suggestions for the design of multimedia messages are based on trying to support the learner's natural learning processes.

The major theme of this chapter is that Web-based instruction should be designed to complement and foster the learner's cognitive processing. Yet, some interesting questions remain: How can we increase the sense of social presence and productive social interaction; how can we best address the problem of high dropout rates in distance learning; and how can we foster metacognitive strategies that online learners need?

It is important to note that a research base is emerging that has direct implications for the design of Web-based instruction (Clark & Mayer, 2003; Mayer, 2001a, 2001b; Sweller, 1999), and that base will continue to expand as researchers continue to look for answers to the remaining questions. On the basis of this growing research base, multimedia instructional messages can be designed in ways that help learners in their efforts to make sense of the presented material.

REFERENCES

Anderson, L. W., Krathwohl, D. R., Airasian, P. W., Cruickshank, K. A., Mayer, R. E., Pintrich, P. R., et al. (2001). *A taxonomy for learning, teaching, and assessing.* New York: Longman.

Clark, R. C., & Mayer, R. E. (2003). *E-learning and the science of instruction.* San Francisco: Jossey-Bass.

Garner, R., Gillingham, M., & White, C. (1989). Effects of "seductive details" on macroprocessing and microprocessing in adults and children. *Cognition and Instruction, 6*, 41–57.

Grice, H. P. (1975). Logic and conversation. In P. Cole & J. Morgan (Eds.), *Syntax and semantics* (Vol. 3, pp. 41–58). New York: Academic Press.

Harp, S. F., & Mayer, R. E. (1997). The role of interest in learning from scientific text and illustrations: On the distinction between emotional interest and cognitive interest. *Journal of Educational Psychology, 89*, 92–102.

Harp, S. F., & Mayer, R. E. (1998). How seductive details do their damage: A theory of cognitive interest in science learning. *Journal of Educational Psychology, 90*, 414–434.

Mautone, P. D., & Mayer, R. E. (2000). Signaling as a cognitive guide in multimedia learning. *Journal of Educational Psychology, 93*, 377–389.

Mayer, R. E. (1989). Systematic thinking fostered by illustrations in scientific text. *Journal of Educational Psychology, 81*, 240–246.

Mayer, R. E. (1993). Illustrations that instruct. In R. Glaser (Ed.), *Advances in instructional psychology* (Vol. 4, pp. 253–284). Hillsdale, NJ: Erlbaum.

Mayer, R. E. (2001a). *Multimedia learning.* New York: Cambridge University Press.

Mayer, R. E. (2001b). Multimedia learning. In B. H. Ross (Ed.), *The psychology of learning and motivation* (Vol. 41, pp. 85–139). San Diego, CA: Academic Press.

Mayer, R. E., & Anderson, R. B. (1991). Animations need narrations: An experimental test of a dual-coding hypothesis. *Journal of Educational Psychology, 83*, 484–490.

Mayer, R. E., & Anderson, R. B. (1992). The instructive animation: Helping students build connections between words and pictures in multimedia learning. *Journal of Educational Psychology, 84*, 444–452.

Mayer, R. E., Bove, W., Bryman, A., Mars, R., & Tapangco, L. (1996). When less is more: Meaningful learning from visual and verbal summaries of science textbook lessons. *Journal of Educational Psychology, 88*, 64–73.

Mayer, R. E., & Chandler, P. (2001). When learning is just a click away: Does simple user interaction foster deeper understanding of multimedia messages? *Journal of Educational Psychology, 93*, 390–397.

Mayer, R. E., & Gallini, J. K. (1990). When is an illustration worth ten thousand words? *Journal of Educational Psychology, 82*, 715–726.

Mayer, R. E., Heiser, J., & Lonn, S. (2000). Cognitive constraints on multimedia learning: When presenting more material results in less understanding. *Journal of Educational Psychology, 93*, 187–198.

Mayer, R. E., Mathias, A., & Wetzell, K. (2002). Fostering understanding of multimedia messages through pre-training: Evidence for a two-stage theory of mental model construction. *Journal of Experimental Psychology: Applied, 8*, 147–154.

Mayer, R. E., & Moreno, R. (1998). A split attention effect in multimedia learning: Evidence for dual processing systems in working memory. *Journal of Educational Psychology, 90*, 312–320.

Mayer, R. E., & Moreno, R. (2003). Nine ways to reduce cognitive load in multimedia learning. *Educational Psychologist, 38,* 43–52.

Mayer, R. E., Moreno, R., Boire, M., & Vegge, S. (1999). Maximizing constructivist learning from multimedia communications by minimizing cognitive load. *Journal of Educational Psychology, 91,* 638–643.

Mayer, R. E., & Sims, V. K. (1994). For whom is a picture worth a thousand words? Extensions of a dual-coding theory of multimedia learning. *Journal of Educational Psychology, 84,* 389–401.

Mayer, R. E., Sobko, K., & Mautone, P. D. (2003). Social cues in multimedia learning: Role of speaker's voice. *Journal of Educational Psychology, 95,* 419–425.

Mayer, R. E., Steinhoff, K., Bower, G., & Mars, R. (1995). A generative theory of textbook design: Using annotated illustrations to foster meaningful learning of science text. *Educational Technology Research and Development, 43,* 31–43.

Moreno, R., & Mayer, R. E. (1999). Cognitive principles of multimedia learning: The role of modality and contiguity. *Journal of Educational Psychology, 91,* 358–368.

Moreno, R. E., & Mayer, R. E. (2000a). A coherence effect in multimedia learning: The case for minimizing irrelevant sounds in the design of multimedia instructional messages. *Journal of Educational Psychology, 92,* 117–125.

Moreno, R., & Mayer, R. E. (2000b). Engaging students in active learning: The case for personalized multimedia messages. *Journal of Educational Psychology, 92,* 724–733.

Moreno, R., & Mayer, R. E. (2002a). Learning science in virtual reality multimedia environments: Role of methods and media. *Journal of Educational Psychology, 94,* 596–610.

Moreno, R., & Mayer, R. E. (2002b). Verbal redundancy in multimedia learning: When reading helps listening. *Journal of Educational Psychology, 94,* 156–163.

Moreno, R., Mayer, R. E., Spires, H. A., & Lester, J. C. (2001). The case for social agency in computer-based teaching: Do students learn more deeply when they interact with animated pedagogical agents? *Cognition and Instruction, 19,* 177–213.

Mousavi, S., Low, R., & Sweller, J. (1995). Reducing cognitive load by mixing auditory and visual presentation modes. *Journal of Educational Psychology, 87,* 319–334.

Paas, F., Renkl, A., & Sweller, J. (2003). Cognitive load theory and instructional design: Recent developments. *Educational Psychologist, 38,* 1–4.

Paivio, A. (1986). *Mental representations: A dual coding approach.* Oxford, England: Oxford University Press.

Reeves, B., & Naas, C. (1996). *The media equation.* New York: Cambridge University Press.

Sweller, J. (1999). *Instructional design in technical areas.* Camberwell, Australia: ACER Press.

9

ENGAGING AND SUPPORTING PROBLEM SOLVING ONLINE

DAVID H. JONASSEN

Problems are everywhere. Employees in corporations, the military, and other agencies are hired, retained, and rewarded for solving these problems. Although many of us prefer not to admit that we have problems, the reality is that we solve many problems on a daily basis. What shall I wear to work? Which is the best route to avoid this traffic jam? How do I prevent my boss from criticizing me? How can I get that new contract? What shall we make for supper this evening? How shall we market this new product to maximize cash flow? What do I have to do to attract recognition in this agency? We are deluged with problems every day. Karl Popper (1999) averred, "All life is problem solving." Unfortunately, we have rarely been taught how to solve problems.

There is little evidence that producers and purveyors of online instruction are aware of the importance of problem solving to learning, except for games, which often represent complex problems. Most online learning course management systems (e.g., Blackboard) function as materials-distribution systems that rely on the same teach-and-test ontology that has dominated K–12 and university education for centuries. Online course packages provide functionalities to deliver lectures, readings, synchronous and asynchronous conferences, and quizzes. These instructional methods make traditional epistemological assumptions about learning and the transmission of knowledge. There are no course management systems that provide any affordances for problem solving. More troubling are the standards for creating and metatagging reusable learning objects. They support only teaching-and-testing of discrete, micro-level lessons that can support problem solving only as prerequisites (Jonassen & Churchill, 2004). Like course management systems, the metatagging schemes are insufficient for representing the informational complexity and interactions necessary to learn to solve problems. Unfortunately, most instruction assumes that if one teaches the prerequisite concepts for solving problems, then students will somehow learn how to solve them, even though they do not engage in problem-solving. Learning to solve problems requires substantially more complex pedagogies than learning about a knowledge domain (Jonassen, 2004).

I believe that the only legitimate goal of professional education, either in universities or in corporate training, is problem solving. Therefore, online instruction should engage and support learning to solve problems. I support this claim with four warrants. First, problem solving is the most authentic and therefore the most relevant learning activity in which students can engage. Second, situated-learning research has shown that knowledge constructed in the context of solving problems is better comprehended and retained and therefore more transferable. Third, students construct better conceptual understanding while solving problems because they must articulate an intention to solve the problem. Meaningful learning cannot occur until and unless learners manifest an intention to learn. Fourth and last, life is short. Because time allocated to learning is always limited, why not make the most of it?

With these factors in mind, in this chapter I first discuss the importance of problem solving as a tool for learning. I then suggest the development of online architectures for creating type-specific problem-based learning environments (PBLEs), and in the rest of the chapter I describe architectures specifically designed for troubleshooting problems and systems analysis problems.

WHAT IS PROBLEM SOLVING?

Problem solving has three critical attributes. First, a problem is an unknown value, process, method, position, or belief that is worth finding an answer to. Second, to find the unknown, problem solving requires the mental representation of the problem; that is, human problem-solvers individually construct or socially coconstruct a representation of the problem, known as the *problem space* (Newell & Simon, 1972). Third, problem solving engages cognitive and social activities that manipulate the problem space, such as model building, hypothesis generation, speculation, solution testing, information gathering, and so on.

Problem solving historically has been treated as a uniform activity. In traditional models of problem solving (Bransford & Stein, 1993), all problems require the same cognitive processes to solve. Contemporary research and theory assert that problem solving is context specific or domain specific; that is, problems in different domains or contexts are solved differently.

Problems and problem solving vary in several ways. Several authors (Jonassen, 1997; Simon, 1978; Voss & Post, 1988) have distinguished well-structured from ill-structured problems and recommended different learning approaches for each. On the one hand, most problems encountered in schools and universities are well-structured problems. Well-structured problems typically present all elements of the problem; engage a limited number of rules and principles that are organized in a predictive and prescriptive arrangement; possess correct, convergent answers; and have a preferred, prescribed solution process.

Ill-structured problems, on the other hand, are the kinds of problems that are encountered in everyday practice. Ill-structured problems have many alternative solutions to problems, vaguely defined or unclear goals and constraints, multiple solution paths, and multiple criteria for evaluating solutions, so they are more difficult to solve.

Problems also vary in complexity. The *complexity* of a problem is a function of the number of issues, functions, or variables involved in the problem; the number of interactions among those issues, functions, or variables; and the predictability of the behavior of those issues, functions, or variables. Ill-structured problems tend to be more complex; however, there are a number of highly complex well-structured problems, such as in chess.

Dynamicity is another dimension of complexity. In dynamic problems, the relationships among variables or factors change over time. Changes in one factor may cause variable changes in other factors. The more intricate these interactions, the more difficult it is to find any solution. Ill-structured problems tend to be more dynamic.

A final dimension of problems and problem solving is *domain specificity*. There is a common belief in contemporary psychology that problems within a domain rely on cognitive strategies that are specific to that domain (Mayer, 1992; Smith, 1991; Sternberg & Frensch, 1991). These are often referred to as *strong methods*, as opposed to domain-general strategies (weak methods). For example, Lehman, Lempert, and Nisbett (1988) concluded that different forms of reasoning are learned in different graduate disciplines. Graduate students in the probabilistic sciences of psychology and medicine perform better on statistical, methodological, and conditional reasoning problems than do students in law and chemistry, who do not learn such forms of reasoning. The cognitive operations are learned through the development of pragmatic reasoning schemas instead of exercises in formal logic. Graduates in different domains develop reasoning skills by solving situated, ill-structured problems that require forms of logic that are domain specific.

How do problems vary within these dimensions? I (Jonassen, 2000) described a typology of problems that vary primarily along a continuum from well structured to ill structured, including puzzles, algorithms, story problems, rule-using problems, decision making, troubleshooting, diagnosis-solution problems, strategic performance, systems analysis, design problems, and dilemmas. This typology assumes that there are similarities in the cognitive processes for solving problems within classes. Within each category of problems that is described, problems can vary with regard to abstractness, complexity, and dynamicity. Because of space limitations, I describe only some of these problem types.

Story Problems

Story problems are the most commonly encountered problems in formal education. From elementary mathematics through graduate-level courses in dynamics, textbooks present story problems to which teachers and professors demonstrate the solutions. Story problems usually embed numerical values needed to solve an algorithm into a brief narrative or scenario. To meaningfully solve story problems, learners must construct and access a problem schema and apply that schema to the current problem. If they access the correct schema, the solution procedure is usually embedded within that schema. However, numerous difficulties occur when students extract the values from the narrative, insert them into the correct formula, and solve for the unknown quantity, because they focus too closely on surface features of the problems (Woods et al., 1997). Why do students use this ineffectual strategy? Because too often that is how they were taught to solve problems. Teachers and textbooks demonstrate procedures for identifying variables, inserting the variables into formulae, and solving for the unknown. This linear process implies that solving problems is a procedure to be memorized, practiced, and habituated and that emphasizes answer-getting, not meaning-making (Wilson, Fernandez, & Hadaway, 2001)

A number of online tutorials support story problem solving, primarily in science courses. In these practice environments, simple feedback is provided to students about the correctness of their responses, but they receive no conceptual instruction. Solving story problems requires that one understand the structure of the problems. Online instruction must integrate the structural components of the problem and its context with the procedures required to solve the problem. Later in this chapter, I propose an architecture for constructing online story problem environments (Jonassen, 2003).

Decision-Making Problems

Decision-making problems are perhaps the most common form of problem solving. For example, how will I dress for a particular event? Which health plan do we select? Which strategy will yield higher earnings? What should I major in? Although these problems have a limited number of solutions, the number of factors to be considered in deciding among those solutions, as well as the weights assigned to them, can be very complex. Decision problems usually require one to compare and contrast the advantages and disadvantages of alternate solutions. Decisions are justified in terms of the weight of those factors.

Numerous theories of decision making exist (e.g., Hammond, Mc-Clelland, & Mumpower, 1980; Kaplan & Schwartz, 1975), as do techniques for supporting decision making (e.g., Pareto analysis, repertory grid, decision trees, force-field analysis, cost–benefit analysis)—far too many to explicate in this chapter. Emanating from information science, management, cybernetics, psychology, and other disciplines, decision theory is a body of knowledge and related analytical techniques of different degrees of formality designed to help a decision maker choose among a set of alternatives. Online support of decision making normally entails a set of tools for isolating alternatives and weighing them. Few online systems are devoted to learning how to solve decision-making problems. To be effective, online environments would have to include a problem description, decision factors, and a conceptual rationale for weighing them, along with tools for assisting in decision making.

Troubleshooting Problems

Troubleshooting is a commonly experienced form of problem solving. Maintaining automobiles, aircraft, or any complex system requires trouble-shooting skills. Debugging a computer program, or finding out why a committee cannot work together requires troubleshooting. The primary purposes of troubleshooting are to make a fault state diagnosis and to replace or repair the faulty part or subsystem. When part of a system is not functioning properly, its symptoms have to be diagnosed and matched with the user's knowledge of various fault states (Jonassen & Hung, 2006). Troubleshooters use symptoms to generate and test hypotheses about different fault states. Troubleshooting unfortunately is too often taught in face-to-face and online systems as a set of diagnostic procedures. Online troubleshooting instruction requires conceptual knowledge of the system and strategic knowledge of when to use tests and methods. Hypothesis generation and testing also are required. Later in this chapter, I describe an architecture for representing and supporting meaningful troubleshooting online that includes a multilayered conceptual model of the system being troubleshot, a case library of experiences, and a troubleshooting simulator.

Systems Analysis Problems

Systems analysis problems are complex, multifaceted situations in which the nature of the problem is not clear. These ill-structured problems are often solved in professional contexts. Solving business problems, including planning production, are common systems analysis problems. Deciding production levels, for instance, requires balancing human resources, technologies, inventory, and sales. Classical situated systems analysis problems also exist in international relations, such as the following: "Given low crop productivity in the Soviet Union, how would the solver go about improving crop productivity if he or she served as Director of the Ministry of Agriculture in the Soviet Union?" (Voss & Post, 1988, p. 273). International relations problems require that decision making and solution generation and testing be done in a political context. Systems analysis problems require the solver to articulate the nature of the problem and the different perspectives that influence the problem before suggesting solutions (Jonassen, 1997). These types of problems are more contextually bound than any kind of problem considered thus far; that is, their solutions rely on an analysis of contextual factors. Justifying decisions is among the most important processes in solving systems problems. Later in this chapter, I describe an architecture for representing and supporting meaningful troubleshooting online that includes problem representation and articulation tools, multiple perspectives, solution generation aids, and argumentation support.

Design Problems

Among the most poorly structured but meaningful problems are *design problems*. Most engineers are paid to design products, processes, or systems. Whether one is designing instruction, an electronic circuit, a symphony, a bicycle that flies, a marketing campaign for a new Internet company, or any other product or system, one must apply a great deal of domain knowledge, along with a lot of strategic knowledge, to create an original design.

The process of designing entails expanding and then constraining a problem space and then expanding and contracting a design artifact. When describing the problem space, designers integrate prior knowledge and analogies with functional requirements to generate multiple solutions. Options are eliminated through an iterative process of constraint analysis. The design model expands as the design and planning process is articulated and later constrained by various optimization processes. From a psychological perspective, design problem solving is still not well understood.

Although design-oriented curricula are being proposed for schools (Kolodner, Crismond, Gray, Holbrook, & Puntambekar, 1998) and used in capstone design courses in engineering, very little in the way of online design instruction exists, because the process is so complex and poorly understood.

Dilemmas

Dilemmas are the most poorly structured kind of problem, because there typically is no solution that will ever be acceptable to a significant portion of the people affected by the problem (Jonassen, 2000). One example of a dilemma is the current dialectic about same-sex marriage. There are many important perspectives on the situation (constitutional, political, social, ethical, evolutionary, and religious), although none is able to offer a generally acceptable solution. The situation is so complex and unpredictable that no best solution can ever be known. Dilemmas are often complex social situations with conflicting perspectives, and they are usually the most vexing of problems. They are almost never taught in face-to-face classes. However, online learning environments are uniquely geared to support this kind of problem solving, which is the hallmark of an informed citizenry. Online debates that are supported by multiple perspectives would be required to engage and support rational analysis of the issues.

LEARNING TO SOLVE PROBLEMS ONLINE

If one accepts the premise that online learning should engage and support learners in solving problems of some kind, then online learning environments and systems must be reengineered to provide the functionalities required to support the learning that is needed to solve different kinds of problems. To engage learners in solving problems, online learning environments must provide learners the intellectual and social support systems required to solve the problems. First and foremost, this means that problems come first and that content instruction, in whatever form it assumes, is provided in support of the problem-solving activity. How can this be accomplished?

There are multiple approaches to designing PBLEs. The most common is to develop environments, such as the well-known SHERLOCK for electronic troubleshooting (Lesgold & Lajoie, 1991), that meet the specific problem-solving needs of a client. These environments are powerful and effective, but they are also costly and not scalable.

The solution I propose in this chapter is the development of online architectures for creating type-specific PBLEs. The architectures are based on the cognitive requirements to solve different kinds of problems. Affordances and support systems for helping learners to construct sufficient domain mental models, adequate problem representations, simulations for testing their models, and alternative conceptual representations of the problems, are part of each architecture. In the remainder of this chapter, I describe architectures for troubleshooting and systems analysis problems. Research to clarify the utility of these architectures is ongoing.

Troubleshooting

Troubleshooting is among the most commonly experienced kind of problem solving in the professional world. Troubleshooting attempts to isolate fault states in a dysfunctional system, from a faulty modem to multiplex refrigeration systems in modern supermarkets. Once the fault has been found, the part or subsystem is replaced or repaired. Troubleshooting is most often taught as a series of decisions that direct the fault isolation. This approach may help novices solve simple troubleshooting problems; however, it is inadequate for training competent, professional troubleshooters, because effective troubleshooting requires more than a series of decisions. Effective troubleshooting requires system knowledge (conceptual knowledge of how the system works), procedural knowledge (how to perform problem-solving procedures and test activities), and strategic knowledge (e.g., search and replace, serial elimination, and space splitting; Pokorny, Hall, Gallaway, & Dibble, 1996). These different kinds of knowledge comprise the troubleshooter's mental model of the process. The troubleshooter's mental model consists of conceptual, functional, and declarative knowledge, including knowledge of system components and interactions; flow control; fault states, including fault characteristics, symptoms, contextual information, and probabilities of occurrence; and fault-testing procedures. This knowledge is integrated and organized by the troubleshooter's experiences. All sorts of troubleshooters, from experienced technicians to medical physicians, organize their knowledge around the troubleshooting problems they have solved. The problems that are most completely and accurately recalled are those that were the most difficult to solve, because the problem-solver was more conceptually engaged in the process. Therefore, the best predictor of a troubleshooter's ability is the number of similar problems that he or she has solved; that is, the primary differences between expert and novice troubleshooters are the amount and organization of system knowledge (Johnson, 1988) based on experience. To solve troubleshooting problems, problem-solvers must do the following:

- Identify the fault state and symptom.
- Construct a model of the problem.
- Describe goal state (e.g., how do you know when the system is functioning properly?).
- Identify the subsystem fault.
- Examine the faulty subsystem.
- Engage in the diagnosis process.
- Think back to previous cases.
- Rule out the least likely hypotheses.
- Generate initial hypothesis and assumptions.
- Test hypotheses based on domain knowledge.
- Interpret results of tests.
- Confirm or reject validity of hypotheses: If a hypothesis is rejected, generate a new hypothesis.
- Implement the solution.
- Test the solution: Is the goal state achieved?
- Record results in a fault database.

Architecture for Online Troubleshooting

To learn how to troubleshoot, novices must engage in problem-solving behavior that is supported by a rich conceptual model of the problem space and by pseudo-experiences. A design architecture for building troubleshooting learning environments (Jonassen, 2004; Jonassen & Hung, 2006) is illustrated in Figure 9.1. The model assumes that the most effective way to learn to troubleshoot is by troubleshooting problems. Learning to troubleshoot problems requires one to present learners with the symptoms of novel problems and require the learners to solve them. The major components of the troubleshooting learning environment (TLE) are a case library of previously solved problems, a diagnostic simulation that enables the learner to practice troubleshooting, and a rich conceptual model of the system being troubleshot. The conceptual model supports the construction of systems knowledge, the troubleshooter supports the construction of procedural and strategic knowledge, and the case library supports the construction of the experiential knowledge that integrates all of the other kinds of knowledge.

Conceptual Model

Learners mentally construct problem spaces by selecting and mapping specific relations from a problem domain onto the problem (McGuinness, 1986). Those relations entail multiple kinds of knowledge that are represented in different ways. Rasmussen (1984) recommended a hierarchy of

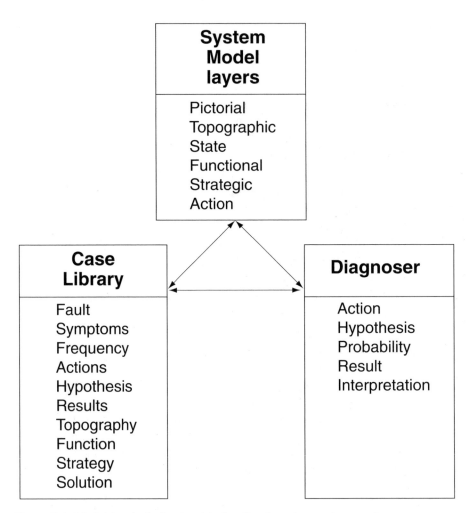

Figure 9.1. Model for designing troubleshooting learning environment.

information types that are needed to diagnose a system, including the following:

- functional purposes (production flow models, system objectives),
- abstract functions (causal structure, information flow topology),
- generalized function (standard functions and processes, control loops),
- physical functions (electrical, mechanical, chemical processes of components), and
- physical form (physical appearance and anatomy, material, and form).

Therefore, learners should have access to a conceptual model of the system that includes multiple representational layers, such as the following:

- The *pictorial layer* contains pictures of the device or system as it actually exists. Associating representations of the system with the actual system is important. Depending on the complexity of the system, it may be necessary to picture different parts of the system. Zooming in from the pictorial layer reveals the topographic layer.
- The *topographic layer* illustrates the components of the system and their interconnections. Zooming in from the topographic layer reveals the state layer.
- The *state layer* includes normal states, fault states, and the probability or frequency of faults. This layer enables the troubleshooter to draw implications about needed actions. If the troubleshooter is unaware of the alternative actions, then he or she can zoom into the strategic layer.
- The *functional layer* illustrates and describes the information, energy, or product that flows through the system, that is, how the system functions. When functions of the system cease, the troubleshooter can zoom into the strategic layer to identify optional actions and tests.
- The *strategic layer* consists of rule-based representations of alternative decisions regarding the states described on the state layer. Zooming in on the strategic layer reveals the action layer.
- The *action layer* includes descriptions of procedures for conducting various tests. The primary purpose of this layer of information is to serve as a job aid or just-in-time instruction for student.

Diagnostic Simulation

The heart of the TLE is a *diagnostic simulation*. This is where the learner troubleshoots new cases. For example, after listening to a description of the symptoms that were present just before a car ceased to work, the learner (like an experienced troubleshooter) first selects an action using a pull-down menu, such as ordering a test, checking a connection, or trying a repair strategy. The novice may be coached about what action he or she should take first, based on the symptomology, or he or she may be free to select any action. Each action the troubleshooter takes shows up in the systems model. For each action taken, the troubleshooter next requires the learner to select, using another pull-down menu, a fault hypothesis that he or she is testing. Requiring the learner to justify his or her actions is an implicit form of argumentation. If the hypothesis is inconsistent with the problem, then feedback can be immediately provided about the rationale for taking such an action. Next, the learner must identify the subsystem in which the fault occurs. If the subsystem is inconsistent with the action, then the learner is immediately sent to the conceptual model so that he or she can better understand the workings of the subsystem that leads to the action or hypothesis. The learner then receives the result of his or her action (e.g., test results, system status) and must interpret those results. If the interpretation is inconsistent with the action, hypothesis, or subsystem, then an error message is triggered. The error-checking function uses a very simple evaluation system.

The simulation requires the learner to think and act like a trouble-shooter. The environment integrates the troubleshooting actions, knowledge types (conceptual, strategic, and procedural), and conceptual systems model with a database of faults that have occurred with the system that the learner and others have solved. Initial instruction in how to use the system is provided by worked examples. As learners solve troubleshooting problems, the results of their practice cases can be added to the learner's case library of fault situations so that the learner can learn from his or her own personal experience.

Case Library

If the diagnostic simulation is the heart of the TLE, then the case library is the head (memory) of the TLE. Discourse is essential to socially negotiating problems, solutions, or meaning. In troubleshooting situations in everyday contexts, the primary medium of negotiation is stories; that is, when a troubleshooter experiences a problem, he or she most often describes the problem to someone else, who recalls from memory a similar problem, telling the troubleshooter about the recalled experience. Stories provide rich contextual information about the subjects in the environment, revealing needs, beliefs, and identity about them. Stories about how experienced troubleshooters have solved similar troubleshooting problems are contained in, indexed by, and made available to learners in a case library (also known as a *fault database*).

The case library or fault database contains as many stories of trouble-shooting experiences as possible. Each case represents a story of a domain-specific troubleshooting instance. Case libraries, based on principles of case-based reasoning, represent the most powerful form of instructional support for ill-structured problems such as troubleshooting (Jonassen & Hernandez-Serrano, 2002). The case library, like the troubleshooter, indexes each case or story according to its system fault, the system or subsystem in which the fault occurred, and the symptoms of the fault. The failure mode, hypotheses or strategies that were tested, the results of those tests, and the lessons learned from the experience are also contained in the case library. The case library represents the experiential knowledge of potentially hundreds of experienced troubleshooters, because troubleshooters almost invariably store their knowledge of problems and solutions in terms of their experiences. The best troubleshooters are the most experienced ones. Their experiential knowledge is precisely what learners do not possess. So, when a learner encounters any difficulty or is uncertain about how to proceed, he or she can access the case library to learn about similar cases, such as what was done and what the results were. The TLE can also be programmed to automatically access a relevant story when a learner commits an error, orders an inappropriate test, or takes some other action that indicates a lack of understanding. Stories are easily collected from experienced troubleshooters by presenting them with a problem and asking them if they are reminded of a similar problem they have solved. Invariably, the experienced trouble-shooters are reminded of similar problems. Hernandez-Serrano and Jonassen (2003) showed that access to a case library while learning how to solve problems improved participants' complex problem-solving performance on an examination.

Systems–Policy Analysis Problems

As described earlier, systems or policy analysis problems are complex, ambiguous, and poorly structured. As such, they represent the antithesis of most formal education, which focuses on correct answers and finding truth. Systems analysis problems often present unknowable phenomena that must be socially negotiated and coconstructed. There never is a single perspective that represents the truth. Solving these problems requires that students accommodate ambiguity. However, tolerance for ambiguity is low among teachers and students. The reason for this has to do with their epistemological beliefs, that is, what people believe that knowledge, truth, and learning mean. People develop their beliefs from simple, black–white thinking, through an exploration of multiple perspectives, to complex, relativistic thinking. The epistemological foundation for most education is what Baxter-Magolda (1987) called *absolute knowing*, whereby individuals believe that knowledge and truth are certain and should be obtained from authorities. Solving case problems requires what Baxter-Magolda called *transitional knowing* (in which knowledge is partially certain and requires logic, debate, and research before it is understood), *independent knowing* (in which knowledge is uncertain and requires independent thinking and open-mindedness), and *contextual knowing* (in which knowledge is based on evidence in context). Because students are most commonly absolute thinkers, they will find case problems very challenging because there is no correct answer. However, if students never face ill-structured case problems, they will probably never develop independent or contextual thinking skills, so some exposure to ambiguity

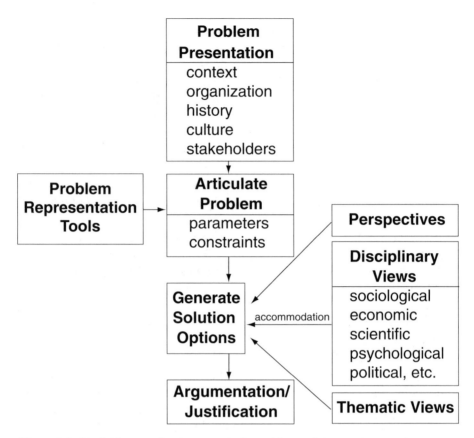

Figure 9.2. Model for case/systems analysis problem-solving environment.

represents a learning experience. A model for designing a case analysis learning environment (Jonassen, 2004) is illustrated in Figure 9.2. I describe these components next.

Problem Representation

Problem representation is too complex a topic to fully explain here. Because systems–policy analysis problems are more context dependent than well-structured problems, it is necessary to develop a more authentic and situated task environment (Voss, 1988). If systems analysis thinking is determined largely by the context and the domain that it represents, then it is important to adequately describe the social, political, and organizational context of the problem. Therefore, a context analysis is needed. The following questions should be asked: What is the nature of the domain? What are the constraints imposed by the context? What kinds of problems are solved in this domain and, equally important, what are the contextual constraints that affect the problem?

Systems and policy analysis problems are often represented by stories, which are better understood, better remembered, and more user friendly than didactic representations of problems. The following excerpt is taken from a policy analysis learning environment on the sociology of welfare that my colleagues and I developed. This particular story introduces the problem in the welfare cycle (seeking assistance, support, welfare to work). The problem has to do with how to help people through the welfare-to-work cycle. Another major goal of the environment was to invoke empathic responses from culturally isolated students at a large state university.

Tuesday, February 2, 1999

My name's Tiffany. I'm on my way to Lewistown with my daughter, Stephanie. Stephanie's almost five, now. I had her when I was eighteen. My home and friends are in Detroit. I can't stay there no more. I got involved with a gang there, selling drugs and dealin'. It took me five years to realize that I didn't want to live like that no more. I was stealin' and doing things I never thought I would. I love my little girl. I realized I would be harmin' her if I stayed with them.

When you've done and seen what I have, there's no point in wanting 'out' unless you're prepared to do it. So I'm leaving, with no cash, no help from no-one. Just Stef and me. Yeah, this has been my "Happy Christmas." I'm lookin' for my natural mother. I know she lived in Lewiston, Pennsylvania, when I was born. Its a long shot, although. I have an address for her for 1992. I ain't never met her. She don't know I'm comin'. I have nowhere else to go—just can't stay in Detroit—no way. I'm near eight months knocked up. I gotta get help, right away when I get there, for the sake of my babies.

Wednesday, February 3, 1999 (5:30 p.m.)

Stephanie ain't never traveled on no Greyhound bus, before. A twenty-hour ride has just about dimmed her enthusiasm—poor baby. Thank God she slept. We left the Howard Street station in Detroit at 10:00 last night and got here at 5:15 today. In this rotten weather, it'll be dark soon. We haven't eaten since we finished our snacks. Jeez, the smell from this Market Street Grill is drivin' me crazy. What have I done? My ticket was $59. That's crazy! Maybe I should o' kept my money.

I ain't got no idea where to go here. The number I have for my mother ain't givin' me no answer. I only have three quarters for the phone. Thirty dollars and my kid and this ol' beach bag with Stef's clothes and beanie babies and some things for myself, that's all I have. And jeez, is this place small, and cold. I know I gotta find us some help. This number still ain't answering. There's no message. Maybe this isn't even the number. . . . It's gettin' late. What are we gonna do?

Representing systems or policy analysis problems in terms of stories is not enough to engage learners in the kind of thinking that is necessary for solving systems or policy problems (Jonassen, 2004). It is equally as important, if not more important, to provide students with a specific, authentic task to solve. In the social welfare problem just described, students were required to counsel this woman, who was seeking to move from welfare to work. Their counseling had to be not only legally correct (the students became very frustrated by the complexity of the forms and the procedures that had to be completed by the recipients) but also empathic.

The task also needs to be fairly specific. The task for a foreign policy analysis problem on the Middle East might require the students to act as foreign policy analysts for the State Department who are tasked with recommending specific policy actions to the Secretary of State about whether Palestinians should be granted independent statehood. There should be a specific kind of outcome (advice) associated with the task, not just a report but a report with specific action items. This does not mean that a particular kind of advice should be given, just a particular form of advice. A systems or policy analysis problem on the political systems in Norway should require recommendations about how to build a parliamentary coalition necessary to pass legislation approving the construction of a gas-fired electrical plant. The more purposeful the task, the more engaging it will be. The same environment with all of its support systems may be altered by redefining the task. Some students may be assigned to an environment that seeks to build a coalition to block the construction of a gas-fired electrical plant. Except for the task, the remainder of the environment may be the same or very similar. In another environment designed for a geography course focusing on the use of maps (see Figure 9.3), students were awarded a contract from the state department of transportation to select an alternate route to bypass a poorly designed highway intersection. In this environment, students had to accommodate the views of motorists, merchants, homeowners, and bureaucrats while using soil, topographic, aerial, and parcel maps to design the most efficient, effective, and acceptable road. As with all design problems, no best solution exists, only better and worse solutions. The task should be as real as possible, and it should be fairly well circumscribed. Too often, problem-solving attempts in the classroom fail because the task is too diffuse. Students are assigned to analyze policy or principles. If the students do not perceive a meaningful purpose for the problem-solving activity, then they are not likely to buy into the problems or their solutions.

Problem Representation Tools

Earlier, I described ways that a problem can be represented to students, including in a narrative format and with concise, authentic tasks. It is

The Problem

Solution Views

Maps

Resources

FAQ's

The Problem

The intersection of I-70 and Highway 63, in Columbia, MO is increasingly busy, and dangerous. During peak traffic times there are traffic jams which cause extended commuting times, high frustration levels, and numerous accidents. Concern about these issues has caused support for a proposed alternate route highway to be built.

Click here for a larger version.

Proponents of this highway hope to lessen the amount of traffic at the I-70 and 63 interchange, with the result of a lower accident rate and less time spent in traffic by commuters. Opponents of this highway have differing concerns, with environmental, social, and standard of living issues cited as causes for alarm.

Figure 9.3. Traffic problem.

important to note that the ways people represent problems to learners in the problem statement affects how problem-solvers mentally represent problems they are trying to solve. That is the goal—to get learners to construct a meaningful, conceptual model of the problems they are trying to solve. However, that problem representation is only one source of influence. The model for engaging learners in systems–policy analysis problems calls for the use of tools by learners to construct their own external representation of the problems. Systems dynamics modeling tools, such as STELLA, PowerSIM, or VenSIM, provide the most powerful tools for representing the dynamic complexities of systems analysis problems. A student-constructed model of the effects of smoking, which was used in a systems analysis of smoking, is represented in Figure 9.4. This model (produced with STELLA) depicts the dynamic relationships among different factors affecting the population. So, if a student's task were to decide whether to impose smoking bans, he or she might begin by building such a model. Systems dynamics tools enable learners to add or subtract factors and test the effects of changes in those factors. These tools also enable the students to test their models by changing parameter values and noticing the effects.

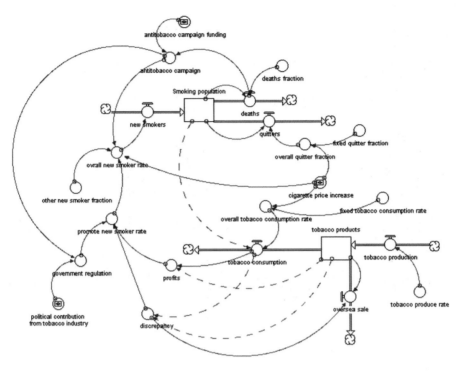

Figure 9.4. Systems dynamics model of smoking population.

Generate Solution Options: Accommodating Multiple Perspectives

The best model for facilitating the consideration of multiple perspectives, an essential process for solving systems–policy analysis problems, is *cognitive flexibility theory* (Spiro & Jehng, 1990). Cognitive flexibility theory stresses the conceptual interrelatedness of ideas and their interconnectedness. Cognitive flexibility environments intentionally represent multiple perspectives or interpretations of the content in the cases that are used to illustrate the content domain. The ill-structuredness of any knowledge domain is best illustrated by multiple perspectives or themes that are inherent in the problems that are represented. My colleagues and I used a cognitive flexibility hypertext in an environment on issues of biodiversity, land use and control, and conflict resolution styles as they have emerged in the controversy surrounding the reintroduction of the Mexican gray wolf into wilderness areas of the American Southwest. The wolf-reintroduction environment (see Figure 9.5) allows the learner to examine the reintroduction issue from the perspectives of a dozen or so people who are affected by the wolves, including ranchers and environmentalists. We also identified various thematic issues interwoven through their comments, including local versus national control of the land, consumption versus conservation, and coopera-

Reintroduction of the Wolf into the Southwest

Long before cowboys roamed, before Spaniards rode in conquest, before even the Apache and Navajo arrived, wolves inhabited the ancient Southwest, but as cattle ranching took hold in the 1800s, the predatory wolf became an obstacle to commerce. By the 1920s it was just about exterminated from the Western landscape. But wolves are making a comeback of a kind in part because of shifting public values.

In January 1995, 19 Canadian gray wolves were released into Yellowstone National Park by the U.S. Fish and Wildlife Service. In January 1996 another 20 were brought to Yellowstone and to Idaho, and in early 1997 the Southwest will get its share. Mexican gray wolves are scheduled to be reintroduced into the wilderness of Arizona and New Mexico, but the battle for public acceptance is still being waged. Should the Mexican wolf be reintroduced? You decide.

For more information, you can read this piece by Sandy Tolan of National Public Radio's Weekend Edition.

To help you make up your mind, you can listen to several people in the area who would be affected by the re-introduction:

- Al Schneeberger of the New Mexico Cattle Growers Association
- A Woman of Catron County
- Man in the Field Interviews
- Charmin Russel
- Dutch Salmon, publisher of High Lonesome Books
- Jim Cook
- Pamela Brown
- The Holders

You can think about some of the major issues involved.

- Consumption vs. Conservation
- Confrontation vs. Cooperation
- National control vs. Local control

Figure 9.5. Wolf-reintroduction environment.

tion versus cooptation. To render a judgment on the continuation of the practice, students had to understand and accommodate these viewpoints. It is essential that students understand the different perspectives that make systems–policy analysis problems complex to generate and evaluate different solutions.

Argumentation

As stated before, ill-structured problems are dialectical in nature. They involve two or more opposing conceptualizations of the problem (different problem spaces) that are used to support different arguments with opposing underlying assumptions (Churchman, 1971). Therefore, it is important that learners are able to articulate the differing assumptions in support of arguments for the solution they recommend. The argument provides the best evidence for domain knowledge that they have acquired. Developing cogent arguments to support divergent thinking (reflective judgment; Kitchener & King, 1981) engages not only cognition and metacognition of the processes used to solve the problem but also awareness of the epistemic nature of the process and the truth or value of different solutions (Kitchener, 1983). In the geography environment there are many possible routes that can be chosen and many possible reasons for choosing any one of them. Requiring students to develop an argument for their choice is tantamount to problem solving; that is, it provides very useful assessment data to help the teacher determine what and how much the learners know. Coaching or prompting can be provided in the form of a series of reflective judgment prompts or questions (Kitchener & King, 1981), such as the following:

- Can you ever know for sure that your position is correct? Will we ever know which is the correct position?
- How did you come to hold that point of view? On what do you base it?
- When people disagree about matters such as this, is it ever the case that one is right and the other wrong? Is one opinion worse and the other better?
- How is it possible that people can have such different points of view?
- What does it mean to you when the experts disagree on this issue?

SUMMARY

In this chapter, I have argued for the supremacy of problem solving among learning outcomes. It is the most common and authentic task performed by most professionals, yet very little problem-solving instruction is provided to students in K–12 schools and universities. Problem solving is even less common in online education, despite the fact that so much of this instruction is aimed at practicing professionals. I have described differences among a typology of problems. I have also provided more detailed descriptions of two kinds of problems—troubleshooting and systems analysis—along with descriptions of architectures for accommodating troubleshooting and systems analysis problems. These conceptual models of online learning environments provide extensive opportunities for research.

CONCLUDING COMMENTS

During several years of research and promoting problem-solving pedagogies, I have discovered that a major impediment to engaging and supporting problem solving is the affective response that problems evoke. Many professionals, especially in corporate training, prefer not to consider or contemplate problems, despite the fact they are being paid to solve problems. They prefer to consider problems as opportunities. I believe that this aversion to problem solving results in part from the affective connotations of the concept of a "problem." Thesauri list many synonyms for *problem*, such as *dilemma, quandary, obstacle, predicament,* and *difficulty,* all of which have heavy affective connotations. Indeed, problems often do represent predicaments, and problems are often difficult. However, regardless of whether problems represent opportunities or obstacles, they need to be addressed in professional education because professionals are hired, retained, and rewarded for solving problems, regardless of what they call them. In this chapter, I have assumed a strong cognitive perspective on problems (i.e., a problem as a question to be solved). I hope that researchers and practitioners will recognize the cognitive importance of problems and regulate their affective responses to better support their learners.

REFERENCES

Baxter-Magolda, M. (1987). Comparing open-ended interviews and standardized measures of intellectual development. *Journal of College Student Personnel, 28,* 443–448.

Bransford, J. D., & Stein, B. S. (1993). *The ideal problem solver: A guide for improving thinking, learning, and creativity.* New York: Freeman.

Churchman, C. W. (1971). *The design of inquiring systems: Basic concepts of systems and organization.* New York: Basic Books.

Hammond, K. R., McClelland, G. H., & Mumpower, J. (1980). *Human judgment and decision making.* New York: Praeger Publishers.

Hernandez-Serrano, J., & Jonassen, D. H. (2003). The effects of case libraries on problem solving. *Journal of Computer-Assisted Learning, 19,* 103–114.

Johnson, S. D. (1988). Cognitive analysis of expert and novice troubleshooting performance. *Performance Improvement Quarterly, 1*(3), 38–54.

Jonassen, D. H. (1997). Instructional design models for well-structured and ill-structured problem-solving learning outcomes. *Educational Technology: Research and Development, 45*(1), 65–95.

Jonassen, D. H. (2000). Toward a design theory of problem solving. *Educational Technology: Research and Development, 48*(4), 63–85.

Jonassen, D. H. (2003). Designing instruction for story problems. *Educational Psychology Review, 15,* 267–296.

Jonassen, D. H. (2004). *Learning to solve problems: An instructional design guide.* San Francisco: Pfeiffer/Jossey-Bass.

Jonassen, D. H., & Churchill, D. (2004). Is there a learning orientation in learning objects? *International Journal on E-Learning, 3*(2), 32–41.

Jonassen, D. H., & Hernandez-Serrano, J. (2002). Case-based reasoning and instructional design: Using stories to support problem solving. *Educational Technology: Research and Development, 50*(2), 65–77.

Jonassen, D. H., & Hung, W. (2006). Learning to troubleshoot: A new theory-based design architecture. *Educational Psychology Review,18,* 77–114.

Kaplan, M., & Schwartz, S. (1975). *Human judgment and decision processes.* New York: Academic Press.

Kitchener, K. S. (1983). Cognition, metacognition, and epistemic cognition: A three-level model of cognition processing. *Human Development, 26,* 222–232.

Kitchener, K. S., & King, P. M. (1981). Reflective judgment: Concepts of justifications and their relationship to age and education. *Journal of Applied Developmental Psychology, 2*(2), 89–116.

Kolodner, J. L., Crismond, D., Gray, J., Holbroook, J., & Puntambekar, S. (1998). Learning by design from theory to practice, Proceedings of ICLS-98, on the web at http://www.cc.gatech.edu/edutech/projects/lbd_icls98/icls.LBD.html

Lehman, D., Lempert, R., & Nisbett, R. E. (1988). The effects of graduate training on reasoning: Formal discipline and thinking about everyday-life events. *Educational Psychologist, 43,* 431–442.

Lesgold, A., & Lajoie, S. (1991). Complex problem solving in electronics. In R. J. Sternberg & P. A. Frensch (Eds.), *Complex problem solving: Principles and mechanisms.* Hillsdale, NJ: Lawrence Erlbaum Associates.

Mayer, R. E. (1992). *Thinking, problem solving, cognition* (2nd ed.). New York: Freeman.

McGuinness, C. (1986). Problem representation: The effects of spatial arrays. *Memory & Cognition, 14,* 270–280.

Newell, A., & Simon, H. (1972). *Human problem solving.* Englewood Cliffs, NJ: Prentice Hall.

Pokorny, R. A., Hall, E. P., Gallaway, M. A., & Dibble, E. (1996). Analyzing components of work samples to evaluate performance. *Military Psychology, 8*(3), 161–177.

Popper, K. (1999). *All life is problem solving.* London: Routledge.

Rasmussen, J. (1984). *Information processing and human–machine interaction: An approach to cognitive engineering.* Amsterdam: North-Holland.

Simon, D. P. (1978). Information processing theory of human problem solving. In D. Estes (Ed.), *Handbook of learning and cognitive process.* Hillsdale, NJ: Lawrence Erlbaum Associates.

Smith, M. U. (1991). A view from biology. In M. U. Smith (Ed.), *Toward a unified theory of problem solving* (pp. 1–21). Hillsdale, NJ: Erlbaum.

Spiro, R. J., & Jehng, J. C. (1990). Cognitive flexibility and hypertext: Theory and technology for the non-linear and multi-dimensional traversal of complex subject matter. In D. Nix & R. J. Spiro (Eds.), *Cognition, education, and multimedia: Explorations in high technology* (pp. 63–201). Hillsdale, NJ: Erlbaum.

Sternberg, R. J., & Frensch, P. A. (1991). *Complex problem solving: Principles and mechanisms*. Hillsdale, NJ: Erlbaum.

Voss, J. F. (1988). Learning and transfer in subject-matter learning: A problem solving model. *International Journal of Education Research, 11*, 607–622.

Voss, J. F., & Post, T. A. (1988). On the solving of ill-structured problems. In M. T. H. Chi, R. Glaser, & M. J. Farr (Eds.), *The nature of expertise* (pp. 261–286). Hillsdale, NJ: Erlbaum.

Wilson, J. W., Fernandez, M. L., & Hadaway, N. (n.d.). *Mathematical problem solving*. Retrieved September 22, 2005, from http://jwilson.coe.uga

Woods, D. R., Hrymak, A. N., Marshall, R. R., Wood, P. E., Crowe, C. M., Hoffman, T. W., et al. (1997). Developing problem-solving skills: The McMaster problem solving program. *Journal of Engineering Education, 86*, 75–92

10

QUESTION-ASKING IN ADVANCED DISTRIBUTED LEARNING ENVIRONMENTS

ROBERT A. WISHER AND ARTHUR C. GRAESSER

Questions arise as a natural part of the learning process in classrooms, tutoring, computer-based training, and other learning environments. Students may request an explanation, a clarification, or a concrete example, or they may make some other form of inquiry that signals uncertainty. Student questions are learner centric because they reflect the learner's lack of specific knowledge or inability to comprehend. The role of student questions is particularly important in computer-based distributed learning, where instruction is available any time, anywhere, for anyone. There needs to be a mechanism for students to get a timely response to a spontaneous question.

An underlying concern, therefore, is the impact of question-asking on learning. How does the process of question-asking and interpreting answers influence learning, performance, and student satisfaction? There is ample evidence that the rate of student question-asking in the classroom is extremely low compared with other learning environments, such as one-on-one tutoring (Graesser, McNamara, & VanLehn, 2005; Graesser & Person, 1994). There is ample evidence that training students to ask good questions can improve the comprehension and learning of technical materials (Craig, Gholson, & Sullins, 2004; King, 1992, 1994; Palincsar & Brown, 1984; Rosenshine, Meister, & Chapman, 1996). How can these findings be beneficially applied to advanced distributed learning environments? Another concern addresses the nature and frequency of the questions that are likely to be asked. To what extent can these questions be anticipated beforehand? What automated mechanisms can be developed to answer them? How important is the capacity for a computer or human to respond quickly? Although mechanisms of answering learners' questions are just as important as the mechanisms of question generation, it is beyond the scope of this chapter to cover the process of question-answering and information retrieval.

A practical concern underlying this chapter is how to incorporate question-generation facilities into learner-centric, advanced distributed learning environments. The term *distributed learning* embraces current practices and common-use technologies, whereas *advanced distributed learning* refers to a future state of technologies and applications (Wisher, 2003). The conventional human–computer interfaces in most electronic environments allow the user to ask questions indirectly by accessing and using facilities such as Help and Frequently Asked Questions. The content of the Help and Frequently Asked Questions facilities is prepared by the design team, often without iterations of user feedback and testing. The content is fixed, closed, and static, so many of the functional questions that users have cannot be answered. Advanced systems allow the user to ask virtually any question in natural language, with answers provided by sophisticated information-retrieval systems that incorporate recent breakthroughs in the field of computational linguistics.

The chapter is intended for a broad audience, including instructors, researchers, designers of learning technologies, and architects who will be charting the future course of advanced distributed learning. The chapter begins with a review of the cognitive underpinnings of question generation and its relation to learning. The primary focus is on *sincere information-seeking (SIS) questions*, those that reflect genuine curiosity, lack of knowledge, uncertainty, and a desire for information to fill such knowledge gaps. Some questions are not SIS questions because the questioner already knows the answer (e.g., a teacher grilling students in a classroom or a lawyer cross-examining a witness in a courtroom) or because the questioner is not particularly interested in the answer (as in rhetorical questions). In the second section, we cover empirical studies of question generation in different learning environments that use various information technologies. In the third section, we discuss practical methods of increasing the frequency and quality of questions.

QUESTION GENERATION

A question-asking facility on a computer allows the user to select or compose a query that the user hopes will be answered by the computer. A question-answering facility is the answer that is delivered to the user who poses the question. The design of question-asking and -answering facilities in any information-retrieval system requires an in-depth analysis of question-generation mechanisms. Such mechanisms specify the representation of the subject matter, the cognitive processes associated with inquiry, and the social context of the communicative interaction. There are many reasons why a question facility can fail in a learning environment or some other information system. This section should help researchers, software designers, and course developers identify some of the potential barriers in addition to gaining an appreciation for sophisticated question-generation facilities.

Impact of Question Generation on Learning

Learning environments that promote question-asking by students have been advocated by researchers in cognitive science and education for a number of years (Beck, McKeown, Hamilton, & Kucan, 1997; Dillon, 1988; Graesser, Langston, & Baggett, 1993; Graesser, McNamara, & VanLehn, 2005; Pressley & Forrest-Pressley, 1985). There are several reasons why question generation can play a central role in learning. The most prevalent is that it promotes active learning and construction of knowledge (Bransford, Brown, & Cocking, 2000). Learners need to construct knowledge actively during learning, and they do so in ways that make sense to them. Otherwise, they become overwhelmed with information that appears unstructured to the learner. Rather than being a mere information-delivery system, an advanced distributed learning environment should serve as a scaffold for the active construction of knowledge, including answering student questions (Edelson, Gordin, & Pea, 1999; Schank, 1986). Constructivist approaches have been so compelling during the past 10 years that they have shaped the standards for curriculum and instruction in the United States, for example, Standards for the English Language Arts (National Council of Teachers of English, 1996) and National Science Education Standards (National Research Council, 1996). Most of these standards apply to education (i.e., reading, mathematics, science) rather than to the training of specific skills and content. Nevertheless, there is no principled reason for doubting the utility of constructivism in training, so we next describe how questions can facilitate learning in training environments.

Question-Generation Learning

Question-generation learning (QGL) is an environment in which learners are encouraged or compelled to ask questions while they study material. For example, questions may be asked after the learner has tried to comprehend each sentence, paragraph, or section in the text. Answers to the questions are provided by an expert immediately (as in synchronous distance learning) or after a delay (as in asynchronous distance learning). Alternatively, there may be no facility that provides satisfactory answers to the questions. The process of formulating a question may itself promote learning, over and above any benefits of an answer to the question. QGL may be effective for several reasons, including the following:

- *Active learning.* Learners actively construct knowledge in the service of questions rather than passively receiving information.
- *Metacognition.* Learners become sensitive to their knowledge deficits and comprehension failures while they attempt to comprehend the material.
- *Self-regulated learning.* Learners take charge of both identifying and correcting comprehension problems.
- *Motivation and engagement.* Because the learning experience is tailored to their own needs, learners are more motivated and engaged in the content.
- *Building common ground with the author.* Learners share more knowledge with the author.
- *Transfer-appropriate processing.* Because learners are normally tested by answering questions, generating questions as part of the learning process should improve the overlap between comprehension representations and test representations.
- *Coding of cognitive representation.* Cognitive representations are more precise, specific, and elaborate when learners generate questions.

It is well documented that improvements in the comprehension, learning, and memory of technical material can be achieved by training students to ask questions during learning (Ciardiello, 1998; Craig et al., 2004; King, 1992, 1994; Rosenshine et al., 1996). The process of question generation accounts for a significant amount of these improvements, over and above the specific information supplied by answers. Moreover, QGL is most effective when students are trained to ask good questions. Exactly what constitutes a good question is discussed later, when we present a taxonomy of questions. Rosenshine et al. (1996) provided a very comprehensive analysis of the impact of QGL on learning in their meta-analysis of 26 empirical studies that compared QGL with learning conditions with appropriate methodological controls. The outcome measures included standardized tests, short-answer or multiple-choice questions prepared by experimenters, and summaries of the texts. The median effect size was 0.36 for the standardized tests, 0.87 for the experimenter-generated tests, and 0.85 for the summary tests.

One informative result of Rosenshine et al.'s (1996) meta-analysis was that the question format was important when training the learners how to ask questions. The analysis compared training with signal words (*who*, *what*, *when*, *where*, *why*, and *how*), training with generic question stems ("How is X like Y?", "Why is X important?", "What conclusions can you draw about X?"), and training with main idea prompts ("What is the main idea of the paragraph?"). The generic question stems were most effective, perhaps because they give the learner more direction, are more concrete, and are easier to teach and apply. This result is informative because it provides guidance in designing question-prompt capabilities for advanced distributed learning applications.

Another informative result pertains to the feedback, comments, and corrections that learners receive in response to their questions. Most of the studies included in the meta-analysis probably provided feedback to the learners on the quality of their questions, but a description of such feedback was absent in most of the reported studies. Therefore, the role of question-asking feedback is an issue for future investigations. Feedback can come from a teacher, a peer learner, or a computer. MacGregor (1988), for example, developed a computer-based instructional format that modeled good questions when the learner appeared to be facing problems in question-asking. Nevertheless, the question of how important it is to have feedback on question quality for learning to occur is not yet settled. Even in the absence of feedback, the process of generating a question may increase the learner's awareness of the gaps in his or her own knowledge and promote deeper self-regulated learning.

Question Facilities in Distance Learning

Question facilities in distance learning applications nearly always deliver answers to questions, as opposed to helping the learner generate questions. It is important to analyze how learning is affected by the technologies that provide answers in addition to the technologies that facilitate the question-asking process. However, as mentioned earlier, the focus of this chapter is on question generation rather than question answering. We are convinced that it is a much bigger challenge to design learning environments to encourage inquiry, curiosity, and question-asking in the learner than it is to provide answers to questions.

Differences between synchronous and asynchronous learning environments are important to questioning mechanisms. Learners receive an immediate answer to their questions in synchronous learning but must wait several hours, or even days, for an answer in asynchronous learning. The available research on QGL has not evolved to the point of having systematic comparisons between synchronous and asynchronous distributed learning environments. As of 2006, no studies have compared questions asked in synchronous versus asynchronous distributed learning environments.

The quality of the answer, in addition to the timing of answer delivery, is no doubt important. The quality of answers has been systematically evaluated in computerized information-retrieval systems that are embedded in learning environments (Graesser, Hu, Person, Jackson, & Toth, 2004). The performance of such systems has been as high as 90% of the answers being relevant and 50% being informative. However, there has been no systematic analysis of the relation between answer quality and amount of learning in such information-retrieval systems. Aside from computerized retrieval systems, there is a large range in the quality of answers supplied by humans. Global social networks of users have been participating in computer-supported collaborative learning (Ogata, Sueda, Furugori, & Yano, 1999; Songer, 1996) and informal peer-help networks (Greer et al., 1998). Users are distributed at various locations and communicate by electronic mail. Learners ask and answer questions of their peers or communicate with designated experts. In some systems, participants in the network score points, or accumulate credits, by helping others and answering questions posed by their peers. Answers generated by an expert are presumably superior to those supplied by peers, but once again, we are uncertain whether gains in answer quality have concomitant gains in learning.

The conclusion that QGL is effective is indisputable, but there are two general concerns that might limit its scope in promoting learning gains. The first is that it is difficult to disentangle three components: (a) the process of asking questions, (b) feedback to the learner on the quality of the question, and (c) the quality of the answer. The comparative impact of these components on learning gains has not been reported in the published meta-analyses. The second concern is that the pragmatic context of question-asking has been unnatural or vague in many of the studies. For example, consider the studies in which the learner is instructed to generate questions while reading. There is no obvious recipient of the question, so it is difficult to determine whether a question is an SIS question or a forced exercise in elaborating the material. Consider the studies in which the teacher models question-asking skills. Most of these questions are not SIS questions because the teacher already knows the answers to the questions. What is needed is an authentic context in which learners are vested in the questions that they ask. In the next section, we address the pragmatics of question-asking and the conditions in which bona fide questions are asked.

Pragmatic Assumptions Behind Question Generation

One could argue that any given task that a person performs is decomposable into a set of questions that a person asks and answers. For example, when an operator encounters a device that malfunctions, the relevant questions are "What's wrong?" and "How can it be fixed?" When an officer reads a situation report, the relevant questions are "Why is this important?" and "What should I do about it, if anything?" When a young adult reads job advertising material, the relevant questions are "What's interesting?" "Do I want to get hired?" and "What are the perks?" The cognitive mechanisms that trigger question-asking and exploration need to be understood to facilitate learning in schools and the workplace.

In contrast to SIS-type questions, the questioner may not particularly care about answers to other types of questions (Graesser & Person, 1994; Van der Meij, 1987). Van der Meij identified 11 assumptions that need to be in place for a question to qualify as an SIS question:

1. The questioner does not know the information he asks for with the question.
2. The question specifies the information sought after.
3. The questioner believes that the presuppositions to the question are true.
4. The questioner believes that an answer exists.
5. The questioner wants to know the answer.
6. The questioner can assess whether a reply constitutes an answer.
7. The questioner poses the question only if the benefits exceed the costs.
8. The questioner believes that the respondent knows the answer.
9. The questioner believes that the respondent will not give the answer in absence of a question.
10. The questioner believes that the respondent will supply the answer.
11. A question solicits a reply.

A question is a misfire (non-SIS question) if 1 or more of these 11 assumptions are not met. For example, when a computer science teacher grills a student with a question in a classroom ("What is RAM?"), it is not an SIS question because it violates Assumptions 1, 5, 8, and 10. When a lawyer cross-examines a witness with a question, it is not an SIS question because it violates Assumptions 1, 3, 4, 5, and 8. A standard lawyer maxim is "never ask a question unless you know the answer." Similarly, the listed assumptions are violated when there are rhetorical questions ("When does a person know when he or she is happy?"), gripes ("When is it going to stop snowing?"), greetings ("How are you?"), and attempts to redirect the flow of conversation in a group (a hostess asks Bill, "So, when is your next vacation, Bill?"). In contrast, a question is an SIS question when a person's computer is malfunctioning and the person asks a technical assistant "What is wrong with my computer?"

These pragmatic assumptions have nontrivial implications from the standpoint of the design of future advanced distributed learning systems. A learner will quickly give up using a system if he or she is unable to articulate the information in sufficient detail to get useful answers (Assumption 2), if the system does not correct misleading presuppositions (Assumption 3), if the system does not supply much useful information in the answer (Assumption 8), if the system has trouble delivering any information (Assumptions 10 and 11), and if the system cannot recognize frivolous or humorous questions posed by the user (Assumptions 1, 4, 5, and 7).

Knowledge Representations and Cognitive Processes

The contrast between shallow and deep knowledge is a fundamental distinction in cognitive psychology (Bloom, 1956; Bransford et al., 2000; Craik & Lockhart, 1972; Snow, 2002). *Shallow knowledge* consists of explicitly mentioned ideas in a text that refer to lists of concepts, a handful of simple facts or properties of each concept, simple definitions of key terms, and major steps in a procedure (not the detailed steps). *Deep knowledge* consists of coherent explanations of the material that fortify the learner for generating inferences, solving problems, making decisions, integrating ideas, synthesizing new ideas, decomposing ideas into subparts, forecasting future occurrences in a system, and applying knowledge to practical situations. Deep knowledge is presumably needed to articulate and manipulate symbols, formal expressions, and quantities, although some individuals can master these skills after extensive practice without deep mastery. Deep knowledge is essential for handling challenges and obstacles because there is a need to understand how mechanisms work and to generate and implement novel plans. Explanations are central to deep knowledge, whether the explanations consist of logical justifications, causal networks, or goal–plan–action hierarchies. It is well documented that the construction of coherent explanations is a robust predictor of an adult's ability to learn technical material from written texts (Chi, de Leeuw, Chiu, & LaVancher, 1994; McNamara, 2004; Webb, Troper, & Fall, 1995).

Researchers in the fields of cognitive science, artificial intelligence, and discourse processes have specified different types and levels of knowledge representation in rich detail (Graesser, Gordon, & Brainerd, 1992; Kintsch, 1998; Lehmann, 1992). In this section, we describe the distinctions that bear on question generation in distributed learning and that clarify the distinction between deep and shallow learning.

The cognitive representations of texts, pictures, and other materials can be segregated into four levels: (a) surface code, (b) explicit propositions, (c) mental models, and (d) pragmatic interaction (Kintsch, 1998). The shallowest level is the *surface code*, which preserves the exact wording and syntax of the explicit verbal material. When considering the visual modality, it preserves the low-level lines, angles, sizes, shapes, and textures of the pictures. The *explicit proposition* representation captures the meaning of the explicit text and the pictures. A proposition contains a predicate (main verb, adjective, connective) that interrelates one or more arguments (noun referents, embedded propositions). An example proposition is "the soldier repaired the computer," represented structurally as [repair(soldier, computer)]. At the deepest level is the *mental model* of what the text is about. For everyday devices, this would include the components of the electronic or mechanical system, the spatial arrangement of components, the causal chain of events when the system operates, the mechanisms that explain each causal step, the functions of the device and device components, and the plans of agents who manipulate the system for various purposes. Finally, there is the *pragmatic interaction* level, which specifies the main messages or points that the author is trying to convey to the learner.

The *types* of cognitive representations are theoretically different from the *levels*. From the present standpoint, there are several types of knowledge representation affiliated with the explicit propositions and mental models. Illustrative examples of the types of knowledge representations that are important for military contexts are listed in Exhibit 10.1. As we discuss later, specific question categories are associated with particular types of knowledge representation.

Cognitive processes vary in levels of depth and difficulty. The major types of cognitive processes that are relevant to an analysis of questions are listed in Exhibit 10.2 (Bloom, 1956). According to Bloom's (1956) taxonomy of cognitive objectives, the cognitive processes with higher numbers are more difficult and require greater depth. Recognition and recall are the easiest, comprehension is intermediate, and Classes 4 through 7 are the most difficult. It is debatable whether there are differences in difficulty among Categories 4 through 7, so in most applications of Bloom's taxonomy they are collapsed into one category.

Question Taxonomies

Schemes for analyzing the qualitative characteristics of questions have been proposed by researchers in the fields of education (Beck et al., 1997; Ciardiello, 1998), psychology (Graesser & Person, 1994), computational

Important Types of Knowledge Representation for the Military

Agents: Organized sets of troops, units, organizations, countries, complex software units, etc. Examples are organizational charts, friend–foe networks, and client-server networks.

Class inclusion: One concept is a subtype or subclass of another concept. For example, an *M1A2* is-a *tank* is-a *weapon system*.

Spatial layout: Spatial relations among regions and entities in regions. For example, *Eagle Base* is-in *Bosnia* is-in *Eastern Europe*. *Bosnia* is-south-of *Germany*.

Compositional structures: Components have subparts and subcomponents. For example, *a computer has-as-parts a monitor, keyboard, CPU, and memory*.

Procedures and plans: A sequence of steps/actions in a procedure accomplishes a goal. Examples are performance steps in disassembling and removing a mine, and the sequence of actions to create a command post filter in the common tactical picture application.

Causal chains and networks: An event is caused by a sequence of events and enabling states. Examples are the stages in firing an artillery round and the chain of events in a battle.

Others: Property descriptions, quantitative specifications, rules, mental states of agents.

linguistics (Harabagiu, Maiorano, & Pasca, 2002), and artificial intelligence (Schank, 1986). Instead of reviewing all of these schemes, we adopt the taxonomy proposed by Graesser and Person (1994). The Graesser–Person taxonomy is both grounded theoretically in cognitive science and has been successfully applied to a large number of question corpora (e.g., human and

EXHIBIT 10.2
Types of Cognitive Processes That are Relevant to Questions

Recognition: The process of verbatim identification of specific content (e.g., terms, facts, rules, methods, principles, procedures, objects) that was explicitly mentioned in the text.

Recall: The process of actively retrieving from memory and producing content that was explicitly mentioned in the text.

Comprehension: Demonstrating understanding of the text at the mental model level by generating inferences, interpreting, paraphrasing, translating, explaining, or summarizing.

Application: The process of applying knowledge extracted from text to a problem, situation, or case (fictitious or real world) that was not explicitly mentioned in the text.

Analysis: The process of decomposing elements and linking relationships between elements.

Synthesis: The processing of assembling new patterns and structures, such as constructing a novel solution to a problem or composing a novel message to an audience.

Evaluation: The process of judging the value or effectiveness of a process, procedure, or entity, according to some criteria and standards.

EXHIBIT 10.3
Adaptation of Question Taxonomy Proposed
by Graesser and Person (1994)

Question category	Generic question frames and examples
1. Verification	Is X true or false? Did an event occur?
2. Disjunctive	Is X, Y, or Z the case?
3. Concept completion	Who? What? When? Where?
4. Feature specification	What qualitative properties does entity X have?
5. Quantification	What is the value of a quantitative variable? How much? How many?
6. Definition questions	What does X mean?
7. Example questions	What is an example or instance of a category?
8. Comparison	How is X similar to Y? How is X different from Y?
9. Interpretation	What concept or claim can be inferred from a static or active pattern of data?
10. Causal antecedent	What state or event causally led to an event or state? Why did an event occur? How did an event occur? How did a state come to exist?
11. Causal consequence	What are the consequences of an event or state? What if X occurred? What if X did not occur?
12. Goal orientation	What are the motives or goals behind an agent's action? Why did an agent do some action?
13. Instrumental/procedural	What plan or instrument allows an agent to accomplish a goal? How did agent do some action?
14. Enablement	What object or resource allows an agent to accomplish a goal?
15. Expectation	Why did some expected event *not* occur? Why does some expected state *not* exist?
16. Judgmental	What value does the answerer place on an idea or advice? What do you think of X? How would you rate X?
17. Assertion	A declarative statement that indicates the speaker does not understand an idea.
18. Request/directive	The questioner wants the listener to perform some action.

computer tutoring, questions asked while using a new computer system, questions asked while comprehending text, questions raised in television news, and questions posed in letters to an editor). The taxonomy is presented in Exhibit 10.3.

The 18 categories in the Graesser–Person taxonomy are defined according to the content of the information sought rather than on question signal words (*who, what, why, how,* etc.). The question categories can be recognized by particular generic question frames (which are comparatively distinctive) but not simply by signal words (which can be ambiguous). As discussed earlier, generic question frames are easier to teach to learners and produce more learning gains than do signal words (King & Rosenshine, 1993;

Rosenshine et al., 1996). Exhibit 10.3 includes the generic question frame for each question category.

Deep comprehension of the material would presumably be expected to inspire questions at deeper levels of processing. Graesser and Person (1994) scaled SIS questions on two different dimensions of depth in their investigations of human tutoring. Of all of the questions that students asked, .28 of the questions were SIS questions. Graesser and Person proposed that some of the categories of SIS questions are associated with deep comprehension and cognitive processes. Specifically, they regarded Question Categories 10 through 15 as deep-reasoning questions because they tapped causal networks, planning, and logical justifications (i.e., answers to *why, how, what-if,* and *what-if-not* questions; see Exhibit 10.3). The proportion of SIS questions that were deep reasoning was recorded for each student in tutoring sessions on research methods and basic mathematics. A separate set of trained judges classified the same sample of SIS questions on depth, using five levels that map onto Bloom's (1956) taxonomy (see Exhibit 10.2). A question depth score, which consisted of the proportion of SIS questions that were in the deeper levels of Bloom's taxonomy, was computed for each student. Graesser and Person reported that there was a .64 correlation between depth score and the proportion of student questions that were deep-reasoning questions. Most of the student questions were shallow (70%) rather than deep (30%). One important result of the study was that, overall, students rarely ask deep-reasoning questions (.30 deep questions × .28 SIS questions = .08 deep-reasoning questions, or 8%). This finding is compatible with one major conclusion in the present report: Getting learners to ask good questions is an uphill challenge.

The majority of student questions (72%) were not SIS questions. Instead, they were questions that simply verify what they already know ("Aren't I supposed to add these columns?" "Doesn't a factorial design have two independent variables?") or that address the social interaction between student and tutor ("Is it my turn?" "What did you say?" "When does this session end?"). We call these *common-ground questions* and *metacommunication questions*, respectively. We expect that these common-ground and meta-communication questions will emerge frequently in synchronous distributed learning, particularly when the learner cannot see the instructor. In contrast, we expect them to be less frequent in asynchronous distributed learning systems because there is a cost in having a delayed answer and because the benefits of such communications are not adequate to justify an unpredictable wait (see Assumption 7 in the list of assumptions behind SIS questions). SIS questions should be more prevalent in asynchronous than synchronous distributed learning because time to reflect and compose a question is not constrained.

Shallow knowledge is sufficient in some educational and training contexts, although it should be recognized that shallow knowledge does not necessarily transfer well to real world practical situations. For example, shallow learning is prevalent when many people learn about the components of a computer, the jargon, and the relevant acronyms. However, this shallow knowledge will not help much when the person needs to apply it in a real-world task of repairing a broken computer. There are occasions when deep knowledge is necessary. Such knowledge involves a different distribution across the cells in the landscape of questions. Such a landscape would be generated when one orthogonally crosses the types of knowledge representation (K; see Exhibit 10.1), the types of cognitive processes (P; see Exhibit 10.2), and the types of questions (Q; see Exhibit 10.3). The KPQ landscape of questions should presumably be considered when designing the question facilities in learning environments and scrutinizing the learning objectives. We believe this landscape of questions will be useful to designers of tests and advanced distributed learning environments because it will expand the horizons on what questions are possible. The vast majority of test questions are shallow in current educational and training practices (Martinez, 1999). Our hope is that the depth and scope of the questions will broaden in advanced learning environments and will thereby improve learning.

Multiple-Choice Question Formats

Test questions can appear in many different formats. The most popular are multiple choice, true–false, matching, short-answer completion, and essay. Multiple choice is the most frequent format and is routinely adopted in tests constructed by the College Board and the Educational Testing Service (e.g., the Scholastic Aptitude Test), the information technology training enterprise (e.g., the certification exams for Microsoft, Cisco, and Novell), and the military (e.g., the Armed Services Vocational Aptitude Battery). Essay questions are sometimes more useful than multiple-choice questions in diagnosing cognitive states and tracing cognitive processes (Dwyer, 2005; Martinez, 1999), but properly constructed multiple-choice items can do an excellent job of tapping complex thought and deep knowledge. There is a rich psychometric tradition in the construction of multiple-choice items on such tests (American Educational Research Association, American Psychological Association, & National Council on Measurement in Education, 1985; Downing & Haladyna, 1997; U.S. Department of Defense, 1983). In this section, we discuss how to construct a good multiple-choice question because this question format is by far the most frequent one adopted in textbooks, e-learning, and schools.

To start, it is important to distinguish between format and content. The *format* refers to the composition of the question elements, methods of circumventing comprehension difficulty, and methods to minimize "giving away the answer" to sophisticated guessers. The *content* refers to the level and type of knowledge tapped (see Exhibit 10.1) and to cognitive processes (see Exhibit 10.2). The following terminology is adopted when describing question format:

- *context*: information that sets the stage and precedes the question stem;
- *stem*: the focal question, without the answer options;
- *key*: the correct answer among the set of alternatives; and
- *distracters*: the incorrect options among the set of alternatives.

In most applications, there are four or five answer options and only one correct answer. It is recommended that the distracter items should vary by degree. For example, one distracter should be the *near-miss*. This is the most seductive distracter that reflects a common misconception that learners have. The discrimination between the key and the near-miss should reflect an important learning objective or pedagogical point rather than being arbitrarily subtle or merely tapping frivolous detail. The *thematic distracter* has content that is related to the topic at hand but is not correct. A learner who quickly scans the learning materials would have trouble discriminating the key, the near-miss, and the thematic distracter. The *unrelated distracter* would seem reasonable to someone who never read the material but is in fact unrelated to the lesson content.

The difficulty of constructing multiple-choice questions perhaps explains one outcome of our literature search on learning through question generation. We were interested in empirical research that tested whether the process of learners generating multiple-choice questions might improve their comprehension of learning material. The process of generating such questions would presumably facilitate test performance because it would prepare them for the sort of tests that they would probably receive (i.e., following the principle of transfer-appropriate processing). We discovered that empirical research on this research question is conspicuously absent. It appears that it is extremely difficult to train learners how to ask multiple-choice questions that satisfy multiple constraints. Indeed, it is also difficult to train teachers and item writers for textbooks how to generate good multiple-choice questions. One promising direction for future research is to develop authoring tools to guide students, step by step, in composing high-quality multiple-choice questions about the material they read. The authoring tool would need to scaffold the learner in constructing questions that follow the particular formats, constraints, and content features discussed in this chapter.

EMPIRICAL STUDIES OF QUESTION GENERATION

There is an idealistic vision that learners are vigorous question-generators who actively self-regulate their learning. They identify their own knowledge deficits, ask questions that focus on these deficits, and answer the questions by exploring reliable information sources. This idealistic vision unfortunately is an illusion because the vast majority of learners have trouble identifying their own knowledge deficits (Azevedo & Cromley, 2004; Hacker, Dunlosky, & Graesser, 1998) and ask very few questions (Dillon, 1988; Good, Slavings, Harel, & Emerson, 1987). Graesser and Person's (1994) estimate of available studies revealed that the typical student asks 0.17 questions per hour in a classroom and that the poverty of classroom questions is a general phenomenon across cultures. The fact that it takes several hours for a typical student to ask one question in a classroom is perhaps not surprising because it would be impractical for a typical teacher to accommodate 25 inquisitive students. The rate of question-asking is higher in one-on-one learning environments. An average student asks 26.5 questions per hour in one-on-one human tutoring sessions (Graesser & Person, 1994). Thus, when there is an attentive question-answerer, the rate of student question-asking goes up 200-fold.

The upper bound in the number of student questions per hour is 135. This estimate is based on college students interacting with Point & Query educational software (Graesser et al., 1993, 2004). The only way that these students could learn about a topic (e.g., woodwind instruments) was by asking questions and by reading answers to their questions. To ask a question, the learner first points to a word, phrase, picture element, or other hot spot on the computer screen in a hypertext system. Second, a menu of relevant questions about the hot spot is presented to the learner (e.g., "What does X mean?", "What does X look like?"). Third, the learner selects one of the question options. Fourth, the answer is presented, and the learner reads the answer. This cycle continues until the learning session is finished. It is extremely easy for a learner to ask a question; it simply involves two clicks of a mouse: one to select the hot spot and the other to select the question. The Point & Query software is similar to some other menu-based question-asking systems (Sebrechts & Swartz, 1991). In this ideal learning environment, the student asks over 700 times as many questions as in a classroom.

Depth of Questions

As we reported earlier, student questions are normally shallow, short-answer questions that recycle through the content and interpretation of explicit material; they rarely tap the deeper levels of knowledge representation and cognitive processes. Students mirror what a teacher does in the classroom: Only about 4% of teacher questions are deep questions (Dillon, 1988; Kerry, 1987). Advanced distributed learning environments have the potential to improve the quality, in addition to the quantity, of student questions. For example, the quality of student questions might improve in Point & Query software that presents only good questions for the students to model. Graesser et al. (1993) found that five times as many deep-reasoning questions were asked when there were deep question options on the Point & Query question menu and the students were given a task that required deep reasoning. Craig, Gholson, Ventura, Graesser, & TRG (2001) presented college students with conversational computer agents that modeled good question-asking behavior. There were dyads of animated conversational agents (i.e., talking heads with synthesized speech) that asked questions and answered each other's questions about topics in computer literacy. In a control condition, the talking heads delivered the same content through monologues consisting of assertions about computer literacy. There were over twice as many deep-reasoning questions in the condition that had the agents model question-asking than in the control condition. Recall for the content was also significantly higher in the question-asking and -answering modeling condition than in the control condition. These findings confirm the conclusions presented earlier that learning gains can be realized by training students in how to ask questions.

Collaborative Question Generation

Group question-asking may provide an environment that enhances learning and question-asking. For example, Adafe (1998) had groups of students generate questions that would appear on an examination. The participants were children, and the topic was mathematics. Each group contributed one or more questions on an examination. This method apparently improved learning because the percentage of grades of C or better increased from 71% to 89% in a group of 30 students. It unfortunately is difficult to determine whether these advantages in learning gains could be attributed to question generation per se or to group learning. Researchers have reported that group learning has several advantages over individual learning (Slavin, 1995; Springer, Stanne, & Donovan, 1999).

Another example of empirical research on collaborative question generation was conducted by the Army Research Institute (Belanich, Wisher, & Orvis, 2003). The research tested the effects on learning of a specialized version of TEAMThink, a novel question-based learning application that stimulates students to actively engage in the creation of questions through small group collaboration over the Internet. The experiments were conducted as part of training programs at three Army schools. The soldiers first completed a Web-based, self-paced tutorial that instructed them on how to write effective multiple-choice questions. The soldiers subsequently generated multiple-choice questions, and then other soldiers critiqued questions authored by their teammates on the same topic. For each question, the four-step procedure was as follows: (a) answer the question; (b) show the proposed correct answer by the author; (c) provide written feedback, such as disagreeing with the author, rewording the question stem, editing the distracters, and so on; and (d) comment on feedback from other teammates on the particular questions. A total of 336 questions were authored across the three schools. The instructors accepted 77% of the questions in terms of technical and doctrinal accuracy. One analysis of learning assessed the percentage of questions answered correctly during a TEAMChallenge, comparing the experimental and control groups. The participants in the experimental group answered 76% of the questions correctly, compared with 68% in the control group. This 8% difference between means was statistically significant, with an effect size of 0.73.

Now that we have covered the theoretical and empirical research on question-asking and learning, we shift the focus to the role of questions in future advanced distributed learning systems. The remaining section should be regarded as informed speculation. It is informed because of the existing body of research reported in the first two sections. It is speculative, however, because research on questions is conspicuously absent in the current distributed learning environments. Existing empirical data are so sparse and fragmented that we have to rely on basic research and theory to support our speculations. This research deficit is not surprising given that there have been few evaluations of distributed learning environments with adequate methodological controls and control groups (Wisher & Champagne, 2000).

PRACTICES FOR INCREASING THE FREQUENCY AND QUALITY OF QUESTIONS

Available research supports a number of conclusions about QGL. As we have expressed repeatedly in this chapter, we know that QGL is effective in promoting learning gains. However, we have also pointed out that learners need to be trained to ask questions because they ask very few questions in most learning environments, and most of the questions are low in quality (i.e., shallow rather than deep). Students clearly need some scaffolding to encourage first, any question at all, and second, deep questions. In this section, we propose methods for increasing the frequency and quality of questions.

Practice 1: Clarify the Learning Objectives and Test Criteria

The learner can evaluate what questions are relevant if he or she knows the objectives and criteria. Without this clarity, there are barriers in the question-generation stages of identifying knowledge deficits and social editing. Some learning objectives, such as assembling a new computer and logging onto a network, require only shallow and procedural knowledge. The test is whether computers get assembled and the learner successfully logs onto the system. Other learning objectives require deep knowledge about causal mechanisms, as in the case of diagnosing and repairing equipment. Designers of learning environments should provide examples of test questions that appropriately map onto the relevant cells in the matrix of questions appropriate to an educational or training program.

Practice 2: Present Challenges That Create Cognitive Disequilibrium

SIS questions are triggered by cognitive disequilibrium (Graesser, Lu, Olde, Cooper-Pye, & Whitten, 2005; Graesser & Olde, 2003); that is, the learner needs to be presented challenges in the form of obstacles to goals, anomalous events, contradictions, discrepancies, obvious gaps in knowledge, and decisions that require discrimination among equally attractive alternatives. Such challenges are most engaging when they are not too easy or too difficult but are at the learner's zone of proximal development (Rogoff, 1990; VanLehn et al., in press; Vygotsky, 1978). This can be accomplished by having the distributed learning system track the learner's mastery of the material and present challenges that are tailored to the learner's profile. The challenges consist of example problems to solve, procedural tasks to execute, and breakdown scenarios to fix.

Practice 3: Give Feedback on Particular Comprehension Deficits

Most learners do not have good comprehension calibration skills, so they do not notice the knowledge deficits that would otherwise drive questions. Feedback on particular knowledge deficits ends up penetrating the "illusion of comprehension" and promoting deeper comprehension and also deeper questions. Intelligent tutoring systems are capable of recognizing bugs, misconceptions, and knowledge deficits at a fine-grained level (Aleven & Koedinger, 2002; Graesser, VanLehn, Rose, Jordan, & Harter, 2001), so the intelligent-tutoring system technology would be one source of implementing this method in future advanced distributed learning environments.

Practice 4: Present Examples of Good Questions

A learner can acquire good question-asking skills by modeling good question-askers (Craig et al., 2004, 2001). Examples of good questions, regardless of format, can be available in relevant cells in the landscape of questions. The learner can observe these question items by pointing to different hot spots on the graphical user interface or in a Help facility. Alternatively, pairs of avatars can exhibit good questions in virtual dialogues. These modeling approaches have proven effective in improving the quantity and quality of questions.

Practice 5: Present Generic Question Frames

Generic question frames (e.g., "What does X mean?", "How do you do X?"; see Exhibit 10.3) guide the user in selecting and articulating questions. They are pitched at a somewhat more abstract level than actual questions, but there is a finite number of frames that are acquired by the learner. The Point & Query interface (Graesser et al., 1993, 2004) adopts these generic question frames and substantially improves the quantity and quality of learner questions. The learner discovers categories of good questions by examining the options on the question menu. The designer of the learning environment can tailor the question options to fulfill the learning objectives and the subject-matter constraints.

Practice 6: Use Conversational Agents to Scaffold the Construction of Questions

Researchers have developed computer-generated, animated talking heads that have facial features synchronized with synthesized speech and appropriate gestures (Johnson, Rickel, & Lester, 2000). These conversational agents have been used as navigators on Web pages, as narrators, as avatars, and as tutors in intelligent tutoring systems. For example, AutoTutor (Graesser et al., 2004; Graesser, Person, Harter, & TRG, 2001) is a conversational agent that teaches students about introductory computer literacy by holding a conversation. Dialogue moves in AutoTutor include backchannel feedback ("Uh-huh," "Okay"), pumps ("Tell me more"), prompts ("Primary memory includes ROM and ____"), assertions, hints, corrections, summaries, questions, and a variety of other speech acts. A turn-by-turn dialogue scaffolds the learner to articulate information.

Conversational agents could be developed to guide learners in articulating questions in various formats, including multiple-choice questions. For example, the agent could follow the following script that guides the user in generating a multiple-choice question: select a question from a cell in the landscape of questions, show an example question in a selected cell, generate a question stem, generate the key, generate a near-miss distracter, generate a thematic distracter, and generate a remote distracter. Each step would be scaffolded by a dialogue manager that allows learners to ask clarification questions (e.g., "What is a stem?"), that answers these questions, that makes suggestions ("At this point, you need to generate a stem"), that gives feedback ("Uh-huh," "That's right," "Okay"), and that gives hints ("Is there an important misconception that motivates this near-miss?"). A conversational agent for question generation is well within the realm of current technologies.

Practice 7: Have Groups Generate Questions Collaboratively

In the TEAMThink project on group question generation, one student generates a multiple-choice question and key, whereas partners in a small group critique the question as well as the proposed distracters (Belanich et al., 2003). Later, the generated questions are used on tests with other small groups. To improve the quality of the questions, researchers could offer feedback from an expert composer before a final question is revised. One other possible augmentation would be to have a competitive game in which groups compete in their generation of questions. A performance-based assessment would be to have other learners, in other groups, answer the questions and to evaluate the questions on discriminative validity (high-performing students answering a question correctly, but with low-performing students missing it). There are other role assignments that might produce more questions, better questions, and/or more learning. One learner could generate the question stem, a second the key, a third the near-miss, a fourth the thematic distracter, and a fifth the remote distracter. Each learner would also justify what is produced from the standpoint of content or question quality. This approach might sharpen important distinctions and yield deeper learning.

Practice 8: Concretize the Author

The author of a document or lesson is normally invisible. Many readers assume that printed text is indisputable truth instead of the best possible account that an author could prepare at a particular point in time. Beck et al. (1997) designed a Questioning the Author method that trains students to imagine an author in flesh and blood and to question what the author says. Why does the author make a particular claim? What evidence is there? How does one idea in a text relate to another idea? The Questioning the

Author method improves questions, comprehension, and metacomprehension. Designers of learning environments can take a significant step in concretizing the author by providing pictures, biographies, and other information about the author.

Practice 9: Reuse of Questions

One goal of the advanced distributed learning initiative (viz., http://www.adlnet.org) is to develop learning content as component units, called *learning objects*, that can be tagged, coded in a repository, identified, and reused or repurposed for other instructional applications. Sharable Content Object Reference Model is a reference model based on emerging e-learning industry standard specifications; it permits interoperability of learning content and learning management systems. The model includes a specification (developed by the IMS Global Learning Consortium for question and test interoperability). The specification defines a standard format that allows interoperability for questions and tests between different computer systems. Computer software that supports question and test interoperability will allow export into and import from this format, so that if a person computerizes questions or tests on one system, then the material will also be usable on another system. This allows exchange of questions between learning management systems, content authors, content libraries, and other forms of question pools.

CLOSING COMMENTS

This chapter provides a rationale for question generation as a viable learning multiplier in future advanced distributed learning environments. On the basis of this review, nine practices were identified for immediate use in both classroom and distributed learning settings. If used properly, question-generation strategies can increase a learner's depth of understanding of content that ranges from shallow facts to the inner workings of a complex system. This is beneficial for both immediate learning and improved retention over time because the degree of original learning is the best single predictor of knowledge and skill retention (Wisher, Curnow, & Seidel, 2001; Wisher, Sabol, & Ellis, 1999). The advantages of question generation in training are particularly important for the future workforce because training is expected to move from the classroom to a learner-centric mode of delivery. Instead of being an afterthought in future advanced distributed learning environments, a question-generation mechanism should be an essential and integral feature.

REFERENCES

Adafe, V. U. (1998). Students generating test items: A teaching and assessment strategy. *The Mathematics Teacher, 91,* 198–202.

Aleven, V., & Koedinger, K. R. (2002). An effective metacognitive strategy: Learning by doing and explaining with a computer-based cognitive tutor. *Cognitive Science, 26,* 147–179.

American Educational Research Association, American Psychological Association, & National Council on Measurement in Education. (1985). *Standards for educational and psychological testing.* Washington, DC: American Psychological Association.

Azevedo, R., & Cromley, J. G. (2004). Does training on self-regulated learning facilitate students' learning with hypermedia? *Journal of Educational Psychology, 96,* 523–535.

Beck, I. L., McKeown, M. G., Hamilton, R. L., & Kucan, L. (1997). *Questioning the Author: An approach for enhancing student engagement with text.* Newark, DE: International Reading Association.

Belanich, J., Wisher, R. A., & Orvis, K. L. (2003). *Web-based collaborative learning: An assessment of a question generation approach* (Technical Report No. 1133). Alexandria, VA: U.S. Army Research Institute for the Behavioral and Social Sciences.

Bloom, B. S. (1956). *Taxonomy of educational objectives: The classification of educational goals. Handbook I: Cognitive domain.* New York: McKay.

Bransford, J. D., Brown, A. L., & Cocking, R. R. (2000). *How people learn: Brain, mind, experience, and school.* Washington, DC: National Academy Press.

Chi, M. T. H., de Leeuw, N., Chiu, M., & LaVancher, C. (1994). Eliciting self-explanations improves understanding. *Cognitive Science, 18,* 439–477.

Ciardiello, A. V. (1998). Did you ask a good question today? Alternative cognitive and metacognitive strategies. *Journal of Adolescent & Adult Literacy, 42,* 210–219.

Craig, S. D., Gholson, B., & Sullins, J. (2004). Should we question them? An investigation into the role of deep questions in vicarious learning environments. In J. Nall & R. Robson (Eds.), *Proceedings of E-learn 2004: World conference on e-learning in corporate, government, healthcare, & higher education* (pp. 1836–1840). Norfolk, VA: Association for the Advancement of Computing in Education.

Craig, S. D., Gholson, B., Ventura, M., Graesser, A. C., & The Tutoring Research Group. (2001). Overhearing dialogues and monologues in virtual tutoring sessions: Effects on questioning and vicarious learning. *International Journal of Artificial Intelligence in Education, 11,* 242–253.

Craik, F. I. M., & Lockhart, R. S. (1972). Levels of processing: A framework for memory research. *Journal of Verbal Learning and Verbal Behavior, 11,* 671–684.

Dillon, T. J. (1988). *Questioning and teaching: A manual of practice*. New York: Teachers College Press.

Downing, S. M., & Haladyna, T. M. (1997). Test item development: Validity evidence from quality assurance procedures. *Applied Measurement in Education, 10*, 61–82.

Dwyer, C. A. (Ed.). (2005). *Measurement and research in the accountability era*. Mahwah, NJ: Erlbaum.

Edelson, D. C., Gordin, D. N., & Pea, R. D. (1999). Addressing the challenges of inquiry-based learning through technology and curriculum design. *Journal of the Learning Sciences, 8*, 391–450.

Good, T. L., Slavings, R. L., Harel, K. H., & Emerson, M. (1987). Students' passivity: A study of question asking in K–12 classrooms. *Sociology of Education, 60*, 181–199.

Graesser, A. C., Gordon, S. E., & Brainerd, L. E. (1992). QUEST: A model of question answering. *Computers and Mathematics With Applications, 23*, 733–745.

Graesser, A. C., Hu, X., Person, N. K., Jackson, T., & Toth, J. (2004). Modules and information retrieval facilities of the Human Use Regulatory Affairs Advisor (HURAA). *International Journal on eLearning, 3*, 29–39.

Graesser, A. C., Langston, M. C., & Baggett, W. B. (1993). Exploring information about concepts by asking questions. In G. V. Nakamura, R. M. Taraban, & D. Medin (Eds.), *The psychology of learning and motivation: Vol. 29. Categorization by humans and machines* (pp. 411–436). Orlando, FL: Academic Press.

Graesser, A. C., Lu, S., Olde, B. A., Cooper-Pye, E., & Whitten, S. (2005). Question asking and eye tracking during cognitive disequilibrium: Comprehending illustrated texts on devices when the devices break down. *Memory & Cognition, 33*, 1235–1247.

Graesser, A. C., McNamara, D. S., & VanLehn, K. (2005). Scaffolding deep comprehension strategies through Point&Query, AutoTutor, and iSTART. *Educational Psychologist, 40*, 225–234.

Graesser, A. C., & Olde, B. A. (2003). How does one know whether a person understands a device? The quality of the questions the person asks when the device breaks down. *Journal of Educational Psychology, 95*, 524–536.

Graesser, A. C., & Person, N. K. (1994). Question asking during tutoring. *American Educational Research Journal, 31*, 104–137.

Graesser, A. C., Person, N., Harter, D., & The Tutoring Research Group. (2001). Teaching tactics and dialog in AutoTutor. *International Journal of Artificial Intelligence in Education, 12*, 257–279

Graesser, A. C., VanLehn, K., Rose, C., Jordan, P., & Harter, D. (2001). Intelligent tutoring systems with conversational dialogue. *AI Magazine, 22*, 39–51.

Greer, J., McCalla, G., Collins, J., Kumar, V., Meagher, P., & Vassileva, J. (1998). Supporting peer help and collaboration in distributed workplace environments. *International Journal of Artificial Intelligence in Education, 9*, 159–177.

Hacker, D. J., Dunlosky, J., & Graesser, A. C. (Eds.). (1998). *Metacognition in educational theory and practice*. Mahwah, NJ: Erlbaum.

Harabagiu, S. M., Maiorano, S. J., & Pasca, M. A. (2002). Open-domain question answering techniques. *Natural Language Engineering, 1,* 1–38.

IMS Global Learning Consortium, Inc. (n.d.). *IMS question and test interoperability specification.* Retrieved December 19, 2006, from http://www.imsglobal.org/question/index.html

Johnson, W. L., Rickel, J. W., & Lester, J. C. (2000). Animated pedagogical agents: Face-to-face interaction in interactive learning environments. *International Journal of Artificial Intelligence in Education, 11,* 47–78.

Kerry, T. (1987). Classroom questions in England. *Questioning Exchange, 1,* 32–33.

King, A. (1992). Comparison of self-questioning, summarizing, and notetaking-review as strategies for learning from lectures. *American Educational Research Journal, 29,* 303–323.

King, A. (1994). Guiding knowledge construction in the classroom: Effects of teaching children how to question and how to explain. *American Educational Research Journal, 31,* 338–368.

King, A., & Rosenshine, B. (1993). Effects of guided cooperative-questioning on children's knowledge construction. *Journal of Experimental Education, 6,* 127–148.

Kintsch, W. (1998). *Comprehension: A paradigm for cognition.* Cambridge, England: Cambridge University Press.

Lehmann, F. (Ed.). (1992). *Semantic networks in artificial intelligence.* New York: Pergamon Press.

MacGregor, S. K. (1988). Use of self-questioning with a computer-mediated text system and measures of reading performance. *Journal of Reading Behavior, 20,* 131–148.

Martinez, M. E. (1999). Cognition and the question of test item format. *Educational Psychologist, 34,* 207–218.

McNamara, D. S. (2004). SERT: Self-explanation reading training. *Discourse Processes, 38,* 1–30.

National Council of Teachers of English. (1996). *Standards for the English language arts.* Urbana, IL: International Reading Association.

National Research Council. (1996). *National science education standards.* Washington, DC: National Academy Press.

Ogata, H., Sueda, T., Furugori, N., & Yano, Y. (1999). Augmenting collaboration beyond classrooms through online social networks. In G. Cumming, T. Okamoto, & L. Gomez (Eds.), *Advanced Research in Computers and Communications in Education, ICCE '99,* (pp. 277–284). Amsterdam: IOS Press.

Palinscar, A. S., & Brown, A. L. (1984). Reciprocal teaching of comprehension-fostering and comprehension-monitoring activities. *Cognition and Instruction, 1,* 117–175.

Pressley, M., & Forrest-Pressley, D. (1985). Questions and children's cognitive processing. In A. C. Graesser & J. B. Black (Eds.), *The psychology of questions* (pp. 277–296). Hillsdale, NJ: Erlbaum.

Rogoff, B. (1990). *Apprenticeship in thinking.* New York: Oxford University Press.

Rosenshine, B., Meister, C., & Chapman, S. (1996). Teaching students to generate questions: A review of the intervention studies. *Review of Educational Research, 66,* 181–221.

Schank, R. C. (1986). *Explanation patterns: Understanding mechanically and creatively.* Hillsdale, NJ: Erlbaum.

Sebrechts, M. M., & Swartz, M. L. (1991). Question asking as a tool for novice computer skill acquisition. In S. P. Robertson, G. M. Olson, & J. S. Olson (Eds.), *Proceedings of the ACM CHI 91 Human Factors in Computing Systems Conference* (pp. 293–299). New York: Association for Computing Machinery.

Slavin, R. E. (1995). *Cooperative learning: Theory, research, and practice* (2nd ed.). Boston: Allyn & Bacon.

Snow, C. (2002). *Reading for understanding: Toward an R&D program in reading comprehension.* Santa Monica, CA: RAND.

Songer, N. B. (1996). Exploring learning opportunities in coordinated network-enhanced classrooms: A case of kids as global scientists. *Journal of the Learning Sciences, 5,* 297–327.

Springer, L., Stanne, M. E., & Donovan, S. S. (1999). Effects of small-group learning on undergraduates in science, mathematics, engineering, and technology: A meta-analysis. *Review of Educational Research, 69,* 21–51.

U.S. Department of Defense. (1983). *Armed Services Vocational Aptitude Battery, Form 12a.* Washington, DC: Author.

Van der Meij, H. (1987). Assumptions of information-seeking questions. *Questioning Exchange, 1,* 111–118.

VanLehn, K., Graesser, A. C., Jackson, G. T., Jordan, P., Olney, A., & Rose, C. P. (in press). When are tutorial dialogues more effective than reading? *Cognitive Science.*

Vygotsky, L. S. (1978). *Mind in society.* Cambridge, MA: Harvard University Press.

Webb, N. M., Troper, J. D., & Fall, R. (1995). Constructive activity and learning in collaborative small groups. *Journal of Experimental Psychology, 87,* 406–423.

Wisher, R. A. (2003). Reaching out after 5 years: Advanced distributed learning moves beyond developing standards. *Training and Simulation Journal, 4*(2), 12–13.

Wisher, R. A., & Champagne, M. V. (2000). Distance learning and training: An evaluation perspective. In S. Tobias & J. Fletcher (Eds.), *Training and retraining: A handbook for business, industry, government, and military* (pp. 385–409). New York: Macmillan Reference USA.

Wisher, R. A., Curnow, C. K., & Seidel, R. J. (2001). Knowledge retention as a latent outcome measure in distance learning. *American Journal of Distance Education, 15*(3), 20–35.

Wisher, R. A., Sabol, M. A., & Ellis, J. (1999). *Staying sharp: The retention of military knowledge and skills* (Special Report No. 39). Alexandria, VA: U.S. Army Research Institute for the Behavioral and Social Sciences.

IV

CONCLUSIONS

11

PROBLEMS AND POSSIBILITIES: STRATEGICALLY PURSUING A SCIENCE OF LEARNING IN DISTRIBUTED ENVIRONMENTS

STEPHEN M. FIORE AND EDUARDO SALAS

Science is about problems and about possibilities—solving problems and realizing possibilities. It is a paradoxically creative act in that one has to generate unique theories and methods that have not existed before to understand a phenomenon that oftentimes has already existed. Thus, scientific discoveries are often the hallmark of creative genius, and history is replete with accolades cast on the lone scientist who has helped us understand our world and our universe in new ways. Yet in the 21st century we are facing problems and possibilities at a level of complexity that we have not considered before. Indeed, it is critical to realize that "the way in which

The writing of this chapter was partially supported by Grant SBE0350345 from the National Science Foundation and by Grant N000140610118 from the Office of Naval Research. The opinions and views of the authors are their own and do not necessarily reflect the opinions of the University of Central Florida, the National Science Foundation, the Office of Naval Research, or the U.S. Government. There is no express or implied endorsement by the U.S. Government of any product discussed herein.

our universities have divided up the sciences does not reflect the way in which nature has divided up its problems" (Salzinger, 2003, p. 3). Addressing this requires not only creativity but also collaboration across disciplines, and the scientific community is recognizing that *multidisciplinarity* is no longer a buzzword but a 21st-century reality. Thus, these problems and possibilities require coordinated scientific efforts cutting across disciplines. To achieve this, researchers need a form of strategic science wherein scientific endeavors are coordinated such that the inherent creativity of science is not stifled but more appropriately channeled to target particular problems and realize particular possibilities.

For the concluding chapter to this volume, we choose to discuss the contributions along this line of strategic thinking in scientific pursuits. We do so because the science of learning is indeed one of the critical problems and unlimited possibilities we are facing in the 21st century. Technological innovation is increasing at a rapid rate, often outpacing worker capabilities in learning. At the same time, the demands for learning more complex material are filtering down earlier into the educational process. As such, we suggest that developing a science of learning for distributed learning and training requires a type of thinking that can target the gaps in our understanding of this complex phenomenon. Moving toward this goal requires a strategic coordination of multidisciplinary approaches whereby cognitive, organizational, and social psychology interact to help us better understand the complex behavioral and technological issues inherent to learning and performance that take place at a distance. To close this volume, then, we choose not to summarize the contributions. Instead, we conceive of how these contributions can be viewed more strategically to support the burgeoning science of learning. Recall that our goal in this volume was to address a subset of the important areas emerging in distributed learning and training. The contributors have helped us substantially by outlining theory and data that address particular questions and provide substantial answers. With this chapter, we now take on the challenge of strategically integrating the ideas within this volume to direct where a science of learning dedicated to distributed learning and training should take us. We offer these ideas to stimulate thinking and to encourage discussion of the science of learning at the highest level.

Strategic thinking in science must necessarily first be conceptualized from a macro-level perspective. Because of this, we outline our ideas through the lens of science policy and discuss how strategic thinking needs to drive scientific funding if we are to truly address the societal needs associated with understanding learning. Toward this end, we describe how the scientific community can pursue a model of strategic science developed through the integration of concepts that have emerged in science policy debates and discussions over the past 10 years. We divide this chapter into two primary sections. First, we summarize some of the broader scientific issues that have been circulating in policy debates so that we can inform readers of the types of ideas that will eventually affect scientific endeavors. Then we outline our conceptualization of a strategic science space where we have integrated a set of concepts that can guide science to better address the complex problems we are facing in the 21st century. This sets the stage for our second part, in which we then discuss the contributions to this volume within the context of our strategic science space to illustrate how the ideas presented in these chapters can be conceptualized as laying the foundation for a science of learning in distributed environments.

SCIENCE POLICY AND THE PURSUIT OF UNDERSTANDING

The 1990s was the beginning of what may turn out to be a fundamental change in the relationship between the scientific and policy communities. To comprehend this change, one must understand the origination of the federal funding model that was so influential in the tremendous gains in knowledge made during the latter half of the 20th century. The foundation of this issue is the fairly simple yet profoundly important distinction that has long been made between basic and applied research. Scientists and historians are beginning to document that fundamental scientific research and applied research are not separate categories (e.g., Bransford, Brown, & Cocking, 2000; Stokes, 1997) and, although a complete discussion of this topic is beyond the scope of this chapter, in this section we briefly review some of these ideas and the conceptual remedies that have been offered to resolve what is increasingly being seen as a policy dilemma.

Stokes (1997) argued that there exists an unnecessary tension because of this dichotomy between basic and applied research. He illustrated how humankind's quest for fundamental understanding, historically considered under the rubric of basic science, and humankind's considerations for use, typically considered applied science, did not originate as mutually exclusive categories of science but rather have been effectively integrated to produce important scientific gains. Others have analogously argued that the commingling of science and technology in basic and applied pursuits be viewed as a seamless web (see also Hoffman & Deffenbacher, 1993; Holton & Sonnert, 1999; Latham, 2001).

Stokes (1997) illustrated how important scientific gains were due to this form of commingling of basic and applied research. He used Louis Pasteur as the model for what he labeled *use-inspired basic research*, showing how Pasteur's groundbreaking studies in microbiology always had a consideration for use (i.e., disease prevention) yet still produced fundamental gains in understanding. On the basis of such examples, Stokes suggested that both science and science policy can benefit from a conceptualization of research as a matrix in which a quest for fundamental understanding is crossed with a consideration of use. Along analogous lines, Holton and Sonnert (1999) argued for a model of Jeffersonian science, based on the writings and actions of Thomas Jefferson. This approach has as its motivation a particular social problem about which people are scientifically ignorant. As Holton and Sonnert explained, the purpose of Jeffersonian research is "to remove that basic ignorance in an uncharted area of science and thereby to attain knowledge that will have a fair probability—even if it is years distant—of being brought to bear on a persistent, debilitating national (or international) problem" (p. 62).

Constructs such as use-inspired basic research or Jeffersonian science are a necessary but insufficient means with which to address the problems inherent in the basic–applied dichotomy. These are for the most part meta-scientific themes used to describe a particular area or form of research in which fundamental questions about a societal problem are investigated. What is lacking is direction about how science can more readily resolve problems of societal importance. This requires that members of the scientific community be marshaled so that they are more systematic in their pursuit of understanding writ large.

Our purpose in providing this brief overview of policy debates is that they effectively illustrate how we can begin conceptualizing models of strategic science dedicated to "understanding" and "use" in the area of distributed learning and training. In particular, the science of learning (see Bransford et al., 2000) exemplifies how an area of study can be effectively researched with varying goals. As we noted in the beginning of this volume, the contributing authors have all been on a "quest for fundamental understanding," that is, following an epistemological path, yet they have all had a focused "consideration for use." We now consider how science can be productively channeled by discussing components of our model of strategic science. These are an amalgam of constructs based on the aforementioned writings. Our goal is to describe how these approaches can be productively integrated to drive a science of learning focused on distributed environments. The components of this model we describe next are illustrated in Figure 11.1.

Research Drivers: Need or Curiosity

We characterize the first dimension of our strategic science space as the *research driver*, that is, the particular motivation behind a given research endeavor. We suggest that a research driver can be characterized as either need or curiosity. In the former case (falling in the left side of our research space), we have a particular societal need. This is contrasted with curiosity-driven science, where the motivation is purely for the sake of understanding

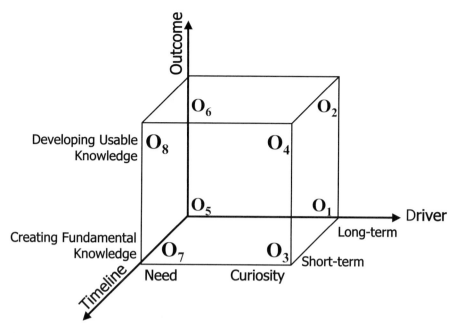

Figure 11.1. A model for strategically managing a science of learning.

a given phenomenon (the right portion of our space). More specifically, solving problems that fall on the left side of our space (i.e., need-driven problems) may more directly lead to viable solutions, but solving problems that fall on the right side of our space (i.e., curiosity-driven problems) may or may not readily produce solutions of more immediate viability.

Research Outcomes: Creation or Development of Knowledge

In his view of scientific research as a matrix, Stokes (1997) considered one dimension to be a quest for fundamental understanding and viewed research as either being on such a quest or not. We view our next dimension somewhat along the same line that Stokes discussed in that it describes research endeavors that either do or do not contribute to foundational (or new) knowledge. Nonetheless, we provide some clarification by suggesting that research outcomes can either lead to the creation of new knowledge (more closely aligned with basic research) or can contribute to the development of extant knowledge for usable purposes (more closely aligned with applied research). To solve certain problems or pursue differing lines of inquiry, members of a scientific field often recognize that there is knowledge that needs to be created and/or gaps to be filled before a research program can move forward. The distinguishing characteristic here is the degree to which research can create either a discrete change in our understanding of a phenomenon by creating new knowledge (lower portion of the space) or more of a continuous change of understanding through development of existing knowledge (upper portion). As such, this provides a descriptive means through which to illustrate that research outcomes can increase our understanding of the world, albeit in differing ways. The value of this dimension, then, is that it identifies the expected outcome of a given endeavor (i.e., creation or development of knowledge) and illustrates the important role that both approaches can play in the scientific process.

Research Time Frame: Short Term or Long Term

For our final dimension, we consider the time frame associated with a given research endeavor. Although risk is sometimes considered in the context of research decision making, the scientific community can more readily gauge the amount of time that needs to be invested in a particular research area to produce an outcome (whether it be creating new knowledge or the development of existing knowledge). Although this may seem like a benign distinction in that it maps easily onto the basic–applied research continuum, its inclusion in our framework serves an important purpose: It allows both the practicing scientific and the policy communities to recognize how projects should be considered in a larger context of strategic research. Furthermore, the concept of a time frame is not lost in writings on science policy. Holton and Sonnert (1999) stated that the goals of research endeavors vary from "practical, and *preferably rapid benefits* [italics added]" to the attainment of "knowledge that will have a fair probability—*even if it is years distant* [italics added]—of being brought to bear on a persistent, debilitating national (or international) problem" (p. 62). In short, because there is strategic value in recognizing the importance of the dimension of time to research decision making, our space considers both short-term and long-term endeavors. From a definitional standpoint, we approximate *short term* as being 6 years or less. This is roughly the time frame for two iterations of the standard 3-year research grant cycle, and one could expect tangible products, be they knowledge or tools, after these cycles. We approximate *long-term* research to be on the order of 9 or more years because the issues being addressed likely are complex enough to warrant several iterative cycles of investigation.

Summary

While fully acknowledging Stokes's (1997) important contributions to our understanding of science policy, here we wish to differentiate our model from Stokes's conceptualization. We view our approach as an adaptation of Stokes's model and not necessarily as a divergence from his approach.

TABLE 11.1
Basic–Applied Matrix of Research Quests

Quest for fundamental understanding	Consideration of use	
	No	Yes
No		Pure applied research (*Thomas Edison*)
Yes	˙ Pure basic research (*Niels Bohr*)	Use-inspired basic research (*Louis Pasteur*)

Note. From *Pasteur's Quadrant: Basic Science and Technological Innovation* (p. 73), by D. E. Stokes, 1997, Washington, DC: Brookings Institution Press. Copyright 1997 by the Brookings Institution. Reprinted with permission.

Recall that Stokes outlined how science and science policy can benefit from considering research not along a single continuum of basic versus applied but within a matrix that crosses a quest for fundamental understanding with a consideration of use (see Table 11.1). As can be seen in Stokes's matrix, although three of the four cells are easily filled, the upper left cell is not easily considered and leaves a conceptual gap in the articulation of the two axes. Our approach differs in several important respects. First, although our "Research Driver" axis is somewhat similar to the "Consideration of Use" axis, it is fundamentally different in that it allows for a clearer understanding of the genesis of research ideas, that is, it allows one to query whether the driving motivation is inherent curiosity or an attempt to solve a realized need. Second, our "Knowledge Outcome" axis differs from Stokes's "Quest for Fundamental Understanding" axis in that it provides a more useful description of the research products or outcomes. Simply stating whether a research project is on a quest for fundamental understanding does not as clearly convey the notion that a research outcome can still contribute to the body of knowledge as it currently exists. Specifically, a project can add to extant understanding on a given topic through what we described as a discrete change in our understanding, that is, something entirely new, or through more of a continuous development of knowledge, that is, by adding to our current understanding in more of a step-by-step process. Third, our axis presents more of a continuum and less of a hard, dichotomous distinction. This allows us to consider how research moves along these continua as concepts or research programs evolve. Fourth, and this is important, when these two axes are considered simultaneously it is natural to see how differing research programs can easily be conceptualized as fitting within the differing areas of these spaces. This allows us to address the blank cell in Stokes's matrix in that we leave no conceptual gaps.

It is important to reinforce that it is the overlap of these concepts that creates the conceptual environment that can guide research, and our approach is devised to allow research decision makers to conceptualize where and how to develop a field of inquiry (i.e., decide on research trajectories) as well as set time frames against these trajectories. We turn next to a discussion of how we implement this strategic science framework within the context of the content of this volume.

CREATING STRATEGIC RESEARCH PORTFOLIOS FOR DISTRIBUTED LEARNING AND TRAINING

As seen in Figure 11.1, we view the dimensions of our strategic science space not as separate but as intermingled. Our goal with explicating the aforementioned dimensions was to set the stage for how a science of learning can support various types of research activity that we describe as *strategic science*. This is described more generally as a type of research activity requiring the systematic and planful coordination of research targeting a particular area of inquiry. In strategic science, the research collectively addresses a problem that is broad in scope. Within such efforts, however, there are individual research projects, which we label *tactical science*, leading to an integrated outcome. In particular, tactical science comprises research activities that do not necessarily require collective activity on an individual basis but, when viewed in total, are addressing problems larger in scope. Policy and funding decisions, then, can be viewed as attempts to create a strategic portfolio of research projects that are tactically devised to address a particular subproblem. A *portfolio*, then, consists of a collection of tactical research efforts that simultaneously and/or systematically investigate a problem larger in scope. It is this type of strategic approach to solving scientific problems that we argue is warranted if researchers are to effectively develop a science of learning for distributed environments.

We turn now to a type of a priori conceptualization of what may comprise strategic portfolios of research endeavors dedicated to a science of learning in distributed environments. On the basis of portfolio models such as those found at the National Institutes of Health and those recently being developed at the Transportation Security Administration (see Fiore, Rubinstein, & Jentsch, 2004; Rubinstein, 2002), we propose a type of thought experiment to speculate on potential future paths for the contributions to this volume. Thus, instead of summarizing the contributions to this volume, given their strong theoretical base, we take them to the next level and ask how these concepts can be leveraged strategically. How can we channel these ideas so that they can begin the important process of helping us understand the complex issues that exist when learning and performance takes place at a distance? We use our strategic science space to enable a conceptualization of research trajectories designed to manage the development and use of knowledge that help us solve problems and realize possibilities. We have adopted this notion of trajectories on the basis of the theorizing of Vicente (2000), who proposed a metascientific model for use in the ergonomic sciences. Vicente convincingly showed how research trajectories within a given project can be outlined such that inquiry and methodologies are predetermined. Thus, Vicente's framework effectively explicates how the practice of science at the project level can be more systematically managed through carefully articulated research trajectories. Our goal is larger than viewing this at the project level; it has more to do with demonstration of how the scientific community can begin to envision a broader form of inquiry based on the theoretical contributions within this volume and how these can be pursued as possible trajectories within a strategic research space. More specifically, we imagine strategic portfolios of research targeting a science of learning in distributed and distance learning environments using the ideas put forth in this volume.

To describe in a concrete manner how our framework can be used to create differing portfolios, we use the language of strategic planning and propose a set of *strategic goals* and candidate *tactical objectives* based on each of the chapters in this volume. Strategic goals are purposely broad in that they develop the policy that guides research by suggesting trajectories for a given endeavor. To specify the nature of the research falling along a given trajectory, one would specify tactical objectives. To illustrate how a tactical objective can be conceptualized, we provide one of many candidate tactical objectives for these strategic goals. The actual policy that would be created to support such goals would have a fairly large number of objectives associated with it. These objectives would drive the development of differing research projects by guiding research efforts to be conceptualized more at the level of the principal investigator. In short, strategic goals would be used to drive policy-level decisions about funding particular areas of inquiry, and tactical objectives would be used to focus research within such areas, perhaps through the generation of requests for proposals or broad agency announcements. To illustrate our thinking on this, we use the contributions from this volume to offer representative examples of what we mean by strategic goals and tactical objectives. The examples we present are by no means exhaustive; we provide them only to encourage a higher level of thinking about a science of learning in distributed environments.

In short, viewing this as a type of armchair exercise, we hope to illustrate to the scientific community how strategic thinking based on sound theory can move us closer to solving significant societal problems while considering the underlying epistemological issues inherent in such research. For ease of explication, we divide our research space into octants (see Figure 11.1), that is, eight sections within the space fitting with the major category labels of our three primary dimensions (see Table 11.2). This allows us to

TABLE 11.2
Defining Dimensions for Octants Within the Strategic Science Space

Octant	Driver	Outcome	Timeline
		Dimension	
1	Curiosity	Creating knowledge	Long term
2	Curiosity	Developing knowledge	Long term
3	Curiosity	Creating knowledge	Short term
4	Curiosity	Developing knowledge	Short term
5	Need	Creating knowledge	Long term
6	Need	Developing knowledge	Long term
7	Need	Creating knowledge	Short term
8	Need	Developing knowledge	Short term

speculatively place the ideas put forth in this volume in differing areas of this space and then offer potential trajectories for their ideas as movement toward differing octants. We organize the differing strategic goals and tactical objectives drawn from each chapter as serving either distributed learning and training models, teams, or processes. We follow the general format of this volume, first discussing the "model" chapters, then the "team" chapters, and then the "process" chapters and illustrating the differing trajectories that can be used to form strategic portfolios within these areas.

Strategic Consideration of Theoretical Models Emanating From Distributed Learning in Organizations

Chapter 2: Kozlowski and Bell

The expansiveness of Kozlowski and Bell's chapter places it within Octant 5 (long-term, need-driven creation of knowledge) of our strategic space. Their model offers a strong theoretical basis for examining how the many components of distributed training can alter learning, and the issues discussed deserve both short- and long-term exploration. Within the broad theorizing presented in their chapter are any number of possible research trajectories that would enable increases in fundamental understanding as well as a more immediate investigation of how extant knowledge can be developed and tested. In our illustration, we present candidate trajectories that would guide research to move relatively quickly but produce differing knowledge outcomes.

> *Strategic Goal 1 (SG1):* Develop policy for the examination of how information richness theories influence organizational effectiveness through research with a short-term perspective while creating fundamental knowledge.

> *Example Tactical Objective*: Support laboratory research in which differing training tasks are investigated in the context of information richness theory.

In the case of SG1, information richness theory could be used as a backdrop against which we could be helped to understand how the associated factors differentially interact with differing training needs and tasks. As such, SG1 moves the research from Octant 5 to Octant 7 and is aimed at developing research that creates fundamental knowledge surrounding training task contexts, but it moves us closer to the implementation of this knowledge (i.e., a short-term outcome) by narrowly focusing on a given area of inquiry (i.e., information delivery).

> *Strategic Goal 2 (SG2)*: Develop policy to investigate organizational learning by means of training technologies research with a short-term perspective while targeting the development of existing knowledge.

> *Example Tactical Objective*: Support field research using simulations within training studies across differing knowledge domains.

To the degree that there is a strategic need to move more toward developing usable knowledge in support of team learning and development, the theorizing presented in Kozlowski and Bell's chapter similarly suggests a number of ways this can be accomplished. With respect to SG2, we suggest a trajectory moving from Octant 5 to Octant 8, with the aim more toward development of existing knowledge by looking at how simulation tools used in field research can alter training outcomes. For example, research funding could support learning within particular content areas (e.g., the biological sciences) to see how training variations, based on their model, increase training efficacy for particular disciplines.

Chapter 3: Brown and Van Buren

Brown and Van Buren demonstrate a creative approach to learning in organizations using theorizing that is based on notions of social capital. Considering how this research was derived, we suggest that Brown and Van Buren's ideas fall within Octant 1 (long-term, curiosity-driven creation of knowledge) of our strategic science space. Specifically, this has been mostly derived from the "what-if" perspective of science, as Brown and Van Buren have pursued their own curiosity to creatively integrate ideas from a number of domains. Furthermore, it is clearly contributing to our fundamental understanding of organizational processes and, as such, is producing new knowledge. Within this context, we present strategic goals that can develop their theory.

Strategic Goal 3 (SG3): Develop policy to investigate organizational learning and productivity through development of social capital research with a short-term perspective while creating new knowledge.

Example Tactical Objective: Support organizational science research to establish the existence of social capital and its relation to organizational productivity.

Considering research goals based on Brown and Van Buren's work, in the case of SG3 we move from Octant 1 to Octant 3 and focus on developing research that seeks to establish an understanding of how social capital may exist within organizations and its potential relation to organizational productivity. For example, this trajectory could move the field more rapidly toward an understanding of social capital theory in the context of organizational learning. Such funding could take the form of research using methods such as field surveys developed to map the existence of social capital (e.g., through analyses of communication networks) yet be flexible enough for the outcomes to be easily translated into parameters for use within models of organizational productivity. Thus, given the relative newness of the model, the research policy decisions would need to first encourage understanding social capital in organizational contexts, and hence our emphasis on the creation of knowledge.

Strategic Goal 4 (SG4): Develop policy to investigate organizational productivity through social capital research with a short-term perspective while targeting the development of existing knowledge.

Example Tactical Objective: Support training research in which social capital is cultivated within or across organizations.

With respect to SG4, here the research trajectory moves us from Octant 1 to Octant 4, supporting a shorter-term perspective to establish training research based on the constructs proposed within Brown and Van Buren's model. For example, considering the propositions Brown and Van Buren put forth, funding could encourage training research examining how social capital can be cultivated at the intra-organizational level (i.e., across organizational departments) and the interorganizational level (e.g., between customers and service personnel). This supports the development of existing knowledge within training theory but integrated within a social capital perspective of organizational learning.

Chapter 4: Kraiger and Jerden

The thorough analysis of the learning literature provided by Kraiger and Jerden has laid the foundation for an extensive line of training research for organizations in the area of learner control. As a meta-analytically based chapter, the ideas fit within Octant 5 (long-term, need-driven creation of knowledge) of our strategic science space; that is, the model presented has elements within it that can be pursued with a short- and long-term focus. It is important to recognize that on the basis of their analyses, a number of important training factors have been articulated that can now be explored through trajectories moving upward as well as continuing with the creation of new knowledge. We can envision funding that supports research examining how adult learners master work-related content when learner control varies and across differing types of tasks.

> *Strategic Goal 5 (SG5)*: Develop policy to investigate how individual characteristics and related factors influence adult learning through research with a long-term perspective while creating new knowledge.

> *Example Tactical Objective*: Support research for adult age learners (post-college) to establish how objective versus preferred learner control moderates comprehension and retention of to-be-learned material.

In the case of SG5, research targeting adult populations (i.e., not research for K–12 or college-age participants) could examine differing forms of learner control to determine how they affect learning at these age levels. We still need to develop the fundamental knowledge within this area of inquiry before we can consider the development of usable knowledge because our understanding of this area has not been completely explored. Hence our trajectory moves us toward the right from Octant 5 to Octant 1.

> *Strategic Goal 6 (SG6)*: Develop policy to help understand how learner control affects organizational productivity through research with a short-term perspective while targeting the development of existing knowledge.

> *Example Tactical Objective*: Support field research within organizations and across industries where training system design factors are examined in the context of learner control to assess efficacy of learning systems.

SG6 serves a more short-term need with the trajectory moving the research from Octant 5 to Octant 8. Here we propose to examine how research in training systems can be pursued across differing industries. This would help the development of existing knowledge by looking at how training systems alter learning outcomes and whether usable similarities can be identified.

Summarizing the Research Portfolio Possible for Theoretical Models Emanating From Distributed Learning in Organizations

What we illustrate in Figure 11.2, and what we have described overall in this section, is a strategic portfolio of research projects. There are two main points to consider with respect to this particular strategic portfolio. First, this can be considered a portfolio with outcomes that cut across much of our strategic science framework. Second, it is critical that this portfolio,

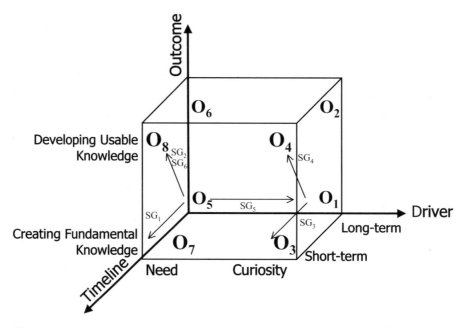

Figure 11.2. Strategic goals for theoretical models of distributed learning and training.

although varied in its outcomes and approaches, still targets a specific area of inquiry within a science of learning focusing on distributed environments. In particular, this portfolio is devised to explore an understanding of a set of theoretical models emerging within distributed learning environments. With respect to Kozlowski and Bell's chapter, we suggest proposing policy supporting short-term outcomes that either create fundamental understanding (SG1) or support the development of extant knowledge (SG2). However, one can see across both of these strategic goals trajectories aimed at a more rapid implementation of findings related to their theory of training systems. With respect to Brown and Van Buren and social capital theory in organizational learning contexts, we can envision trajectories also supporting a more rapid attempt to develop new understanding (SG3) or trajectories supporting the development of extant knowledge (SG4). In both instances, their theory of social capital is pursued with differing endpoints. On the one hand would be the creation of knowledge surrounding organizational understanding, and on the other hand would be the refinement of our understanding of how social capital knowledge within organizations can be disseminated through training programs. Finally, conceptualizing a research program in adult learning contexts based on Kraiger and Jerden's theorizing can have somewhat divergent endpoints. In particular, we can consider these objectives broadly, to support the creation of knowledge associated with metacognition in adult learners (SG5), but we can also suggest a more rapid pursuit of knowledge development through policy supporting short-term outcomes (SG6). It is the confluence of these goals and their respective trajectories that we argue creates a strategically based portfolio of research projects. This portfolio, therefore, is based on a sound body of extant theory and supports societal needs through the pursuit of knowledge creation and development within the organizational sciences.

Strategically Considering Distributed Teams and Distributed Team Training

Chapter 5: Goettl, Ashworth, and Chaiken

Within the context of distributed team training research, Goettl, Ashworth, and Chaiken describe an impressive line of theoretically driven studies in distributed training for the military. On the basis of the focus of their research, we suggest that their approach falls within Octant 7 (short-term, need-driven creation of knowledge) of our strategic science space. Specifically, this line of inquiry has a clear basis of need, but it is still contributing to fundamental understanding of distributed team training. Finally, the time frame of this research is more short term in that their studies have used testbeds with sufficient fidelity to enable a relatively quick translation of findings. Viewing this work from the perspective of movement within our strategic science space, there exist possibilities for trajectories leading both upward as well as toward the right. In particular, the ideas put forth by Goettl et al. suggest some important issues to explore more from a curiosity-driven perspective (i.e., movement from Octant 7 to Octant 3 or 8), and they open the door for a rich area of study.

> *Strategic Goal 7 (SG7)*: Develop policy to examine how transfer can be supported through development of advanced technologies research with a short-term perspective while creating new knowledge.

> *Example Tactical Objective*: Support modeling and simulation research to examine how forms of fidelity alter retention and transfer in complex tasks.

When considering SG7, we propose a trajectory moving from Octant 7 to Octant 3 to target the development of research that may be able to establish how it is that the differing forms of fidelity enabled in technology-based training contexts can facilitate transfer. Such funding would support research to help us understand the complex learning processes involved in transfer of training. This has been an area of inquiry present since the inception of the psychological sciences (e.g., Thorndike & Woodworth, 1901), and our understanding of this in complex tasks, and the specifics of how fidelity alters learning, can still be expanded, particularly in the context of simulation-based training.

Strategic Goal 8 (SG8): Develop policy to investigate skill acquisition and expertise through research with a short-term perspective while targeting the development of existing knowledge.

Example Tactical Objective: Support training research examining the impact of fidelity variation on learners differing in expertise levels.

For SG8, our trajectory suggests a rapid pursuit of knowledge but targets a more specific focus by proposing research that examines skill acquisition across levels of expertise. This would be a trajectory moving upward from Octant 7 into Octant 8 in that it would explore how fundamental findings in fidelity can translate to a particular domain or experience level. For example, one can imagine a particular line of study devised to ascertain how what we find on skill acquisition using laboratory studies where fidelity was varied, scaled to complex process control research (e.g., industrial power plants), but across personnel with varied levels of experience.

Chapter 6: Fiore, Johnston, and McDaniel

In their analysis of team training using distributed simulation-based exercises, Fiore, Johnston, and McDaniel put forth an area of inquiry that has already seen considerable implementation in a variety of other domains. The narrative form in particular has been leveraged in the computational sciences for many years and has been part of teaching pedagogy for even longer. On the basis of the nature of their theorizing, we place it within Octant 5 (long-term, need-driven creation of knowledge) of our strategic science space. Their framework contributes to fundamental gains in our understanding of how teamwork may be better understood through narrative theory, but it has a clear need in mind (i.e., improving distributed training for the Navy). Given the complexity of such research, the time frame associated with this theorizing is more long term; that is, its utility in distributed training, particularly those as complex as distributed simulations, requires much study.

Strategic Goal 9 (SG9): Develop policy to examine how narrative theory can be supported in distributed team research in general through research with a long-term perspective while creating new knowledge.

Example Tactical Objective: Support research on the narrative form within distributed teams to examine its impact on team development and evolution.

In consideration of SG9, the research trajectory moves from Octant 5 to Octant 1 and suggests exploration and development of research examining how narrative theory affects our understanding of the evolution of distributed teams in general. This would be funding that supports studies investigating the basic tenants of narrative theory, for example, across differing types of teams to determine how the theoretical constructs can be reified within a framework for understanding team process. Such research might determine whether team development is fostered through a more principled incorporation of narrative–story into the learning process.

> *Strategic Goal 10 (SG10)*: Develop policy to investigate how multidisciplinary research can incorporate narrative theory into training system design through research with a short-term perspective while targeting the development of existing knowledge.

> *Example Tactical Objective*: Support research in computational and psychological sciences to examine how narrative systems can influence learning and performance in teams.

When considering SG10, policy could encourage multidisciplinary research on narrative. Here we have an instance in which it may be feasible to move from Octant 5 to Octant 8 (i.e., toward the front and the top of the space). Such funding could, for example, support multidisciplinary research and development in which the computational and psychological sciences collaborate to explore the utility of techniques such as object-oriented programming in narrative systems developed for training. Funding also could support development of narrative-based technologies that better integrate pre-, in-, and postprocess learning content, that is, material used in the preparation for, execution of, and reflection on the overall learning experience.

Chapter 7: Cooke, Gorman, Pedersen, and Bell

Through an investigation of team cognition developed within the training sciences, the work of Cooke and colleagues has helped us understand how cognitive processes are affected by, and alter, process when teams interact either in a colocated setting or at a distance. Given that this is a type of research that creates fundamental knowledge within the context of understanding teamwork in military contexts, it falls within Octant 5 (long-term, need-driven creation of knowledge) of our strategic science space. Even though it has more of a long-term emphasis because it is laboratory based, given the cognitive fidelity present in their research it is possible to consider trajectories aimed toward the front of this space. Therefore, funding can encourage both long-term (e.g., continued laboratory studies) and short-term outcomes (e.g., by taking these laboratory findings and supporting training systems research that examines these findings in the field). Thus, Cooke, Gorman, Pedersen, and Bell's principled approach to examining team cognition and coordination opens a number of intriguing areas for research.

> *Strategic Goal 11 (SG11)*: Develop policy to investigate how distributed interaction alters teamwork through research with a long-term perspective while creating new knowledge.

Example Tactical Objective: Support laboratory research in distributed teams to understand how communication processes are altered by, and subsequently alter, distributed team process and performance.

In the case of SG11, our trajectory takes us from Octant 5 to Octant 7, with research possibilities for examining factors surrounding the nature of communication in distributed teams. Here, a shorter-term trajectory would allow for examination of some of the fundamental issues that Cooke et al. uncovered in their research. For example, the degree to which differing communication patterns and forms (e.g., explicit vs. implicit) lead to common understanding in distributed teams could be examined. This could in turn lead to specific principles for use by researchers developing distributed training systems.

Strategic Goal 12 (SG12): Develop policy to understand how training technologies can support team adaptation through research with a long-term perspective while targeting the development of existing knowledge.

Example Tactical Objective: Support research on distributed teams in which training systems are examined regarding their impact on individual and collaborative cognitive processes.

Conversely, SG12 defines a trajectory that takes us from Octant 5 to Octant 6 and supports a long-term need where research in training systems can be pursued to help us better understand technology's impact on distributed team cognition. This would enable the development of existing knowledge by looking at how such systems influence cognitive processes and alter collaboration and the concomitant effect this may have on team adaptation. For example, research could examine how adaptation is fostered or hindered by shared-display technologies and how this may differ in colocated versus distributed teams. Because this is a complex undertaking, we suggest that a longer-term perspective is warranted.

Summarizing the Research Portfolio Possible for Distributed Teams and Distributed Team Training

As with the prior section, we have presented (and illustrated in Figure 11.3) a strategic portfolio of research projects. This portfolio has outcomes cutting across our strategic science framework, yet it targets a specific area of inquiry within a science of learning. Specifically, this strategic portfolio explores distributed teams and distributed team training through a number of research trajectories. For example, Goettl et al.'s productive research program can be further developed into research trajectories that support the creation and development of knowledge. Specifically, these lines of inquiry could support both the creation of greater understanding of training

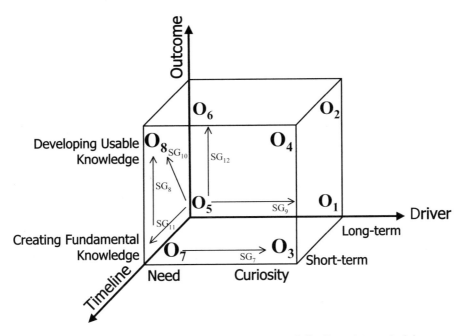

Figure 11.3. Strategic goals for distributed teams and distributed team training.

transfer within teams (SG7) and the development of existing knowledge within skill-acquisition research focusing on teams (SG8). With respect to Fiore et al.'s approach to melding narrative theory with distributed team training, this could be pursued in such a way that differing knowledge outcomes are supported. Specifically, multiple trajectories would allow the narrative concept to be explored in a way that potentially produces new knowledge (SG9) or develops usable knowledge in support of team learning and development (SG10). Last, we have suggested how team cognition research, as presented in Cooke et al.'s chapter, can be supported with different trajectories in pursuit of short- and long-term research outcomes. Specifically, the strategic goals articulated for the theory put forth by Cooke et al. more broadly allow for the pursuit of knowledge associated with cognition and communication, and the differing trajectories can encourage both a deeper understanding of the issues they have uncovered (SG11) and the application of their findings (SG12). Considered in combination, the goals we have articulated and the trajectories we have illustrated help us conceptualize what can be a strategically based portfolio for distributed teams. In this way, we are able to move our understanding of distributed teams forward through simultaneous consideration of scientific and societal needs.

Strategic Consideration of Cognitive Processes and Products in Distributed Learning Environments

Chapter 8: Mayer

Mayer effectively demonstrates the important empirical and theoretical strides made in our understanding of how multimedia implementations influence the learning process. On the basis of the nature of this research, we suggest that Mayer's work in multimedia and cognition falls within Octant 7 (short-term, need-driven creation of knowledge) of our strategic science space. Specifically, this has clearly been a need-driven approach in that Mayer has attempted to understand how multimedia implementations influence learning. Yet it is undoubtedly contributing to our fundamental understanding of this topic; that is, it is producing, or has produced, new knowledge related to learning. Finally, this work, although based on a long line of laboratory studies, is specific enough to support a shorter turnaround. As articulated in this volume, Mayer's ideas are ready for movement in differing directions of our research space, as the short-term outcomes that could be derived from his theory are apparent.

> *Strategic Goal 13 (SG13)*: Develop policy to transition multimedia learning theory to curiosity-driven research with a short-term perspective but aimed at creation of new knowledge.

> *Example Tactical Objective*: Support laboratory studies using multimedia learning theory in brain imaging research.

Considering the potential strategic goals based on Mayer's work, in the case of SG13 we propose a trajectory that moves multimedia theory from Octant 7 to Octant 3. In particular, this theoretical approach can be used to investigate brain-based processing distinctions in the context of multimedia learning. Mayer's theorizing is supported by a broad set of behaviorally based studies. When this theory is coupled with recent methodological advances in neuroscience, we may be able to develop a fuller understanding of the neurophysiology associated with learning when multimedia implementations are involved. For example, recent work in understanding working memory and its underlying neurology can be considered in the context of the burgeoning discipline of neuroergonomics (e.g., Hancock & Szalma, 2003; Parasuraman, 2003). An overarching goal of neuroergonomics is to use our knowledge of brain function to better design learning and performance systems. In particular, "knowledge of how the brain processes visual, auditory and tactile information can provide important guidelines and constraints for theories of information presentation and task design" (Parasuraman, 2003, p. 6).

> *Strategic Goal 14 (SG14)*: Develop policy to transition multimedia learning theory to research with a short-term perspective that targets the development of existing knowledge.

Example Tactical Objective: Support e-learning field research such that technologies based on multimedia learning theory are tested in complex industry-based training.

With respect to SG14, we suggest research that moves from Octant 7 to Octant 8. We have proposed Octant 8 as a target for this trajectory because the extant knowledge manifest in this theory has many components ready to be refined and shaped within specific areas so that it can become usable knowledge (e.g., e-learning training and/or technology specifications for a given domain).

Chapter 9: Jonassen

Jonassen eloquently argues in his chapter for the importance of understanding the nature and process of problem solving and lays out the theoretical issues that would support such research. On the basis of this theorizing, we place the ideas presented by Jonassen within Octant 5 (long-term, need-driven creation of knowledge) of our strategic science space. This theorizing contributes to fundamental gains in our understanding of problem solving, but it has a clear basis for need (i.e., better training of a competent problem-solving workforce). Within the context of understanding problem solving, we have trajectories leading the research community to short- and long-term time frames but with differing knowledge outcomes.

Strategic Goal 15 (SG15): Develop policy to support research on problem solving across a variety of task contexts through research with a long-term perspective while creating new knowledge.

Example Tactical Objective: Support laboratory studies that examine problem-solving learning environments across well-structured and ill-structured task contexts when interacting takes place in distributed environments.

In considering the potential strategic goals with SG15, our trajectory moves us from Octant 5 to Octant 1. In this instance, research on problem-solving learning environments is encouraged across task contexts. Furthermore, this research is targeted for laboratory settings so that factors could be varied for the purposes of developing an understanding of how they alter problem-solving processes and address fundamental issues that are generalizable to distributed problem solving overall.

Strategic Goal 16 (SG16): Develop policy to investigate how technologies affect problem-solving effectiveness through research policy with a short-term perspective while creating usable knowledge.

Example Tactical Objective: Support field research investigating how decision-support software can be used in problem-based learning environments in distributed engineering.

With respect to SG16, the trajectory takes us from Octant 5 to Octant 8. With this trajectory, we have problem-based learning environments still as a research focus, but the aim is to explore how technologies can be developed to augment the learning and performance factors surrounding learning theory in these environments. The notion is that this is a clear setting through which to support a shorter turnaround and development of potentially useful knowledge.

Chapter 10: Wisher and Graesser

On the basis of a strong foundation of research coming out of cognitive psychology, Wisher and Graesser present an important area of study on question-generation processes and how query-based systems are developable for more complex learning environments. Because their approach illustrates longer-term possibilities, they fall within Octant 5 (long-term, need-driven creation of knowledge). Specifically, their theory pursues fundamental under-standing in the area of learning systems, and its translation requires added and varied forms of research. Nonetheless, they elaborate on a coherent set of research questions that, from the policy perspective, can be developed to help us understand the design and development of efficacious distributed learning environments. More specifically, question generation represents an important area of inquiry requiring both increases in fundamental under-standing and a more immediate investigation of how extant knowledge can be developed and tested. As such, we have trajectories that can guide researchers along both short- and long-term time frames, each with differing knowledge outcomes.

> *Strategic Goal 17 (SG17)*: Develop policy to examine question genera-tion through research with a short-term perspective while creating new knowledge.

> *Example Tactical Objective*: Support laboratory research investigating agent-based technologies that support social-cognitive processes during distributed learning.

When considering candidate strategic goals with SG17, we propose a trajec-tory moving from Octant 5 to Octant 7. This would support research wherein question generation could be explored through more focused study, for example, on intelligent agents that support the type of guidelines and recom-mendations put forth by Wisher and Graesser. Specifically, SG17 is aimed at creating fundamental knowledge in that it would enable an understanding of automated pedagogical agents capable of interacting within the question-generation processing rubric. Nonetheless, it would move us closer to implementation in that it could produce research outcomes more directly translatable in the shorter term.

Strategic Goal 18 (SG18): Develop policy to investigate how computational systems can support question generation through research with a long-term perspective while creating usable knowledge.

Example Tactical Objective: Support information sciences research on intelligently managing question processes in distance learning.

With respect to SG18, the trajectory moves us from Octant 5 to Octant 6. In this case, a broader line of study would be developed such that information sciences research could examine the numerous issues surrounding how the question-generation process would be managed and controlled within distributed learning.

Summarizing the Research Portfolio Possible for Cognitive Processes and Products

With respect to this section and what we illustrate in Figure 11.4, we see a strategic portfolio of research projects tailored to understanding a specific area of inquiry within a science of learning focusing on distributed environments. In particular, this portfolio is devised to explore an understanding of the cognitive processes and the cognitive products emerging within distributed learning environments. Thus, with the trajectories devised for Mayer's theory of multimedia implementations we have the potential

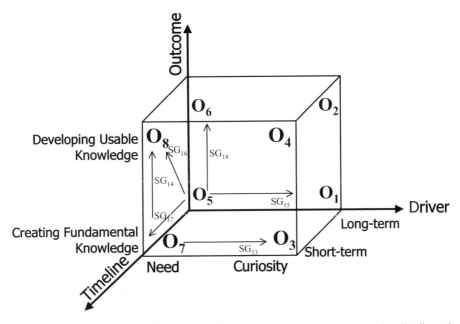

Figure 11.4. Strategic goals for cognitive processes and products in distributed learning environments.

for research to produce knowledge in a short- and long-term time frame. In this way, the practicing education and training communities are supported through the development of policy that examines differing outcomes targeting the creation of new knowledge (SG13) as well as the development of knowledge (SG14). With respect to the trajectories suggested for the theory put forth by Jonassen, there is an important distinction to consider. Specifically, the difference would be that SG15 supports research that will contribute to creating fundamental understanding, whereas SG16 pursues the development of extant knowledge in technologies relating to distributed engineering as a specific context. Finally, with respect to the theorizing of Wisher and Graesser, the user communities can benefit more rapidly through policy that supports short-term outcomes (SG17), but the science of learning in distributed learning and training would still examine more complex issues requiring a longer-term focus (SG18). By strategically conceptualizing a set of targeted goals and respective trajectories, we create a portfolio built on the basis of strong theorizing and that enables the solving of both scientific and societal goals.

SOME CONCLUDING THOUGHTS ON STRATEGIC THINKING IN SCIENCE AND TRANSLATING RESEARCH INTO PRACTICE

We close this chapter with, again, a broader perspective, this time on the intimate relation between science and society and how research can help meet societal needs. It is important to note that many of the chapters in this volume tend to cluster within particular octants of our space. This is not surprising given that the nature of the funding that is supporting much of this research—that is, funding primarily provided by mission agencies—was targeting identified needs. Nonetheless, our goal with illustrating these within our research space was to illustrate how such funding not only helps us understand a given phenomenon but also provides innovative ideas that support the development of additional research trajectories throughout the strategic space. In particular, research beginning in a particular octant does not preclude movement in any direction out of that octant. To foster such movement, the scientific, educational, and industry communities should pursue a more integrated collaboration in the investigation of a science of learning in distributed environments. Within the context of our strategic research space we can begin to imagine how interaction between policy-makers and stakeholders can provide input to this space and help guide resource allocations. From this broader perspective, Sarewitz (1997) described how democratic ideals need to be infused into the way researchers formulate their scientific endeavors and translate scientific findings to help meet societal goals. He called arguments that only scientists are qualified to identify scientific problems and societal priorities self-serving and politically unconvincing. Describing how activists have influenced biomedical research, he noted that "there is ample evidence that when scientists work cooperatively with knowledgeable activists from outside the research community, science as well as society can benefit" (p. 30).

More specifically, we consider the suggestions of Guston (2000), who encouraged the pursuit of a reciprocal relationship whereby the communities that need their problems solved (e.g., education, industry) allow the scientific community to consider their problems in detail, while the scientific community is more willing to understand their problems and provide that help. Without the creation of legitimate mechanisms to allow public and/or user input into research and development priorities, this goal remains out of reach. To better serve society Guston argued for what he called *collaborative assurance*, a process requiring the input of organizations and institutions that enlist and/or include nonscientists. Guston suggested that the broader community of stakeholders needs to be better integrated into the federal research model. This is an important point, and the lack of stakeholder involvement may be an explanation for the poor translation of research findings in areas such as the science of learning. Specifically, the translation of research results in the psychological sciences in general, and the cognitive and learning sciences in particular, have been far weaker than the magnitude of data produced would suggest. Indeed, in an important article supporting a better application of the science of learning, Newcombe (2002) suggested that the ways we teach and learn need to be more informed by laboratory experimentation in human cognition just as the practice of medicine is informed by laboratory studies in biology. The fault lies not only with the user communities—that is, educators and trainers in need of a science of learning—but also with the learning science communities, perhaps for not adequately enlisting input from what Guston described as *boundary organizations*: "institutions that sit astride the boundary between politics and science and involve the participation of nonscientists as well as scientists in the creation of mutually beneficial outputs" (p. 34).

The writings of Guston and Sarewitz (e.g., Guston, 2000; Sarewitz, 1997) go further and argue that even models based on Stokes's (1997) notion of use-inspired research and Holton and Sonnert's (1999) view of Jeffersonian science are still firmly entrenched in dated views of science policy (i.e., nondemocratic, patronage forms of thinking about funding). Although we rely on the thinking of Stokes and the likes of Holton and Sonnert, our approach is not necessarily at odds with notions of what Guston (2000) termed "collaborative assurance" or Sarewitz's (1997) democratic ideals for science policy. In particular, we do not espouse any form of patronage funding system. Furthermore, nonscientists from user communities or boundary organizations would play an important role in helping to define programs within, or move research toward, what we have conceptualized as need-based projects. In short, our aim was more to get the practicing scientific community as well as those in policy circles to think about science and society within the context of a science of learning for distributed environments and offer guidance as to how to work together to form scientific projects that are broad in scope. Thus, our strategic science space is merely one step in the direction of a conceptual structure for use by the scientific community and boundary organizations. Only by providing a structure that encourages translation of research will scientific gains be more probable. We have tried to illustrate how to redress problems of input and translation by suggesting different ways a science of learning in distributed learning can be conceptualized.

An important additional point to recognize for a strategic approach to science is that a generation of scientists must be trained to both understand and embrace such a model. This is best explained in a recent report by Sabelli and Dede (2001) on how to integrate research and practice. Although discussed in the context of education research and practice, their points speak to a much broader range of science. In particular, they support a shift such that "the impact of research on education practice goes beyond 'transfer' and 'action research' toward reconceptualizing the relationship between scholarship and practice as instead a scholarship of practice" (p. 2). We fully agree with this, as it resonates with our strategic science space and attempts to link research programs to the user communities. However, Sabelli and Dede are not the only people arguing for a sturdier bridge between research and practice. Branscomb, Holton, and Sonnert (2002) similarly asked how it is that we can

> get a cumulative knowledge base on thinking and learning, and make it accessible to practitioners? We need new avenues for capturing the wisdom of practice, and we need *a new kind of professional who can bridge the worlds of research and practice* [italics added]. (p. 409)

Perhaps by taking notions such as "collaborative assurance" in conjunction with funding models such as our strategic science space, and by ensuring that graduate education embraces such a culture of thinking, we can increase the probability that science and practice become indistinguishable.

Finally, a necessary complement to developing graduate training that encourages this type of worldview is a fundamental shift in the way academic scientists themselves are rewarded. Just as funding sources must dictate general research areas and even encourage partnerships for disciplinary integration, university administrations must also become involved for real research translation to at least begin. This requires more than reliance on rewarding publications in oftentimes esoteric journals in which important ideas and findings are presented only to a small group of like-minded individuals. For example, university tenure review panels can begin to make research outreach (e.g., working with user communities and boundary organizations to facilitate translational components of one's findings) a serious part of the tenure-granting process. Similarly, professional organizations can become involved by providing outlets where fundamental research is considered in the light of particular societal needs. This includes continuation of publications such as the American Psychological Association's *Journal of Experimental Psychology: Applied* and the Association for Psychological Science's *Psychology in the Public Interest*. In short, what is required is for the academic, professional, and funding communities to nurture, encourage, and reward thinking in both understanding and use.

Although this chapter was merely an armchair exercise in strategic thinking about a science of learning in distributed environments—that is, a type of what-if question using the contributions to this volume—our goal was really nothing more than this. Writing the concluding chapter to edited volumes provides one with a unique opportunity to question and expand on the variety of ideas presented. We hope we have stimulated the thinking of a number of important constituencies—current and future scientists, department chairs, policymakers, and even user communities—with the result being that some or all of these people are thinking more strategically about a science of learning in distributed environments. We all must recognize that modern scientists need to understand the intimate relation between science and society as well as how the knowledge they produce fits into the larger societal picture. This must be provided through training in graduate school and supported by the academic and funding communities. Within this context, as we stated at the beginning of this chapter, the scientific problems we are currently facing require multidisciplinary approaches. Within our strategic science space we have proposed trajectories devised in such a way that they require multidisciplinary teams if they are to meet the stated strategic goals; that is, they require coordinated scientific efforts cutting across disciplines. Only when such teams can be formed, and these issues are beginning to be addressed, can a science of learning begin the important process of solving the problems of, and realizing the possibilities for, the 21st century.

REFERENCES

Branscomb, L. M. (1999, Fall). The false dichotomy: Scientific creativity and utility. *Issues in Science and Technology, 16*(1), 66–72.

Branscomb, L. M., Holton, G., & Sonnert, G. (2002). Science and society. In A. H. Teich, S. D. Nelson, & S. J. Lita (Eds.), *AAAS science and technology policy yearbook* (pp. 397–433). Washington, DC: American Association for the Advancement of Science.

Bransford, J. D., Brown, A. L., & Cocking, R. R. (2000). *How people learn: Brain, mind, experience, and school.* Washington, DC: National Academy Press.

Fiore, S. M., Rubinstein, J., & Jentsch, F. (2004). Considering science and security from a broader research perspective. *International Journal of Cognitive Technology, 9,* 40–42.

Guston, D. H. (2000, Summer). Retiring the social contract for science. *Issues in Science and Technology, 17*(1), 32–36.

Hancock, P. A., & Szalma, J. L. (2003). The future of ergonomics. *Theoretical Issues in Ergonomic Science, 44,* 238–249.

Hoffman, R. R., & Deffenbacher, K. A. (1993). An analysis of the relations of basic and applied science. *Ecological Psychology, 5,* 315–352.

Holton, G., & Sonnert, G. (1999). A vision of Jeffersonian Science. *Issues in Science and Technology, 16*(1), 61–65.

Latham, G. P. (2001). The reciprocal effects of science on practice: Insights from the practice and science of goal setting. *Canadian Psychology, 42,* 1–11.

Newcombe, N. S. (2002). Biology is to medicine as psychology is to education: True or false? In D. F. Halpern & M. D. Hakel (Eds.), *Applying the science of learning to university teaching and beyond* (pp. 9–18). San Francisco: Jossey-Bass.

Parasuraman, R. (2003). Neuroergonomics: Research and practice. *Theoretical Issues in Ergonomic Science, 44,* 5–20.

Rubinstein, J. (2002). Aviation security long-term theoretical human factors research. *International Airport Review, 6,* 49–54.

Sabelli, N., & Dede, C. (2001). *Integrating educational research and practice: Reconceptualizing goals and policies. How to make what works, work for us?* Retrieved March 5, 2004, from http://www.virtual.gmu.edu/ss_research/cdpapers/policy.pdf

Salzinger, K. (2003, Summer). Moving graveyards. *Psychological Science Agenda, 16*(3), 3.

Sarewitz, D. (1997, Summer). Social change and science policy. *Issues in Science and Technology, 13*(4), 29–32.

Stokes, D. E. (1997). *Pasteur's quadrant: Basic science and technological innovation.* Washington, DC: Brookings Institution Press.

Thorndike, E. L., & Woodworth, R. S. (1901). The influence of improvement in one mental function upon the efficiency of other functions. *Psychological Review, 9,* 374–382.

Vicente, K. J. (2000). Toward Jeffersonian research programmes in ergonomic science. *Theoretical Issues in Ergonomics Science, 1,* 93–113.

AUTHOR INDEX

Numbers in italics refer to listings in the references.

Govindasamy, T., 17, 18, *36*
Grabowski, B. L., 68, *84*
Graesser, A. C., 209, 211, 214, 215, 216,
        217, 218, 220, 223, 224, 226,
        227, *230*, *231*, *232*, *233*
Gray, J., 191, *206*
Gray, S. H., 67, 68, *86*
Green, A. S., 27, *38*, 54, *62*
Greer, J., 214, *231*
Grice, H. P., 179, *183*
Gully, S. M., 34, *38*
Guston, D. H., 261, *264*
Guzley, R. M., 27, *37*

Hacker, D. J., 223, *232*
Hackman, J. R., 48, *61*
Haladyna, T. M., 221, *231*
Hall, E. P., 192, *206*
Hamid, A. A., 16, 33–34, *37*
Hamilton, R. L., 211, *230*
Hamm, H., 34, *38*
Hammond, K. R., 189, *205*
Hancock, P. A., 256, *264*
Handoe, L., 122, *145*
Hanna, B., 49, *62*
Hannafin, M. J., 66, 67, 78, 79, 82, *86*
Harabagiu, S. M., 218, *232*
Harel, K. H., 223, *231*
Harp, S. F., 178, *183*
Harpin, P., 81, *89*
Harris, D. M., 57, *60*
Hart, S. G., 101, *115*
Harter, D., 226, 227, *231*
Hartley, L. L., 122, *143*
Harward, H., 122, *141*
Hassett, M. R., *86*
Hatano, G., 22, *37*
Healy, A. F., 95, *115*, *116*
Hedberg, J., 66, *89*
Hedges, L. V., 69, *86*
Hedlund, J., 151, 153, *166*
Heiser, J., 178, *183*
Heller, M. A., 152, *166*
Hemphill, L., 123, *143*
Herman, D., 125, 126, *143*
Hernandez-Serrano, J., 196, *205*, *206*
Herrnstein-Smith, B., 137, *143*
Higginbotham-Wheat, N., 69, *84*
Hill, L. A., 48, *61*
Hinsz, V. B., 147–148, *166*

Hintze, H., 68, *86*
Hirumi, A., 125, *143*, *144*
Hodson, R., 49, *61*
Hoffman, R. R., 239, *264*
Hoffman, T. W., *207*
Holbrook, J., 191, *206*
Hollenbeck, J. R., 151, *166*
Hollingshead, A. B., 27, *38*
Holton, G., 239, 240, 242, 261, 262,
        263, *264*
Holyoak, K. J., 22, *37*, 101, 102, *115*,
        116
Homans, G. C., 57, *61*
Howell, A. W., *86*
Hrymak, A. N., *207*
Hsin-Yih, S., *86*
Hu, X., 214, *231*
Huff, M. T., 27, 31, *37*
Huffcutt, A. I., 71, *86*
Hughes, C. E., 124, *143*, *145*
Hughes, R. G., 97, *114*
Hung, W., 189, 193, *206*
Hunter, J. E., 69, 72, *86*

Idzikowski, C., 95, *116*
Ilgen, D. R., 151, *166*
IMS Global Learning Consortium, Inc.,
        232
Ingaki, K., 22, *37*

Jackson, T., 214, *231*
Jacobson, M. J., 79, *89*
Jeffries, P. R., 71, *86*
Jehng, J. C., 202, *206*
Jensen, P. J., 122, *143*
Jentsch, F., 6, *11*, 120, *142*, 244, *264*
Johnson, M. M., 31, *37*
Johnson, S. D., 192, *205*
Johnson, W. L., 227, *232*
Johnston, J., 120, *142*
Jonassen, D. H., 69, *86*, 186, 187, 188,
        189, 190, 191, 193, 196, 198,
        200, *205*, *206*
Jones, W. E., 97, *114*
Jordan, P., 226, *231*

Kalyuga, S., 33, *37*
Kanfer, R., 22, *37*, 79, *86*, 98, *114*

McClelland, G. H., 189, *205*
McCormick, E., 103, *115*
McDaniel, R., 120, 121, 126, 139, *142, 143, 144*
McGrath, J. E., 27, *38*
McGrath, D., 87
McGuiness, C., 193, *206*
Mckenna, C., 125, *144*
McKenna, K. Y. A., 27, *38, 54, 62*
McKeown, M. G., 211, *230*
McLendon, C. L., 44, *60*
McNamara, D. S., 209, 211, 216, *231, 232*
McPherson, J. A., 120, *144*
Meagher, P., 214, *231*
Meisel, S., 27, *38*
Meister, C., 26, *39*, 124, *144*, 210, *233*
Merrill, M. D., 67, 79, *88*
Metcalf, D. S., 120, 121, *143, 144*
Meyer, T. N., 99, *116*
Micikevicius, P., 124, *145*
Milanovich, D. M., 162, *167*
Milheim, W. D., 66, 67, 68, *88*
Miller, T. M., 99, *116, 117*
Minsky, M., 126, 127, *144*
Mitchell, T. R., 44, *62*
Moe, M. T., 5, *12*
Mohr, H., 68, *86*
Molfino, M. T., 79, *85*
Monty, R. A., 77, *88*
Moore, C., 67, *84*
Moreno, R., 33, *38*, 178, 180, *184*
Morrison, E. W., 43, 52, *60, 62*
Morrison, G. R., 67–68, *88*
Morrow, D. G., 122, *141*
Moshell, J. M., 124, *145*
Mousavi, S., 181, *184*
Mullich, J., 6, *12*
Mullins, M. E, *38*
Mumpower, J., 189, *205*
Murphy, M. A., 68, *88*

Naas, C., 179, *184*
Nahapiet, J., 44, 45, *62*
Nason, E. R., *38*
National Council of Teachers of English, 211, *232*
National Council on Measurement in Education, 221, *230*
National Research Council, 211, *232*

Newcombe, N. S., 261, *264*
Newell, A., 186, *206*
Newlin, M. H., 5, *12*
Niemiec, R. P., 67, 69, *88*
Nisbett, R. E., 187, *206*
Noe, R. A., 19, *38*
Norman, D., 122, *144*
Novick, L. R., 102, *116*

O'Donnell, A. M., 26, *38*
Oehlert, M. E., 90
Ogata, H., 214, *232*
Ohlsson, S., 21, *38*
Olde, B. A., 226, *231*
O'Leary-Kelly, A. M., 52, *60*
Olkin, I., 69, *86*
Olson, G. M., 53, *62*
Olson, J. S., 53, *62*
Ong, J., 79, *88*
Orlikowski, W. J., 54, *62*
Orvis, K. L., 224, *230*
Oser, R. L., 131, *142, 143*

Paas, F., 29, 33, 34, *38*, 181, *184*
Page, W., 124, *143*
Paine, J. B., 44, *62*
Paivio, A., 177, *184*
Palincsar, A. S., 210, *232*
Parasuraman, R., 256, *264*
Park, O. C., 66, *90*
Park, S., 78, *88*
Parks, M. R., 54, *62*
Parsons, J. A., 69, *88*
Parush, A., 34, *38*
Pasca, M. A., 218, *232*
Pattanaik, S. N., 124, *143*
Patterson, M., 72, *87*
Pea, R. D., 211, *231*
Penner, L. A., 163, *167*
Pennings, J. M., 43, *62*
Perkins, M. R., 122, *141*
Perlmuter, L. C., 77, *88*
Person, N. K., 209, 214, 215, 217, 218, 220, 223, 227, *231*
Phillips, J., 5, *12*
Phillips, P. P., 5, *12*
Philopoulos, A., 26, *36*
Pintrich, P. R., 81, *88*
Podsakoff, P. M., 44, *62*

SUBJECT INDEX

ABOUT THE EDITORS

Stephen M. Fiore, PhD, holds a joint faculty appointment with the University of Central Florida's Cognitive Sciences Program in the Department of Philosophy and the Institute for Simulation and Training. He earned his PhD (2000) in cognitive psychology from the University of Pittsburgh, Learning Research and Development Center. He maintains a multidisciplinary research interest that incorporates aspects of cognitive, social, and organizational psychology in the investigation of individuals and teams, and he has published in the area of learning, memory, and problem solving. Dr. Fiore has received research funding from organizations such as the National Science Foundation, the Transportation Security Administration, the Office of Naval Research, and the Air Force Office of Scientific Research.

Eduardo Salas, PhD, is professor of psychology at the University of Central Florida (UCF) where he was selected as a Trustee Chair Professor and holds an appointment as program director for the Department of Human Systems Integration Research at the Institute for Simulation and Training (IST). Previously, he was the director of UCF's Applied Experimental and Human Factors PhD Program. Before joining IST, he was a senior research psychologist and head of the Training Technology Development Branch of the Naval Air Warfare Center Training Systems Division for 15 years. During this period, Dr. Salas served as a principal investigator for numerous research and development programs, including the Tactical Decision Making Under Stress program, which focused on teamwork, team training, decision making under stress, and performance assessment. Dr. Salas has coauthored over 300 journal articles and book chapters and has coedited 19 books. His expertise includes assisting organizations in how to foster teamwork, design and implement team training strategies, facilitate training effectiveness, manage decision making under stress, and develop performance measurement tools. Dr. Salas is a fellow of the American Psychological Association, the Human Factors and Ergonomics Society, and a recipient of the Meritorious Civil Service Award from the Department of the Navy.